P9-EDN-649

Jerry Baker's HERBAL PHARMACY

www.jerrybaker.com

Other Jerry Baker Books:

Grandma Putt's Home Health Remedies
Jerry Baker's Supermarket Super Remedies
Jerry Baker's The New Healing Foods
Jerry Baker's Cut Your Health Care Bills in Half!
Jerry Baker's Amazing Antidotes
Jerry Baker's Anti-Pain Plan
Jerry Baker's Oddball Ointments, Powerful Potions, and Fabulous Folk Remedies
Jerry Baker's Giant Book of Kitchen Counter Cures

Jerry Baker's Supermarket Super Gardens
Jerry Baker's Dear God...Please Help It Grow!
Secrets from the Jerry Baker Test Gardens
Jerry Baker's All-American Lawns
Jerry Baker's Bug Off!
Jerry Baker's Terrific Garden Tonics!
Jerry Baker's Backyard Problem Solver
Jerry Baker's Green Grass Magic
Jerry Baker's Terrific Tomatoes, Sensational Spuds, and Mouth-Watering Melons
Jerry Baker's Great Green Book of Garden Secrets
Jerry Baker's Old-Time Gardening Wisdom

Jerry Baker's Backyard Birdscaping Bonanza
Jerry Baker's Backyard Bird Feeding Bonanza
Jerry Baker's Year-Round Bloomers
Jerry Baker's Flower Garden Problem Solver
Jerry Baker's Perfect Perennials!

Jerry Baker's Can the Clutter!
Jerry Baker's Cleaning Magic!
Jerry Baker's Homespun Magic
Grandma Putt's Old-Time Vinegar, Garlic, Baking Soda, and 101 More Problem Solvers
Jerry Baker's Supermarket Super Products!
Jerry Baker's It Pays to be Cheap!

To order any of the above, or for more information on Jerry Baker's amazing home, health, and garden tips, tricks, and tonics, please write to:

Jerry Baker, P.O. Box 1001, Wixom, MI 48393
Or, visit Jerry Baker online at:
www.jerrybaker.com

Jerry Baker's HERBAL PHARMACY

1,347 Super Secrets *for Growing and Using Herbal Remedies*

by Jerry Baker,
America's Master Gardener®

American Master Products, Inc.

NOTICE

All efforts have been made to ensure accuracy. This is a reference volume only, not a medical manual. Although the information presented may help you make informed decisions about your health, it is not intended as a substitute for prescribed medical treatment. If you have a medical problem, please seek competent medical help immediately. Jerry Baker assumes no responsibility or liability for any injuries, damages, or losses incurred during the use of or as a result of following this information. Herbal research is still in its infancy, and the interaction between herbs and pharmaceutical products remains largely unknown. Herbal remedies and nutraceuticals can have effects similar to those of pharmaceutical products. As a result, they are not without risk. They can interact with each other or with conventional medications, and some people may experience an allergic reaction or other adverse effects when starting an herbal or nutraceutical regimen. That's why you should always check with your doctor before you use them. Women who are pregnant or breastfeeding and children under age 18 should not use herbal or nutraceutical products without their doctor's specific recommendation.

IMPORTANT — Study all directions carefully before taking any action based on the information and advice presented in this book. When using any commercial product, always read and follow label directions. When reference is made to trade or brand names, no endorsement by Jerry Baker is implied, nor is any discrimination intended.

Executive Editor: Kim Adam Gasior

Published by American Master Products, Inc. by arrangement with Storey Communications, Inc., Pownal, Vermont 05261
Contributing Writer: Arden Moore
Editors: Gwen W. Steege, Maryann Teale Snell, and Eileen M. Clawson
Cover Design: Betty Kodela
Text Design: Mary B. Minella
Text Layout: Eileen M. Clawson, Betty Kodela, and Jennifer Jepson Smith
Illustrations by: Laura Tedeschi on pages 2, 3, 6, 9, 14, 16, 21, 22, 27, 30, 37-40, 42, 48, 49, 53, 56, 58, 60, 64, 71-74, 76, 78, 82, 104, 109, 124, 148, 151, 173, 188, 227, 341, 355
Additional illustrations by: Cathy Baker, Beverly Duncan, Brigita Fuhrmann, Charles Joslin, Alison Kolesar, Mallory Lake, Frank Riccio, Mary Rich, Louise Riotte, Ralph Scott, Hyla Scudder, Elayne Sears, Laura Tedeschi, and Brian Whitehurst
Indexer: Nina Forrest, Looking Up Indexing Services
ISBN 978-0-922433-37-7

Printed in the United States of America
4 6 8 10 9 7 5 3 hardcover

Contents

Herbs: Grow 'em, Love 'em, and Use Their Power to Heal

My dear garden friends: You are about to embark on a wonderful journey, and I am proud to be your guide. The path we're about to take will start out in and around your garden and from there meander into your kitchen and pantry. We will continue on to your natural health food store, drugstore, and supermarket, and there will be a few other stops along the way, including your bathtub!

As we progress on our journey, you will learn all about the fascinating, wonderful ways herbs enrich our lives. By touching, tasting, smelling, and feeling the power of herbs, you and your family will appreciate the bounty of benefits they offer you.

Herbal Renewal: They're Everywhere!

Nowadays, herbs are literally everywhere. Take a moment to look around, and you'll see them in the darndest places. Hundreds of varieties bloom with eye-catching beauty outdoors in gardens and indoors in windowsill containers. Herbs fill your spice racks and the crisper drawers inside your refrigerator. They share space inside your medicine cabinet with old standbys like aspirin and cough syrup. And countless manufactured herbs line supermarket and drugstore shelves in tea, tincture, and capsule forms.

May I Introduce You To . . .

In this book, I'm going to share with you the knowledge and expertise I've gained through the years working with herbs. You're going to learn how to grow and harvest herbs, and I'll even let you in on my cooking secrets and mouthwatering recipes. Plus, I'll shed some light on how to tap the potent medicinal powers of herbs safely and effectively so that you can keep on growing and going like me, well into your 70s, 80s, and even 90s!

The journey begins, naturally, in one of my all-time favorite places on earth — the garden. As a little boy, I was fortunate to be my Grandma Putt's enthusiastic gardening apprentice. She would take my small hand and guide me up and down her garden rows, introducing me to all of her blooming and beautifying friends. Grandma Putt would talk to her herbs just like she would her neighbors — always with kindness and respect.

Jerry's Words of Wisdom

I've been a huge fan of herbs ever since I was knee-high to the proverbial grasshopper. Why, my Grandma Putt showed me how to use the thick, slippery liquid in aloe leaves to soothe the numerous scrapes and cuts I always seemed to get. Later on, when I started adding herbs to my own garden, I discovered their healing powers all over again. It seems that the older I get, the more I learn, and the more I learn, the more herbs amaze me!

Grandma Putt's Old-Time Wisdom

- Grandma Putt taught me the value of plotting out a garden on paper before making my first plunge into the soil with a shovel.
- She told me to think in terms of themes, start small, and slowly expand as I grew more comfortable with her herb friends.
- She also kept a weather eye out, warning me to be prepared and to "never let Jack Frost bring any harm to them."

I'm happy to say that my Grandma Putt gave me a terrific foundation to grow on. Although I didn't know it then, she gave me a priceless gift: her old-time herbal wisdom that has withstood the test of time. To this day, I consider the herbs that I was introduced to at Grandma Putt's place to be among my closest friends. I've learned how to give them the best soil and just the right amount of water and light. I've also gotten pretty good at giving them the right "haircut" and even relocating my herbs when they put on a growth spurt. Then, come harvesttime, I'm almost a natural when it comes to knowing where to snip, pinch, tug, or pull at their peak of perfection.

It's Thyme for Lunch

From the garden, our herbal journey will take us into my favorite room in the house — the kitchen! Now, just stop for a moment, and try to imagine food without herbs. Talk about . . . well, there would be nothing to talk about. Pesto isn't pesto without basil and garlic. A potato is a plain old spud without freshly chopped chives. And I can't even imagine a nice, tall, soothing glass of iced tea without sprigs of fresh peppermint in it.

See what I mean? Herbs tantalize our taste buds and fill our bellies full of flavorful goodness. You'll be able to experience the goodness for yourself once you try my easy-to-make recipes. Why, I have no doubt that your family will be begging for seconds!

Sink or Swim: Bathing with Herbs

Once we're out of the kitchen, we'll venture into the bathroom. Just think — for a little liquid relaxation (the kind you don't drink), you can treat yourself to an aromatic herbal bath scented with chamomile, which is a well-deserved treat at the end of a long day. On the other hand, to rev up your engines and prepare yourself for a hectic day of activity, a nice hot ginger bath does the trick.

Herbs That Heal

Herbs can work wonders, so the final stop on our little journey together will bring us to Healthy Junction. That's right — herbs not only look great, taste great, and smell great, but when used correctly, they can also make us feel great, inside and out! How can you beat that? *You can't!*

With all the fuss and hype nowadays about the medicinal wonders of herbs, you'd think we had just discovered their healing powers. In fact, we're simply "rediscovering" natural remedies that have healed folks for thousands of years! My Grandma Putt knew all about them, as did her mother, as did her mother, and so on. We are simply living in what I call the Renaissance Age of Natural Healing.

Many people today are suddenly discovering the calming aroma of lavender and using it to cope with the stress-filled, hectic pace of the 21st century. But how many of you know that this fragrant herb was already the top choice among frantic European socialites in the 17th century? Ginseng is another "new" wonder, heralded as a memory-enhancer. Believe it or not, it's been helping to sharpen memories for over 2,000 years.

I could go on and on, but that's what the rest of this book is for. I've got over 1,300 herbal tips, tricks, and tonics to share with you that'll make you feel happy and healthy, and enrich your life.

So, are you ready to start the journey toward becoming a better gardener, a more resourceful cook, and a healthier person? If so, roll up your sleeves and let's get going!

A BLAST FROM THE PAST

Long before chemists and pharmacists began toiling inside high-tech laboratories to create modern-medicine breakthroughs, ancient Chinese women soothed irritated skin with calendula petals, 16th-century Europeans healed wounds with St. John's wort flowers, and North American natives fought colds with echinacea tea. And way before we had prescriptions to lower blood pressure and cholesterol levels, ancient physicians knew of the cholesterol-reducing abilities in garlic cloves.

CHAPTER

1

Getting Started in the Garden

Although I've been gardening for more than 50 years, I never get bored sowing, growing, weeding, and harvesting herbs. In fact, I get a little giddy each new planting season, just thinking about what herbs I'll grow and where I'll put them. Part of the fun and adventure comes in deciding what kind of herb garden I want to have this year.

I've found that the dead of winter is an ideal time to start making a plan. You can sit down at your dining room table with paper, pencil, and a few catalogs, and map out a spring garden, plant by plant, row by row. As you're doing this, think of yourself as an herbal horticultural architect, building a bountiful bevy of blooming beauty!

Dream of Themes

If you need some motivation to help you plan your garden, try a theme, or plan it to match a specific area of interest: If you love to cook spicy or tasty dishes, consider planning a garden that's loaded to the gills with basil, chives, cilantro, and thyme. These herbs will produce a bounty of flavor-filled leaves, flowers, and seeds. If you're a big tea sipper, why not grow your own teatime batch of peppermint, chamomile, and lemon balm?

An Inside Job

Whatever you decide, tender herbs deserve all the protection and TLC you can give them. That's why I recommend you start them from seed and grow them indoors, where you'll definitely have more control over the environment. After all, unless you have a roofless house, there's no need to worry about violent thunderstorms, scorching sun, or icy frosts coming in and destroying your seeds!

I recommend that you sow seeds indoors about 6 to 8 weeks before they'll be ready to transplant to your outdoor garden. This is where timing is critical. Check an almanac, and find out when the final spring frost in your area is predicted. Then count backwards 6 to 8 weeks on the calendar, and put an "X" marks the spot on your calendar — that's your date for starting seeds indoors.

Steppin' Out for Sprouts

Your seeds will sprout and grow into strong seedlings if you follow my foolproof, 10-step plan:

Step 1. Select quality seeds. Until you can harvest your own seeds, my number 1 rule is to only buy quality seeds from local nurseries or mail-order companies. Check out the expiration dates on the seed packets before plunking down your hard-earned cash. If they're too old or a bargain basement, pass them by.

Step 2. Choose loose soil. By this I mean top-quality soil, free of bugs and other thugs. You want soil that drains well. You can use either a pasteurized commercial soil mix or vermiculite, which is a soil-free, weed-free product. Both of these choices are delicate enough for seedling roots to stretch out in. And don't forget dessert! A half-cup of balanced organic fertilizer mixed into 5 gallons of the soil mix will help your seedlings grow up big, strong, and healthy.

Step 3. Provide a good home. If you're planning on planting an army, start your seeds in store-bought nursery flats. For smaller projects, use plastic pots, small clay pots, or even small, washed-out yogurt containers. Whatever you choose, make sure that there are drainage holes in the bottom; if they didn't come that way, you'll have to poke your own.

Step 4. Row, row, row your seeds. Space large seeds evenly in rows. Cluster itsy-bitsy, teeny-weeny seeds in little bunches. Gently push seeds into the soil with your thumb or forefinger, a pair of tweezers, or even a pencil until you can't "seed" them anymore.

Step 5. Be shady. Place the trays of seedlings somewhere out of direct light, where the temperature stays between 65 and 75°F; the top of the refrigerator is usually a pretty good place to start seeds.

Step 6. Water lightly. Going overboard on the H_2O will make the soil soggy and not very hospitable for your tender tykes. So use a fine-mist sprayer to keep the soil moist, but never soaked.

Step 7. Gimme shelter. To trap in moisture and warmth, cover the flat with a pane of glass, a sheet of plastic wrap, or an old, dampened towel.

Step 8. Give 'em some air. As soon as you see some sprouts sticking their little heads above the soil, remove the glass or plastic wrap. This will allow air to circulate, and keep your seedlings free of disease.

Step 9. Head for the sun. Young seedlings need plenty of sun to grow; most prefer a minimum of 6 hours of light each day, preferably in the form of sunlight streaming through a window. Fluorescent lights will also work, especially if you live in an area with lots of overcast, cloudy skies.

Step 10. Coax them outdoors. When you celebrate your seedlings' 8-week birthday, you can gradually start introducing them to the great outdoors. Shoot for a couple of hours a day for the first few days, then work your way up to 24 hours of outdoor exposure before you actually transplant them.

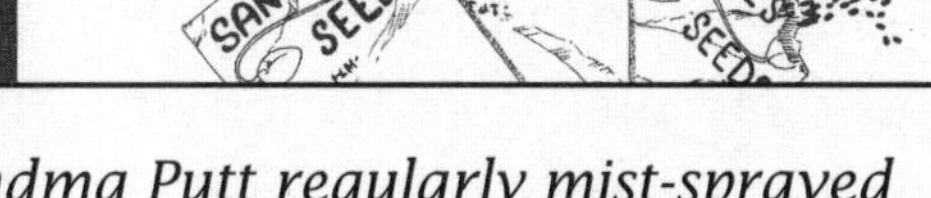

Seed Starter Tonic

After planting her seeds, Grandma Putt regularly mist-sprayed them (and later, her seedlings, too) with this super tonic:

¼ cup of Barnyard Booster*
¼ cup of soapy water
¼ cup of tea water

Stir the ingredients into 2 gallons of water, and then pour into a mist sprayer. Your seedlings will love you for it!

*For an ample supply of Barnyard Booster, mix 5 lbs. of manure, 5 lbs. of peat moss, 5 lbs. of gypsum, and 2½ lbs. of garden food, and set aside to "age" until you're ready to use it!

Operation: Transplant

Once your seedlings are old enough to be moved outdoors, it's time to transplant! Just make sure that Jack Frost's final chill has long gone. Also, pick a cloudy day to perform this operation, my fellow garden doctors — it will be less stressful on your little green friends! You can also transplant in the evening, when the sunshine starts to fade. Just make sure you have enough light to see what you're doing, or you're liable to end up with rows that are as crooked as the day is long — oops!

Tips for the Impatient Gardener

Don't want to mess with sowing seed by hand? Or you're new to gardening and don't want to bother? Then it's time for Plan B — head to your local nursery and pick up a bunch of pregrown bedding herbs. But Buyer Beware! Just remember, as with anything else, you get what you pay for. This is no time to head for the bargain table in the back of the store. A droopy-looking seedling has two strikes against it, and there's virtually no chance of it making a fighting comeback in your garden.

Healthy herbal youngsters, on the other hand, should look the part — fresh and vibrant. They will if they've been given just the right water, light, and soil care. The little bit of TLC the grower gave the plants makes them definitely worth the price. Ask when new plants are going to be delivered, and then be the first in line.

It should go without saying that the soil should be clear of all weeds, old roots, clods of dirt, and stones. Then take a trowel and scoop out a hole wide enough so that the roots of your transplanted seedlings won't feel like their elbows are stuck in their ribs. Place a seedling into the ground, straight and tall like a soldier, and gently firm the soil around it with your fingertips. Finish the operation by watering the seedling with a gentle mist from your garden hose or a sprinkling from a watering can.

Scouting Around for Garden Real Estate

Once you've decided which herbs you're going to grow, then you must determine where you're going to grow them. Again, the key is location, location, location! The two biggest selling points (and the difference between success and failure) in the herb gardening world are the amount of sun and the drainage of the soil.

Sun and soil determine how many different types of herbs could thrive in your garden. Obviously, properties that have different soil conditions as well as shady and sunny areas can grow a wide variety of herbs. For best results, consult my handy-dandy chart on page 8 to learn where some of the more popular herbs grow best.

Who Loves the Sun and Who Doesn't

Sun-Lovin' Herbs

- Anise hyssop ☼
- Bee balm ☼
- Calendula ☼ ◐
- Chamomile ☼ ◐
- Fennel ☼
- Lavender ☼
- Rosemary ☼ ◐
- Sage ☼ ◐
- Thyme ☼ ◐

Made-in-the-Shade Herbs

- Angelica ◐
- Chervil ◐
- Mints ☼ ◐
- Parsley ☼ ◐
- Sweet woodruff ●

Cool-Climate Herbs

- Chives (Zones 3–9)
- Cilantro (Zones 2–9)
- Garlic (Zones 5–11)
- Sweet cicely (Zones 3–7)
- Yarrow (Zones 2–8)

Warm-Climate Herbs

- Aloe (Zones 9–11)
- Basil (annual)
- Ginger (Zones 9–11)
- Lemon verbena (Zones 9–11)
- Marigold (annual)

Legend full sun ☼ partial shade ◐ shade ●

Don't Be Foiled by Poor Soil!

Some folks are born with cavity-free teeth, 20/20 eyesight, and a strong heart. If that's you, then you should rejoice in your good genes and good fortune; we should all be so lucky! If you are that lucky, then you just may have inherited healthy soil, too. But if you're like most of us, you've got a mixed bag of dirt that needs anywhere from a little to a lot of tending.

Think of soil as Mother Nature's Boardinghouse — your herbs' food provider. Herbs need a healthy, balanced diet of nitrogen, phosphorus, and potassium. To find out how healthy your soil is, just give it my old-fashioned squeeze test. Simply grab a handful of moist garden soil and gently squeeze it. Then open your hand. If the ball of soil crumbles easily, you've got loamy or sandy soil. A lot of herbs dig this type of soil.

If the soil stays as hard as a baseball, then it is high in clay, or maybe silt. Clay soil drains poorly, holding too much water during wet spells and drying or cracking during dry times. Either way, it can spell D-E-A-T-H for your herbs.

But don't give up: Make a raised bed by raking the soil 4 to 8 inches deep above ground level and adding a 2- to 3-inch layer of compost on top of it. Raised beds provide excellent drainage, are easy to maintain, and enable many herbs to thrive in places where they'd have no more than a snowball's chance in h-e-l-l of surviving!

Test Your Soil

Next, you need to figure out if your soil is acidic or alkaline. Take a soil sample to your local county Cooperative Extension Service, or buy a home test kit at

Know Your Zone!

When it's cold outside, we reach for an overcoat, hat, and gloves. When it's sizzling hot, we slip into tank tops and shorts, and smear on the sunscreen. Unfortunately, herbs aren't able to adapt to climate changes as easily as we do. So they must rely upon the kindness of strangers — *you!*

What can you do? Plan ahead, and learn all about how herbs are ranked by "hardiness." It's simple, really: the hardier the herb, the better it can tolerate extreme cold temperatures. The United States is divided up into 11 different temperature zones when it comes to herb growing. Hot spots like southern Florida and southern California rank as 10s and 11s (temperatures rarely fall below 40ºF), while cold places like northern Minnesota and North Dakota fall into the 2 and 3 Zones (temperatures reach minus-40ºF). So before you plant, KNOW YOUR HARDINESS ZONE!

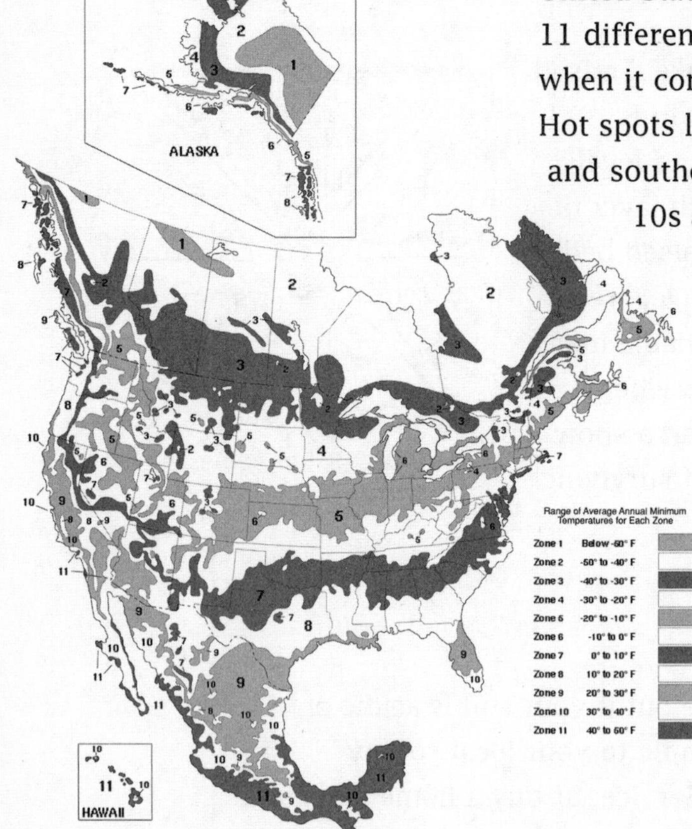

your local garden center or from one of the mail-order catalogs. The acidity of soil is measured by its pH ("potential of hydrogen"), on a scale of 0 to 14. The midpoint, or 7, is neutral and tells you that your soil is neither acidic nor alkaline. Anything above 7 is alkaline soil; anything below 7 is acidic soil. Most herbs prefer a pH that's between 5.5 and 7.5.

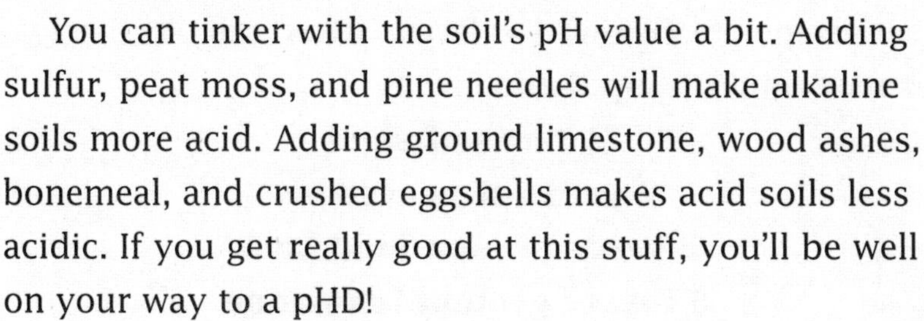

You can tinker with the soil's pH value a bit. Adding sulfur, peat moss, and pine needles will make alkaline soils more acid. Adding ground limestone, wood ashes, bonemeal, and crushed eggshells makes acid soils less acidic. If you get really good at this stuff, you'll be well on your way to a pHD!

All-Purpose Organic Fertilizer

This is how my Grandma Putt made her fabulous All-Purpose Organic Fertilizer:

1 part dehydrated manure
1 part bonemeal
3 parts granite dust
5 parts seaweed meal

She mixed these ingredients up in a large, old wheelbarrow. Then come chow time, she wheeled it out into the garden and put it into action!

The Direct Approach

Sowing seeds directly into your outdoor garden is the easiest way to grow many herbs, especially calendula, caraway, dill, fennel, and summer savory.

Before you plant, prepare the soil by raking it free of rocks and other debris. If your site is less than ideal, then before planting, you should condition the soil. For smaller areas, mix up a batch of my Soil Booster Mix (see recipe box below). For larger areas, call out the artillery and mix up the following:

2 yards of sand
2 yards of peat moss
2 yards of shredded bark
5 lbs. of ground limestone
5 lbs. of 5-10-10 fertilizer
1 lb. of iron sulfate

This will give you about 5 inches of soil in an area measuring 25 sq. ft. Work it into the soil, and then let it set for several months before planting.

Soil Booster Mix

Here's a super Soil Booster Mix that'll really send your herbs a-flyin':

5 lbs. of lime
5 lbs. of gypsum
1 lb. of 5-10-5 garden food
½ cup of Epsom salts

Work this mix into each 50 sq. ft. of herb garden area to a depth of 12 to 18 inches, and then let it set for 7 to 10 days.

For small seeds, sprinkle them about an inch apart in straight rows over the soil. For large seeds, space them out a couple of inches, and use your thumb to gently push them about 1/8 inch into the soil. Then cover the seeds with a thin layer of soil.

Once you've finished planting, wet the seedbed with water from a watering can or a hose with a fine misting spray. Be careful — you don't want to accidentally wash the seeds away. Give them a drink every day or so, except when Mother Nature provides the water.

Feed 'em Fertilizer

Always remember that your herbs need a spring feeding at the start of the growing season. In most cases, an inch-thick layer of well-made compost is all herbs need. But some plants need an extra boost. In those cases, apply Grandma Putt's All-Purpose Organic Fertilizer (see page 11) to the planting beds.

After that initial feeding, feed your herb garden every 6 weeks with my Herb Booster Tonic (see the recipe on page 14). But don't forget that you should avoid heavy or frequent applications of fertilizer during the growing season. This can cause low oil production or leggy growth.

Jerry's Words of Wisdom

"A gardener must weed what he sows, so never plant more herbs than you can weed!"

Herb Booster Tonic

Make this fabulous Herb Booster Tonic by combining:

1 bottle of beer

½ cup of Murphy's Oil Soap

1 cup of ammonia

½ cup of corn syrup

Mix these ingredients in a 20 gallon hose-end sprayer jar, then spray all of your herbs thoroughly.

Multiply the Little Guys!

Just like your hair needs regular grooming, so does your herb garden. Regular rejuvenation will boot out old, dying plants and make way for healthy, young ones. There are many different ways to "thin the ranks," as we say professionally. Here are some of the more common tactics:

- **Divisions.** You can stop aggressive spreaders or replace older plants by digging them up and separating them into several smaller clumps. Replant the healthiest sections and discard any dead, diseased, or dying portions. Mint and chives are two herbs that thrive when you divide them.
- **Cuttings.** This method involves growing new herbs from pieces of roots or stems of established plants. Rooted cuttings are little

clones of their parent herbs. Taking cuttings is easy to do; simply use pruning shears to make a slanting cut just below the lowest set of leaves of a 3- to 4-inch terminal shoot. Plant the cuttings in moist potting mix. Bee balm, lavender, lemon verbena, mint, rosemary, and thyme are ideal cutting candidates.

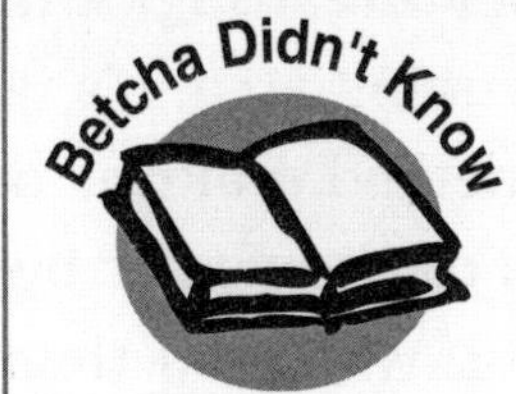

Rosemary, winter savory, sage, and thyme can all be layered.

• **Layerings.** This works well for semi-woody herbs. If you're going to try this, allow long shoots to develop roots while they are still attached to the parent plant. Simply make a small nick in the stem where you want roots to grow, and pin the stem to the ground using a stick or large paper clips. Once a sturdy set of roots develops, cut the layered shoot free from the parent plant, just beyond the roots, and replant it.

Herbal Rejuvenation

About midway through the growing season, all herbs need a helping hand unloading old flowering tops and dead leaves. That's where you come in. Here are some ways to keep your herbs shipshape with fresh foliage all season long:

• **Pinching.** For both tender annuals and perennial herbs, pinch off the soft growth by using your thumb and forefinger.

• **Deadheading.** Although the term sounds ghastly to the uninitiated, it's really for your herbs' own good. This method removes the faded flowers with garden shears or clippers or by pinching them off with your thumb and forefinger, to encourage new flowers to form. You can do this on any flowering herb, including bee balm, calendula, and echinacea.

• **Staking.** For tall herbs like borage, dill, and fennel, you'll need to stake them up to keep them from becoming top-heavy. You should initially stake plants when you set them out using twigs, bamboo, wire, or plastic. Make sure the stakes will be 6 inches shorter than the mature height of the plant, place them behind the plants, and sink them into the ground. Loosely secure the plant to the stake with strips of old panty hose, Velcro, twist ties, or plant clips.

Keeping Insects and Diseases at Bay

You can make your garden as safe and secure as Fort Knox when it comes to undesirables. Over the years, I've learned a thing or two about how to manhandle the bad bugs and keep garden diseases away. Here are a few of my secrets.

Good Bug, Bad Bug

Some herbs can be mighty powerful protectors of the rest of your garden against bad bugs and critters. These include anise, borage, cilantro, dill, scented geranium, mint, rosemary, and sage.

Other herbs actually have a way of recruiting beneficial insects like lady beetles, parasitic wasps, and lacewings. What happens is that a mini–Neighborhood Watch program develops — the good bugs take care of the bad bugs, and the garden plants benefit. These good neighbor herbs include anise, chamomile, dill, fennel, mint, and yarrow.

And it always pays to use good old common sense — if you notice that pests are picking on a particular type of plant, don't just sit there, bring on the herbal allies! How? By surrounding the plant with different herbs that give off a range of fragrances that will confuse the pest.

Natural Bug-Busting Juice

Keep varmints out of your garden with my Natural Bug-Busting Juice:

¼ cup of marigold flower tops
¼ cup of geranium flower tops
¼ cup of garlic cloves, minced

Chop these ingredients finely and thoroughly mix them in 5 gallons of warm water. Let the mix set overnight, add it to your watering can, and sprinkle it over your garden.

All-Season Clean-Up Tonic

To keep your herbs happy and healthy, bathe them every 3 weeks until the first hard frost with my All-Season Clean-Up Tonic:

1 cup of liquid dish soap

1 cup of chewing tobacco juice*

1 cup of antiseptic mouthwash

Mix these together and pour them into the jar of a 20 gallon hose-end sprayer, filling the balance of the jar with warm water.

*Tobacco juice: ½ handful of chewing tobacco wrapped in a piece of old panty hose and soaked in 1 gallon of hot water until the mix is dark brown. Strain and store until ready to use.

Disease Prevention

You can keep your herb garden virtually disease-free by practicing these three habits:

1. Provide good air circulation among the plants so that they have enough room to grow. This reduces mildew, leaf spot, and stem rot.

2. Maintain well-drained soil to steer clear of root, crown, and stem rot.

3. Go easy on the fertilizer. Herbs that OD on nitrogen become easy prey for slugs, snails, rot, and other garden thugs.

So, my dear gardening friends, as you can see, a healthy crop of herbs year after year is just a few short, simple steps away. And the best part is your reward — a bounty of tasty goodness for many years to come!

CHAPTER 2

Growing Great Indoor Companions

Want to know a surefire way to never let the bitter cold or sun-baked heat affect your herbs? Grow them inside! Yep, that's right — many herbs are ideally suited for indoor life. They can add flavor and color to your kitchen, living room, and even your bathroom! So with that said, welcome to the world of indoor landscaping!

Whether you're a city-dwelling herb-lover living in a high-rise apartment or a displaced gardener going back-to-the-land in the cold tundra of Alaska, you don't have to toss in the trowel. You can set up your own little garden plot right there in the comfort and safety of your own home. So vegetate no more!

Herbs, Contain Yourself!

Growing herbs in pots has become quite popular, and for good reason. You can easily move them around to different locations in the house, and you can establish mini "theme" gardens — for kitchen wizardry, for medicinal use, or just to delight your senses with fragrance and greenery. Why, you can even mix and match to do all three at once!

Decisions, decisions. With so many herbs to choose from, which ones should you plant in pots? It's certainly up to you, although if you're stumped for ideas, consult the chart on page 21 for some of my favorite picks.

If you want to feel like you've just inhaled a breath of fresh air each time you step inside your house or open a window, consider framing your kitchen window, front door, or back door with container pots of chamomile, lavender, pennyroyal, and sage. Their scents are just delightful!

Choosing Herbs to Grow Indoors

Sow from Seed

- Basil
- Chervil
- Cilantro
- Dill
- Oregano
- Parsley
- Summer savory

Create from Cuttings

- Basil
- Mint
- Oregano
- Rosemary
- Sage
- Thyme

Transplant from the Garden

- Chives
- Lavender
- Lemon verbena
- Mint
- Rosemary
- Sage
- Summer savory
- Thyme

Picking Perfect Pots

Bigger is better when it comes to choosing pots and containers for your fast-growing herbs. You'll benefit as well, because larger pots (14 inches or more) don't require as much attention as smaller ones, and they're easier to work with. Plus, there's the obvious advantage that they'll accommodate more plants.

Ideally, you should have an ample supply of pots of varying sizes on hand, so that when your herbs get too big for their britches, you can transplant them to bigger pots. I always keep several different sizes kicking around the old potting shed

A Sure Fit

The depth and the width of the container you choose should always be considered when determining the best pot for your herbs. Use these general guidelines.

- **4-inch container:** ideal for basil seedlings, sweet marjoram seedlings, and young thyme divisions
- **6-inch container:** perfect for mature basil, clumps of chives, oregano, summer savory, and thyme
- **8-inch container:** your best bet for marigolds, dill, and sage
- **12-inch container:** home-sweet-home for scented geraniums, catnip, fennel, lavender, mints, and rosemary
- **14-inch or larger container:** just right for bay tree and lemon verbena

"just-in-case" . . . just-in-case I get back from vacation and find a friend gone wild, just-in-case the dog runs over and breaks one of the pots, and just-in-case I feel like puttering around in my indoor herb garden. As you can see, "just-in-case" is a pretty darn important reason; remember it the next time your significant other trips over the important stuff that we gardeners tend to accumulate.

Sizing Up the Situation

A little forethought goes a long way: Matching the right herb to the right-size container will prevent a lot of problems down the road. Shoehorning herbs into tight quarters creates unneeded risk for getting their overgrown roots tangled up in knots and starving from not enough nutrients in their soil. We all experience growing pains, but please, these pains will seem like torture!

Teatime

If you're a true tea-totaler, keep your favorite blends close at hand. In separate containers, keep these herbs "brewing" in and around your kitchen:

- **Chamomile**
- **Lemon balm**
- **Lemon verbena**
- **Peppermint**

Container Explainer

Containers come in all different types of materials, including plastic, terra cotta, and clay. Herbs do best in clay pots, which come closest to reproducing the natural conditions of growing in good old Mother Earth.

You can also insert these "work shoes" into decorative plastic, glass, metal, ceramic, or wood containers ("dress shoes") to match the decor of your home. *Terra cotta,* which is Italian for "baked earth," is usually reddish orange in color; clay pots come in many colors. The thing that's good *and* bad about these pots is that they are porous, so they breathe, but they also lose a lot of water. Herbs in particular are very water sensitive, so you have to keep a close eye on them to make sure they don't die of thirst.

Whether you opt for plastic, clay, or other containers, make sure the pot has at least one drainage hole in the bottom. Otherwise, excess water may collect there and cause roots to rot — or even the whole plant to die. To keep water from running out the bottom when you water, place a few pebbles or small pieces of broken

Keep-'em-Clean Tonic

Sometimes the insides of my pots develop a slimy film from algae or a white residue of salt leaching out from the soil. Before reusing clay or plastic pots, wash them first in this easy-to-make solution that'll prevent slimy buildup. Just combine all of the ingredients in a large plastic bucket, let the pots soak for 15 minutes or so, then scrub them clean with one of those dishwashing scrubber pads. Rinse well!

½ oz. of bleach
1 oz. of liquid dish soap
1 tbsp. of instant tea
½ oz. of hydrogen peroxide
½ oz. of antiseptic mouthwash
1 qt. of warm water

pottery to partially cover the drainage hole before adding the soil.

Don't forget to put the right type of saucer or tray under indoor containers! Moisture seeping through unglazed clay can damage tabletops and floors, so you're better off with plastic, glass, rubber, china, or other nonporous catchers. A layer of small pebbles in the saucer will keep the container's drainage holes above water.

The Soil Reason for Success

As tempting as it may seem, you can't simply go out to your garden and scoop up some soil to use for your indoor herbs. It may seem like a great idea, but garden soil is usually too heavy for indoor plants — it's about as comfortable as having a 150-pound bull mastiff sitting in your lap. Trust me, you don't want to go there!

If you're only planning to grow a handful of herbs, you may prefer to buy a bag of commercially prepared professional potting soil. But if you plan on creating an herbal jungle inside your home, you can save a lot of time and money by making your own supply of potting soil. Here's what you should do.

First, just dig up a bunch of the best soil from your garden. Then add some peat moss to clay or sandy soils, which will help absorb moisture. While you're at it, throw in some finished compost, too. Finally, add clean coarse sand, vermiculite, or perlite — all of which are readily available at most garden centers. Vermiculite and perlite are mineral particles that have a consistency like popcorn, and they help to keep the mixture porous yet moist.

I told you to use containers that have adequate drainage holes in the bottom, and now you may be wondering how to keep the potting soil from falling out. Well, that's easy: Just moisten the mix before you put it in the container!

Jerry's Potting Soil

My perfect blend of soil for growing indoor herbs is made by mixing:

1 part sharp sand

1 part clay loam

1 part organic matter

Per peck of soil mixture, I add ½ cup of Epsom salts, ½ cup of dried coffee grounds, and 4 eggshells, dried and crushed into a powder. Come and get it!

A Little TLC

You certainly won't need to use a rake or garden hose on your indoor potted herbs. In fact, you won't need to roll up your sleeves or get anywhere near as dirty as you might if you had an entire garden plot to dig in. But that doesn't mean it's any less fun to grow herbs in your home. Here are some of my "insider's tips" on how to make them thrive.

Water Works

Stick your forefinger out straight and determine where it measures an inch from the tip. Maybe it's your first knuckle, maybe not. Just remember where it is, because you've just made your first indoor gardening tool — a handy-dandy, never-to-be-misplaced water marker.

Every couple of days, check to see if your herbs are thirsty by pushing your finger into the soil about an inch. If the top soil in that inch range is dry, then you know that it's time to water.

Once a month, I want you to treat your plants to a steam bath in the loo. Take a large bucket and fill it with steaming hot water. Then lay a narrow wooden board (or a couple of chopsticks, if the bucket isn't too

Healthy Herb Tonic

Here's a tonic I first learned from Grandma Putt. To keep her herbs healthy, she mist-sprayed them every week or so with this tonic:

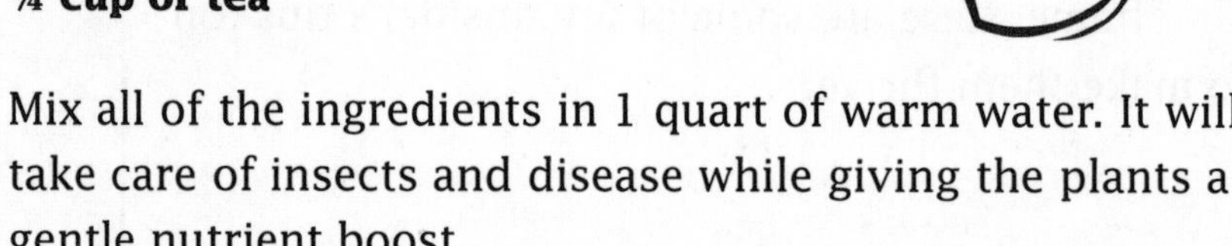

1 tbsp. of liquid dish soap

1 tbsp. of antiseptic mouthwash

1 tbsp. of ammonia

¼ cup of tea

Mix all of the ingredients in 1 quart of warm water. It will take care of insects and disease while giving the plants a gentle nutrient boost.

wide) across its top. Carefully place the potted plant on top of the board. Shut the bathroom door and let the herb enjoy a 5-minute, private sauna. It'll do wonders for its delicate complexion, not to mention its outlook on life!

For the sake of having healthy plants (and a healthy you!), you should consider investing in a humidifier for the dry winter months. Herbs prefer humidity levels of 50 percent or higher when they're indoors. You'll appreciate the added moisture, too — you'll be less likely to get those shocking, static electricity zaps created by walking on the carpet.

Be Wise and Fertilize

Since indoor plants have only a small amount of soil to draw moisture and nutrients from, it's up to you to feed them regularly by mist-spraying them once a week or so with Grandma Putt's Healthy Herb Tonic (see page 28).

But if you're thinking you can't be bothered, you might try using time-release fertilizers at potting time. They come as small sticks that you sink into the soil or tiny beads you spoon onto the soil surface. Or, every couple of weeks you can add fish emulsion or diluted liquid fertilizer to your watering can. Just follow the instructions on the label.

Let There Be Light . . . and Warmth

Most herbs need at least 6 to 8 hours of sunlight a day to grow their very best. If you're caught in a week's worth of rainy days, old-style fluorescent lights and 60-watt lightbulbs make adequate light substitutes. Better yet, the next time you're at the hardware store, pick up a grow-light or full-spectrum fluorescent light and keep it handy for just such emergencies.

Temperature-wise, indoor herbs prefer daytime temperatures that range from 65 to 70°F and nighttime temperatures above 55°F.

Vacation Tip

We all need to take a break from our job every now and then and enjoy a little R and R. So if that means heading for warmer climes for a 2-week vacation, you can always persuade a relative, friend, or neighbor to "plant-sit" and leave him or her watering instructions for your herbs.

But sometimes you can't find anybody. If that's the case, then there's another way to take care of your indoor potted pots from a distance — by putting them in your bathtub! Here's what you should do.

Cut a length of glass lamp wicking (available from craft stores) for each herb plant. Bury the wick in the soil and place the other end in a large bucket of water that has been elevated (you can just set it on a crate or some other sturdy box). Get this all set up a few days before you head out, to make sure everything's in working order. Test it out by touching the exposed part of the wick. If it's wet, the wicking's working! If it's not, then what? After a little trial and error, you'll discover that a large bucket of water is enough to keep several plants quenched for up to 3 weeks. Isn't that neat?

Don't Stew about Pruning

Even indoor plants need to be tamed to keep them from growing wild. I tell folks that plants, just like fingernails, need occasional manicures. Here's how to properly give your herbs a much needed "plant-i-cure."

Regularly remove old flower heads to trigger growth in younger buds. Also, use your finger and thumbnail to pinch off the tip of the main and side leaf shoots, which will encourage new growth. Pinching helps you control the growth and promotes a compact, bushy look, which is actually best for the plant.

For more-involved pruning, you'll need a sharp knife or scissors. A word of warning — make sure they are sharp! How would you like it if your hairdresser or barber cut your hair with a dull pair of scissors? I know I wouldn't! Prune by making your cuts just above a bud pointed in the direction you want the new shoot to grow. Pruning gets rid of diseased portions of a plant and clears the way for healthy tissue to grow and bloom.

Jerry's Words of Wisdom

"Always disinfect your pruning tools with rubbing alcohol before using them — and when you switch to another plant — to keep from spreading germs among your herbs."

Moving Plants Indoors in the Fall

Just about the time you find yourself reaching for a sweater before the first fall frost is your cue to move your outdoor herbs inside for the winter. Dig up as many plants as you want to keep indoors, and put them in pots; but heed these words of caution:

Keep the relocated outdoor plants far away from your year-round, indoor plants!

These newcomers have spent the entire summer being exposed to insects, pests, and possibly diseases, and the last thing you want to do is spread any of these things to your healthy indoor plants. So even before you bring the plants into your home, give them a thorough exam. Check the underside of the leaves, and hose them down with Knock-'em-Dead Insect Spray (see my easy-as-pie recipe below).

Knock-'em-Dead Insect Spray

To make this potent brew, mix:

6 cloves of garlic (chopped finely)

1 small onion (chopped finely)

1 tbsp. of cayenne pepper

1 tbsp. of dish soap

Add this fiery combination to 1 quart of warm water, let it sit overnight, and then mist your plants with it. But be careful — you've got yourself one heck of a weapon against pesky insects!

As for moving specific outdoor herbs indoors, I always trim mature plants such as geraniums, lavender, and sweet marjoram back by one-third their full height, to make them more manageable. Place them inside containers that are slightly bigger than their roots, and then fill in the rest with your potting soil mix. Then don't panic if your lemon verbena or other herbs suddenly shed some of their leaves when you move them indoors. That's only a sign of hibernation. Keep them cool, watered, and fertilized, and they will grow back as good as new!

Moving Plants Back Outdoors in the Spring

The key to moving indoor herbs outdoors for their summer vacation is patience. You've pampered your plants all winter long, protecting them from Mother Nature's wrath. So come spring, reintroduce them to the great outdoors gradually. Take your plants out for a couple of hours each day, kind of like recess when you were in school. Over the course of a week to 10 days, build up their outdoor time to a full day. Just before they're outside for good, give them one final bath with my Super Send-Off Spray (see below). Then they'll be suited down to the ground!

You've just gotta love the great indoors! As I've told you in this chapter, herbs make terrific roommates if you treat them right, no matter where you live. So just keep sowing and growing, and soon you'll have one great big happy green family!

Help Your Herbs See the Light

All plants lean into the sunlight, so every few days, give the container a quarter turn so all sides of the herb can see the light.

Super Send-Off Spray

This spray will help your herbs "stand tall" against the toughest yard and garden bullies:

1 tbsp. of Murphy's Oil Soap
1 tbsp. of antiseptic mouthwash
1 tbsp. of ammonia
1 tbsp. of instant tea

Mix all of these ingredients in a gallon of warm water. Add it to your sprayer and sprinkle it over your herbs once they're in their summer vacation homes.

CHAPTER 3

Picking, Stocking, and Storing Herbs

Harvesting your herbs is a perfect way to celebrate your botanical bounty. Unlike working in the fields, when it's time to harvest herbs, you can sleep in, but just don't stay in the sack until noon!

The ideal time to gather herbs is mid-morning, just after the dew has dried but before the beaming sun makes everything hot and wilted. This is the time of day when the plants' essential oils are greatest. Plucking leaves, flowers, and flowering tops in mid-morning just about guarantees that you will get them at their peak, in terms of both flavor and medicinal goodness.

The Dos and Don'ts of Harvesting

Here are a few things to keep in mind when gathering ripe-and-ready herbs from your garden:

- **Do** snip flowers and leaves with a pair of scissors or pruning shears for clean cuts.
- **Don't** rip off flowers and leaves with your bare hands. The jagged ends can weaken the rest of the plant.
- **Do** cut the stem just above a leaf where you want to encourage new, healthy growth.
- **Don't** harvest moldy, bug-infested, diseased, or wilted parts of the plant.
- **Do** use a spray bottle or fine-mist setting to gently remove bugs, dirt, and other debris from the harvested herbs.
- **Don't** collect more than you can use. Remember the old saying, "Waste not, want not!"
- **Do** keep harvested herbs in brown paper bags that "breathe" while drying them.
- **Don't** try to dry herbs in plastic bags. They encourage mold and mildew.
- **Do** pat dry cleaned herbs with paper towels before hanging them up to dry.

When to harvest — well, that depends on the herb and the climate. But generally, roots are best harvested in the spring or fall. Leaves from plants with volatile oils — such as lemon balm and mints — should be gathered in the spring, when the flowers are budding. Stems should be collected once the flowers start to open.

Harvesting is fun, and it can be as simple as snipping a sprig of rosemary and dropping it in a glass of wine. So grab your pruning shears or garden scissors, along with an easy-to-tote basket, and let's head out to the garden!

Drying Herbs

Yes, fresh is best — the flavor is intense and the aroma is tantalizing. But there are times when dry can be mighty fine! If you dry and store garden-grown herbs the right way, you can keep their medicinal and culinary magic alive year-round. And you're in luck because I'm here to show you how!

Picture yourself in the cold, dark, depressing depths of winter. The temperature's about minus 20°F, the wind's a-howlin', and you can't remember the last time you saw the sun. But you're inside your cozy home, treating yourself and a friend to a pot of relaxing chamomile tea. You know the tea will taste

great because you grew the herbs and harvested and dried them yourself.

Or you're ready to season the salmon fillets you're serving to your guests, and no ordinary spice will do. You reach for your homegrown supply of dried thyme, garlic, and basil, and your mouth starts to water! Believe you me, it doesn't get any better than that. There are many ways to dry fresh-picked herbs; I'll describe some of my favorites and let you decide what's best.

Air-Drying

No, not hair-drying, although this method is by far and away the most common. To air-dry, collect leafy stalks in small bunches, rather than one gigantic bunch. If you think small, the herbs will dry quickly. If you think you will save time by drying all of your harvest in one big clump, guess again! Not only will it take ages to dry this way, it will probably get moldy in the process. Yuck!

Once you've got your collection in neat, small bunches, tie them together with rubber bands or string. Find a dry, dim location in your home. If you have an herb rack, just attach the bunches with the rubber bands right on the rack. Or if you have ceiling beams, hang the herb bundles from them, using thumbtacks.

Be sure to hang the bundles upside down, with the stems pointing up. You'll find that herbs like chamomile, lavender, and mint have stems that serve as especially convenient handles for air-drying.

Leave the herbs hanging for anywhere from 5 days to a couple of weeks. Take the bundles down when the herbs are just barely dry — in other words, don't wait until they are so dry they fall into crumbs at the mere touch of a finger and thumb! Gently remove the leaves from the stems and store them in an airtight glass container. You can crumble the herbs more finely when you're ready to use them.

Plan Ahead

You can also keep a week's supply of fresh cooking herbs inside the crisper drawer of your refrigerator. Just put the clean, towel-dried herbs in resealable plastic baggies, to lock the flavor in and keep the flavor-sapping moisture out.

Screen-Drying

Some flowering herbs, such as calendula, are better if they're dried on screens rather than hung from rafters. For these herbs, use an old window screen and place the four corners on some boards, cement blocks, or thick books. (Finally! a use for those hardcover dictionaries or encyclopedias that you've been holding onto for years!)

You need some space between the screen and the ground to allow air to circulate in and around the plants. Pick a well-ventilated place out of direct sunlight. Then place the flowers and leafy stems in rows, being careful that they don't touch each another (overlapping leaves will not dry evenly). In a few days, gently flip them over, so that you expose all surfaces to air for even drying.

Brown-Bag Drying

I'm the king of recycling stuff, and there's no better way to reuse brown lunch bags than as delightful mini-dryers for harvested herbs. Save 'em up, and just before the killing frost, tuck small bunches of herbs into each bag. Be careful not to overstuff them — give the herbs a little elbowroom, so that air can circulate around them. Then use a marker pen to record the name of the herb and the date you collected it. That way, you don't have to rely on your memory. Place the bags in a dry, shaded area, and check on them in about a week. If they are still a bit moist, you can spread them out on newspapers for a day or so until they're completely dry.

Microwave Power

Got to prepare dinner for the boss, and you're in a super rush? Microwaving herbs can speed up the drying process. But you need to be careful not to "overzap" your harvested herbs, or you'll end up with a bunch of "crispy critters."

Although the drying time will vary from herb to herb, as a general rule it takes 1 to 3 minutes to dry a small bunch of herbs. I like to set my microwave at its lowest setting for 30-second intervals so that I can check the herbs and make sure that they're crisp but not overdone. Parsley is an ideal herb to dry in the microwave, especially on your "practice run"!

Dehydrators

If you're lucky enough to have a food dehydrator, put it to good use. Just place your herbs flat on the racks. In a matter of 2 to 3 hours, you can dry a whole bunch of freshly picked herbs. I've found that basil and other herbs sporting large, fleshy leaves make ideal candidates for the dehydrator. But just like with the microwave, don't try to get too far ahead of yourself — dry only one type of herb at a time.

Strip Those Stems

Don't just throw the herbs into the microwave oven — strip them from the stem. Then place them flat on a paper towel or paper plate. And microwave only one type of herb at a time.

Freezing Herbs

Don't give your harvested herbs the cold shoulder — just give them a little chill to keep them powerful and potent! All you need are some pint-size plastic freezer bags (resealable ones are best) and ID labels.

Once you've harvested the herbs, mist them clean with a fine spray and gently pat them completely dry. Place them in the plastic bags, and be generous with the space — don't try to stick too many herbs in one bag. Then, don't forget to label the bags!

You can also put sprigs of some herbs in ice-cube trays and fill them with water. The next time you want to enhance the flavor of iced tea, for instance, drop a few pepperminted ice cubes into the glass. You won't believe that you never thought of this trick before!

Frozen herbs keep their flavor for a very long time. Why, I've got some 2-year-old parsley in the freezer that tastes as good as it did the day I harvested it. If I had to choose, these are herbs that I think freeze the best: basil, chervil, dill, lemon balm, lemon verbena, marjoram, parsley, peppermint, rosemary, sage, spearmint, tarragon, and thyme.

For a less chilling experience, you can also keep a week's supply of fresh cooking herbs inside the crisper drawer of your refrigerator. Again, just put the clean, towel-dried herbs in resealable plastic baggies, to lock in their flavor and keep out flavor-sapping moisture.

Storage Containers

Once the harvested leaves, flowers, or other parts of the plant are completely dry, strip them from the stems by gently running your index finger and thumb from top to bottom. You're now ready to store them.

If you don't already have a supply of canning jars on hand, remember this: Throughout the year, save those glass pickle jars! Ditto for empty mayonnaise bottles and jelly jars. They all make ideal storage containers for dried, harvested herbs. Before using them, scrub the jars and lids with hot soapy water, rinse them thoroughly to remove any residue, and let them air-dry.

I've found that, ideally, dark-colored glass jars or bottles work best because they seal in the flavor *and* shut out the light. Just don't make the same mistake that I once did, and try to store your herbs in plastic containers; air and moisture can wiggle their way in and zap the herb of its flavor and potency.

Cooking Tip

To substitute dried herbs for fresh ones in recipes, reduce the amount by one third to one half to compensate. So if your recipe calls for 3 teaspoons of fresh dill, substitute 1 to 1½ teaspoons of dried dill.

Storage Conditions

The cabinet right above your stove may seem like an ideal place to stash containers of dried herbs. After all, it's right within eyesight, plus they'll be easy to reach. But that's actually about the worst place to store your herbs! Just like Kryptonite and Superman, the heat from the stovetop will render them powerless in no time at all.

I also tell folks to keep herbal containers away from windowsills, fireplaces, and ashtrays. The same goes for places that get sprayed a lot with air fresheners. Sunlight, smoke, and air fresheners can rob stored herbs of their healing properties faster than you can say P.U.!

Temperature-wise, you don't need to build a wine cellar to keep your herbs fresh and flavorful. But while we're on the subject, if you have one, it does make a great storage place! Otherwise, just find a place in the house that's generally cool, such as a pantry, and never hot. Temperatures that consistently register above 85°F are too hot for your tender herbs.

Now when harvesttime rolls around, you'll be all set to reap a hearty, healthy bounty. You've got your pick of drying methods, and I've given you the low-down on the best ways to freeze and store your garden herbs. So in a few words — get ready to enjoy!

Careful with the Merchandise!

Each time you handle a dried herb, it loses some flavor. Try to store whole, dried leaves, and crumble them only when you're ready to use them.

CHAPTER 4

How to Buy Herbs That Heal

If there isn't a single green thumb in your entire household, or you simply don't have the time or inclination to grow and cultivate herbs, relax. I'm here to help. Why, in my 50-plus years of gardening, I've learned a thing or two about buying as well as growing herbs.

So, here's my brief Herb-Buying 101 course that'll prepare you for your next trip down the medicinal herb aisle. I'll take you step-by-step so that you'll have the confidence and the know-how to pick the right herb, in the right form and at the right price, to meet your own personal needs.

Ready? Set? Let's go!

Pick Your Packaging

With the explosion of medicinal herbal products on the market these days, herbs and natural remedies come in just about all shapes and sizes, potency and prices. Here's the lowdown on the most popular forms, complete with their pluses and minuses.

The Big Teas

Sip, savor, smile. Ahhh, there's something relaxing, inviting, and downright healing about brewing a cup of herbal tea, letting it steep to perfection, and then slowly drinking it. I love to wrap my hands around the warm, steaming cup and feel the warm all over. Buying tea is as easy as deciding whether you want bulk herbs, tea blends, or tea bags.

+ **Pluses:** Aromatic; inexpensive; gentle on your tummy; easily absorbed by your body.
– **Minuses:** Short shelf life (usually less than 1 year); needs preparation (boil the water, steep the leaves); lacks the medicinal punch of tinctures and capsules.

Try a Tincture

Tinctures (sometimes called extracts) are potent liquid botanicals that are packed in tiny glass bottles with eyedroppers. Their motto: A little goes a l-o-o-o-n-g way!

+ **Pluses:** Long shelf life (about 5 years on average); convenient (one gulp usually does the trick); reliable (usually offers a concentrated extraction of the herb's medicinal compounds); easy to pack and store.
– **Minuses:** Pricey; needs to be diluted (to avoid stinging your tongue); some types contain small amounts of alcohol.

Pop a Capsule

Capsules are made from herb powders. Some have a special coating that helps the herb slide down your throat and pass through your stomach unaltered. That way, the entire capsule dissolves in your intestines, increasing its effectiveness.

+ **Pluses:** Convenient (one swallow); tasteless; easy to tote; good shelf life (2 to 4 years).

– **Minuses:** Hard to swallow for those who gag taking their daily multivitamin; takes longer to act (must first go through your digestive system); questionable potency (some unscrupulous manufacturers load each capsule with up to 65 percent filler).

Other Options

In addition to the Big Three, medicinal herbs can also work their healing magic in these forms:

Poultices. Ground herbs are dampened to form a paste and then tucked inside a moist, double layer of cotton or a muslin pad. The poultice is then placed on the area of skin that needs tending, and it's held in place with rolled gauze or some white adhesive tape from your first-aid kit. They're terrific for drawing out pus and easing swelling.

Compresses. Hot, wet cloths soaked in liquid herbs are placed on skin to relieve bruises, insect bites and stings, and swelling.

Syrups and lozenges. Thick, sweet-tasting syrups tame sore throats and coughs. Lozenges are like hard candy that makes you feel dandy!

Salves and ointments. Cream forms of herbs can be gently rubbed onto troubled skin.

Throat sprays. Herbal medicines can be diluted with distilled water and stored in a spray bottle. Then just open your mouth wide, squirt the back of a sore throat, and say ahhhhh.

Herbal chewing gum. Give your jaws a good workout while you chew your troubles away! Some contain flavors such as peppermint to aid in digestion.

Be a Savvy Shopper

When you're browsing the herbal aisles, wondering how in the world you're going to decide what to put in your basket or cart, don't panic. It's not as difficult and confusing as it looks. Here are some things to keep in mind to ensure that you're always buying premium herbal products.

Set Some Standards

Whenever possible, especially when you first start shopping for medicinal herbs, remember that you can cut through all of the confusion and hype if you stick to buying products bearing the "standardized" seal on them. That's your guarantee that the product contains a notable amount of the herb's major active ingredients.

You see, the potency of herbs can vary from plant to plant and batch to batch. By buying standardized, you eliminate any guesswork. You get the same amount each and every time. I know it sounds a bit low-down, but a manufacturer can list the product as, say, "ginkgo," even if it contains only an itty-bitty amount of ginkgo, not enough to truly do the job.

Now, you'll probably pay a bit more for standardized herbs, but like everything else, you get what you pay for. To me, it's worth the price because I'm paying for quality. Also, standardized herbs tend to maintain their potency a whole lot longer; and they're fairly easy to find in most health food stores, in drugstores, and even in supermarkets.

Choose Organic

Check the label for the phrase "certified organic" — that means this herbal product was made free and clear of any nasty chemicals. The plant was grown in clean soil and naturally turned into medicine.

Speak Latin

OK, I know it's a dead language, but in the world of herbs, it's very much alive. Herbs go by two names: their common names (like our nicknames) and specific botanical names (the proper Latin title). Some herbs bearing the same common name actually bear litle relationship to each other. That's why you need to know their specific botanical names. It's just like a personalized ZIP code.

For example, Asian ginseng and Siberian ginseng are completely different plants. Botanically, Siberian ginseng isn't ginseng at all, but has similar medicinal properties.

Ask "How Old Are You?"

That's not an impolite question when it comes to buying herbs. Just like when you buy a carton of milk, check the herbal product's label for an expiration date. Unlike fine wines, herbal tincture, capsules, teas, and other products don't get better with age. In fact, the older they get, the less potent they are, and the less good they'll do you.

Find the Dose

It can be a little tricky determining exactly how much herb you should take each day. Not all packages include clear directions like you find on aspirin bottles or those over-the-counter cold medications. I say, stick with herbal products that do provide recommended daily dosages on the labels.

Some Shopping Dos and Don'ts

One word of advice: Just to be on the safe side, only buy herbal products that sport safety seals. Beyond that, here are some other tips.

- **Do** choose the herb or herbs that are right for you. Jot down their names, just like you do for grocery shopping.
- **Do** recognize the limitations of herbs. If you have diabetes, you probably need insulin. If you break a leg, you need surgery. Herbs can only assist in taming the pain and in hastening the healing.
- **Don't** feel overwhelmed by the wide selection of herbs. Just focus on the particular herbs you need.

They should also clearly let you know if you're better off taking the herb with meals or in between meals.

Some of us have allergies, so it's always best to read the entire label to make sure the herbal product doesn't contain anything that won't sit too well with you. Also, check the label to see if the product is packed with fillers or preservatives. All they do is add needless bulk.

Don't Mingle; Go Single

To truly reap the benefits of the herb, buy single-herb products. You may think you're saving money by buying multi-herb products (some even come with vitamins); but chances are, there isn't enough of any of those herbs in a single dosage to make a real impact on your health. So if you want to stick with your multivitamin, that's fine; but don't try to take some 5-in-1 herbal combination!

Have Some Reliance on Science

Stick with proven brands that provide scientific research results right on their labels. Steer clear of any herbal product that claims it contains a "miracle cure" or "secret formula."

If it sounds too good to be true, like that old saying goes, it probably is. The more forthright a manufacturer is on the label, the safer and better I feel in choosing and using it.

Keep Your Herbs Safe and Sound

Everyone and everything has a weakness. No one and nothing is invincible. For that mythical Greek strongman Achilles, it was his heel. For Superman, the Man of Steel of comic-book fame, it still is Kryptonite. For store-bought herbs, it is heat, light, and oxygen. Exposed to any or all three, the herb will quickly lose its potency.

Fortunately, you don't need super strength or super powers to protect your store-bought herbs. All you need is a little common sense.

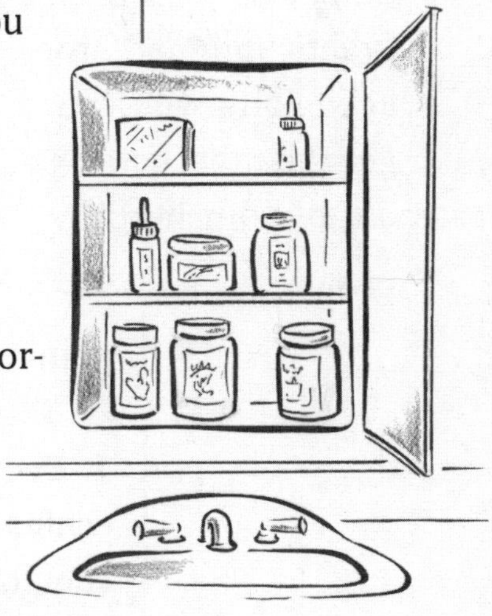

Keep Your Cool

Store medicinal herbs in cool, dry places. Ideal storage locations include the top drawer of your bedroom nightstand, a shelf inside your bathroom medicine cabinet, or a cupboard in your kitchen far from the hot stove or sun-filled windows.

Just don't tuck them away in such a good hiding spot that you forget where they are and neglect to take them!

Put a Lid on It

As for the oxygen issue, don't dilly-dally when you open the bottle. Open, take the dose you need, and seal

A Word on Lastability

How long herbs remain effective depends on the type of product and on you. As a general rule of thumb, tinctures last the longest, followed by capsules or pills, and then teas. By practicing good storage habits, you can get the most mileage out of your herbs!

it shut — pronto! If you have a large container, keep a clean cotton ball inside it to minimize the oxygen around the herbs, or transfer the herbs to smaller containers as your supply dwindles. If you have dried herbs for teas, keep them in airtight glass containers, and seal them tight after each use. If you want tinctures, I recommend buying them in dark glass bottles that help shut out the sunlight.

Use Herbs, Don't Abuse Them!

So you've mastered the art of shopping for herbs and are always careful how to store them. Now, I want you to keep these five points in mind whenever you use herbal medicines:

1. Everything in moderation. Some herbs, such as echinacea, are what I refer to as "on-call" herbs. They should only be used when the need arises. Echinacea is most effective when taken at the onset of a cold to take out its punch. If you take echinacea every day, thinking you'll never get a cold again, think again. Taking echinacea every day actually *lessens* its effectiveness. Kava is best for only those times you feel stressed, anxious, or on deadline. It helps you regain your focus.

2. More is not better. There is a valid reason why manufacturers list recommended dosages on the label. Doubling up on the dosage won't improve your condition twice as fast. Although herbs are generally safe, taking excessive amounts over prolonged periods of time can do you more harm than good.

3. Know when to say when. Some herbs work in cycles. They perform best if you take them daily for 2 weeks, take a break for a week or so, and then start taking them again. The label should tell you, but if not, check with your doctor or herbalist. Also, always stop if your condition worsens, and let your doctor know immediately.

4. Be patient. Don't expect miracles. It may take months for you to notice results from some herbs. Eating well-balanced foods and exercising regularly are also needed to keep you in tip-top shape.

5. Tell your doc what's up. Let your doctor know what you're taking — herbs as well as over-the-counter medications. Some herbs and medicines work together like a team. Others act like squabbling siblings. And some herbs can actually cancel out the intended benefit of a needed prescriptive medication. By keeping your doctor informed, you can avoid any possible harmful herb-drug interactions.

Get a Second Opinion

Sometimes, it seems easier to wade through a mucky lake than make it out of your local health food store with the right product. But fear not! You can get lots more reliable information by checking with knowledgeable folks at these nonprofit organizations. You'll find all the information you need to contact them beginning on page 356 in the back of this book.

American Botanical Council
American Herb Association
The American Herbalists Guild
Herb Growing & Marketing Network
Herb Research Foundation
The Herb Society of America, Inc.
International Herb Association
United Plant Savers

Congratulations! You've passed my crash course in herb buying, and now you're a savvy selector of store-bought herbs. All gardeners like to share, so please pass these tips on to your friends and neighbors!

CHAPTER 5

Cooking, Cleaning, Healing: How to Use Herbs

Here's to your good health — and there's no better way to maintain it than with herbs. They provide natural medicine at its best! In backyard gardens, rustic woods, windowsill boxes, and indoor containers, herbs rise up from good old Mother Earth to stimulate, relax, and even heal us.

Long before there were any pharmaceuticals, people all over the world successfully used herbs to treat countless conditions. They trusted and prized herbs. I'm happy to say that as we are entering a new millenium, more of us are finding the value of returning to our "healthy roots," so to speak. We recognize the important role herbs play in keeping us fit and feeling fine for life!

In this chapter, I'm going to introduce you to the many ways herbs can be part of your life. From sipping teas to soaking in baths, from savoring herb-seasoned dishes to shooing away pesky bugs, herbs come through for us time and time again.

Rescue You

No home should be without what I call a "Green First-Aid Kit," which includes the following:

- **Aloe vera.** The gel from this plant's leaves help relieve pain and heal minor burns and cuts — pronto! Keep a tube handy or, better yet, an actual aloe plant. Remember: This one's for external use only!

- **Arnica.** Take the blues and other colors of the rainbow out of bruises with this healing gel, also for external use only.
- **Calendula.** A supply of dried leaves made into tea serves as an effective cleaner for minor scrapes and cuts.
- **Chamomile.** Keep a stash of fresh or dried leaves and brew a tea to treat indigestion, anxiety, and even insomnia.
- **Echinacea.** Tame the common cold as well as the flu with capsules of this herb.
- **Gingerroot.** This gnarly herb is the top pick to ease nausea and motion sickness. Taken as a tea or in capsules, it settles stomachs and relieves headaches. That's why Mom gave you ginger ale!
- **Witch hazel.** Keep a bottle of this handy to stop infections and to heal minor burns and rashes.

Jerry's Words of Wisdom

"I call the time you spend creating your hot cup of medicinal warmth the **brew-aha.**"

Good-for-You Brew

Contrary to popular belief, all herbal teas are not created equal. To get the full flavor — as well as the full medicinal punch — you need to know which parts of the plant to brew. Some recipes call for fresh or dried leaves or flowers; others, for roots, seeds, or stems. Once you've decided on the right parts for the recipe you want to brew, the next part is easy. Add hot water, steep for a few minutes, then sip your health worries away!

Tea Tech

Basically, herbal teas are brewed one of two ways: *infusions* and *decoctions.* To end any confusion, we'll discuss infusions first.

An infusion. This is the more traditional method of making tea. You've probably done it countless times and never realized it bore such a distinctive title (hey, you learn something new every day, and this is it for today!). Any time you've brewed loose tea leaves in a real teapot, you've created an herbal infusion. Leafy or flowering herbs like chamomile and mint work best with this brewing method. Here's how to make an infusion:

Step 1. Measure a specified amount of dried or fresh herbal leaves (most recipes call for 1 to 2 teaspoons of dried herbs, or a handful of fresh herbs, for a pint of water). Put the dried leaves into a tea ball, brewing tea spoon, infuser, or tea bag. If you're in a hurry, you can drop in some loose leaves, but you'll just have to strain them out later.

Step 2. Pour water into a teapot or saucepan and bring it to a boil. Remove from heat.

Step 3. After the water no longer shows signs of boiling, add the herb leaves to the teapot or saucepan, and cover with a lid to keep the herb's essential oils from leaking out in the steam. Depending on the herb, steep for 5 to 20 minutes.

Step 4. Strain out the herbs (if your leaves have been free-floating), pour the tea into a cup or mug, and then sit back and enjoy!

A Decoction. Now, let's get to the *root* of making a decoction. This type of brew uses the tougher parts of the herb — like the roots, the bark, the seeds, or dried berries. Ginger, cinnamon, and licorice are popular herbs for this brewing method. Here's how to make a tea decoction:

Step 1. For woody herb parts, grate, chop, or bruise the parts using a grater, knife, or coffee grinder. This helps release the medicinal benefits of these toughies.

Step 2. In a saucepan, add a pint of water and the herbs (usually 1 to 2 ounces per cup). Cover with a lid and simmer 20 to 60 minutes, depending on the herb.

Step 3. Pour the decoction into a separate container, trapping the herbs with a coffee filter or fine-mesh plastic strainer. As a bonus, save the used herbs because they are mighty enough to give you another round of tea. Store any extra tea in a sealed glass jar in the refrigerator; it will last up to 2 days.

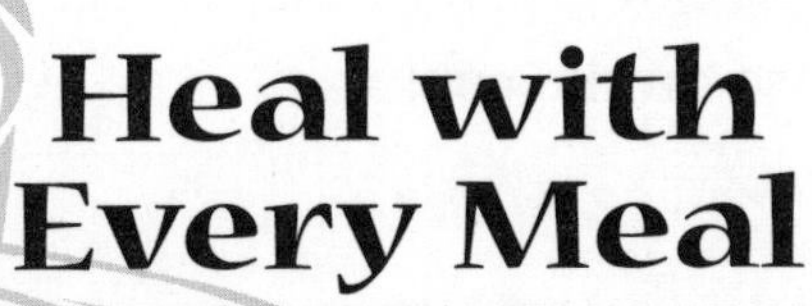

Heal with Every Meal

A world without herbal spices and seasonings would be a very bland-tasting world indeed. I can't even imagine lasagne without basil or garlic, a fresh tossed salad without tarragon and parsley, or grilled salmon without garden-grown dill and thyme. But beyond seasoning, herbs can heal with each and every meal.

Better Butter

Dress up the looks — and the flavor — of pats of butter with herbs! Here are a couple of ways to "butter up" any meal:

- **Basil butter.** Allow 1 cup of butter to soften at room temperature. In a medium-size mixing bowl, use a wooden spoon to thoroughly blend the butter with 2 tablespoons of fresh or dried basil leaves. Using aluminum foil or plastic wrap, shape the butter into a decorative log and store it in the refrigerator. For a special treat, spread it on freshly baked bread. This butter is downright deeelicious!
- **Melted medley.** In a small mixing bowl, beat at high speed 1 cup of butter, 1 teaspoon each of thyme, rosemary, and marjoram leaves (dried is best), along with a pinch each of basil, garlic, and sage powders. Beat till it's fluffy. Store the butter in a covered container until you're ready to brush it on steaming hot green beans, broccoli, or my top choice: corn on the cob!

Vim and Vinegar

Just saying the word *vinegar* makes me pucker up, imagining its sour taste. For you science buffs, the acetic acid in vinegar is what gives this fermented liquid its deep, strong taste. But you and I both know that vinegar not only helps preserve and tenderize food, but it can also pump up the flavor for a whole lot of meats, vegetables, and salads.

Herbal vinegars can bring out the best gardener and chef inside of you. Most homemade vinegars are made from white or red wine or apple cider, plus the herb of your choice. As for the particular herb or herbs, that's the beauty of it — you decide! The more the merrier, I say, and you can hardly ever go wrong!

So if you've never made herbal vinegar, I'm here to show you how. First, though, you need to visit your backyard herb garden. And don't forget to bring your pruning shears!

Let's say you want to create a flavor-enhancing vinegar to top a garden-fresh salad. Snip fresh leaves from your herb garden, wash them, and pat them dry. (Or you can use dried herbs for your vinegar, if you choose.)

Tuck a handful or so of the fresh herbs into a glass jar and use a wooden spoon to bruise them slightly (I said bruise, not beat them silly!). Pour red wine vinegar into the jar, right up to the top. Seal the jar tightly, and tuck it into a dark spot for about a week. Every day or so, give the jar a few good shakes. After a week, give it a sample sip. If it tastes the way you like it, strain out the herbs and reseal the vinegar. Otherwise, taste-test it every few days until you get the flavor you desire. It's that easy!

Best Herbs for Vinegar

Snip fresh leaves from any of the following herb plants to create a great herbal vinegar:

Basil
Cilantro
Rosemary
Tarragon

Wash and pat them dry with a paper towel. Or you can use dried versions of these same herbs instead.

Make a Healthier Salt

If you're looking for a healthy substitute for salt (and who isn't?), I've got just the thing! Dump the salt out of your shaker, get out your coffee grinder, and grind up this herbal blend: 3 tablespoons each of dried basil, marjoram, parsley, and thyme; 4 teaspoons of chives; and 2 teaspoons each of onion powder, paprika, and rosemary. Now refill your salt shaker with this tasty, better-for-you seasoning!

Mix 'n' Match

Here's a handy guide to let you know which herb goes best with which type of vinegar:

Herb	Part of herb	Vinegar
Basil	Leaves	White wine
Cilantro	Leaves	White wine
Dill	Seeds	Red wine
Fennel	Seeds	Red wine
Garlic	Cloves	Red wine
Lovage	Root	Red wine
Mint	Leaves	Cider
Oregano	Leaves	White wine
Rosemary	Leaves	White wine
Sage	Leaves	Red wine
Salad burnet	Leaves	White wine
Tarragon	Leaves	White wine
Thyme	Leaves	White wine

Jammin' Jellies and Pleasin' Preserves

Once you get started, herbs will find their way into many of your kitchen creations, including jellies and preserves. To me, they really dress up a piece of toast or a peanut butter sandwich. Some folks spread these herbal delights right on hot biscuits, muffins, or scones as an alternative to high-fat butters and unhealthy margarines. Yum, yum!

To help you get the right flavor combination, here are some of my favorite herb, fruit juice, and vinegar combinations that work well together:

- Sage leaves, apple cider, and cider vinegar
- Lavender flower petals, cherry juice, and white wine vinegar
- Mint leaves, strawberry juice, and white wine vinegar
- Rosemary leaves, orange and cranberry juices, and white wine vinegar
- Thyme, apple juice, and white wine vinegar

Natural Health and Cosmetics

They say beauty is in the eye of the beholder, so lo and behold! I say that herbs can make you feel beautiful inside and out! Whether you realize it or not, when you grow herbs, you have a living spa growing in your

Simply Jellyicious

As I always say, with a little jelly in your belly, there's yummy in your tummy. Here's an easy recipe that will produce 5 half-pints of some of the best jelly to hit your tastebuds:

2½ cups of fruit juice
1 cup of fresh herbs
¼ cup of vinegar
4 cups of sugar
3 ounces of liquid pectin (omit when using apple juice)

1. Put the fruit juice in a large pan and bring to a boil. Add the herbs, cover with a lid, and let steep on medium heat for about 30 minutes.

2. Strain out the herbs, and then add the vinegar and sugar. Turn the heat back on high and stir with a wooden spoon until the mixture boils. Then stir in the liquid pectin and let boil for a couple more minutes. Skim off any foam, and discard.

3. Use a soup ladle to pour this liquid into half-pint canning jars. Leave about a quarter of an inch of space at the top. Attach two-piece canning lids, or seal with paraffin. You're rounding the corner and heading toward the homestretch!

4. Place the jars on a rack in a deep kettle half full of boiling water. Add some more boiling water — enough to cover the lids by about 2 inches. Cover the kettle, bring the water to a full boil, and let it bubble for about 15 minutes.

5. Use tongs to remove the jars from the kettle, and let them cool before removing the bands and labeling them. Store them in a cool, dark place for a month to let the flavors blend together. Then your jellies are ready to rumble! After you open them up, just store them in the refrigerator.

backyard. Many of the garden goodies can help you feel better physically, mentally, and emotionally. In their many forms, herbs can heal wounds, mend broken hearts, and even restore youthful vibrancy to your skin. Sounds like a dream come true!

So are you ready to view the world of herbs beyond the kitchen and medicine cabinet?

Aromatherapy: Healing Scents

Your nose knows because smelling is believing! Since the days of Cleopatra (the queen of the Nile and *beguile* supposedly won the heart of Mark Antony by scenting her barge sails with jasmine), herbal essential oils have wafted their way into healthy healing. Aromatherapy, simply put, is the art of putting fragrance to good use. It literally means "treatment using scents."

Aromatherapy uses essential oils — that is, extracts distilled from an herb's flowers, leaves, bark, roots, fruit, and resins. So, you say, where are these essential oils located? Well, it all depends on the herb. For instance, you'll find essential oils in lavender's petals, in basil's leaves, in ginger's roots, and in myrrh's resins. Some plants are loaded with essential oil from root to flowers. When applied to the skin or inhaled, aromatic herbal oils help relieve a bundle of physical and emotional woes.

WHOA!

I want you to remember that essential oils are very potent, so they should never be ingested! They should only be inhaled or dabbed on the skin when diluted with vegetable oils such as grapeseed, sweet almond, sunflower, or olive oil. (The notable exception is lavender essential oil, which can be applied directly onto burns.)

Essential oils are used in massage, steam inhalation, compresses, creams, lotions, shampoos, gels, and antiseptic mouthwashes. Here are some of the more popular herbs used in aromatherapy:

- **Chamomile.** This oil is beautiful to behold, with its bright, cobalt-blue hue. When inhaled, it works wonders for migraines, PMS, and frayed nerves. A few drops on a damp washcloth will help shoo away headaches and speed healing of minor cuts.
- **Lavender.** This is by far the most versatile, adored, and medicinally used of all essential oils. Simply sprinkle a few drops on your pillow at night, and you'll be in dreamland in no time at all! The sweet floral scent of lavender can also help you feel more relaxed in stressful situations. Just dab a couple of drops on a tissue, inhale, and soon you will feel yourself calm down and relax.
- **Oregano.** Diluted with olive oil, this essential oil takes away the rainbow colors of a bruise and the red stings of a minor burn. It is warming and pain-relieving, making it terrific for those muscle sprains and strains you get after toiling long hours in your garden.
- **Thyme.** The essential oils, gleaned from its leaves and tiny purple flowering tops, deliver a fresh green scent that kills germs and settles upset tummies. Its uplifting fragrance has even been known to turn that frown to a smile when you're feeling a bit blue.

FAST FACT

You need 12 pounds of lavender flowers to produce just 1 ounce of lavender essential oil.

Soak Yourself

When your muscles ache, your head throbs, or your energy has been zapped after a long hectic day, turn your bathtub into a pampering palace. Bathing with herbs is a perfect way to feel refreshed and renewed.

How to Make Your Own Bath Oil

Even though herbal essential oils range from calming to energizing, the recipe for bath oils is basically the same. The only difference is the specific herbs you use. To make herbal bath oils, put about 30 drops of essential oil for every ounce of vegetable oil (best choices are sweet almond, grapeseed, safflower, and apricot) into a plastic squirt bottle. Give a couple of healthy squirts of this herbal blend into warm (not hot), running bathwater. A hot, steaming bath will cause the essential oils to evaporate too rapidly and possibly leave your skin parched.

After you've filled your tub and slipped in, you may notice a thin layer of oil on top of the water. This layer delicately coats your skin as you soak. When you emerge from the tub, be sure to *blot* yourself dry with a nice thick towel. Rubbing can cause dry skin, especially during the winter months.

Although you can stick with just one essential oil, I prefer to use combinations in my bathtub. Here are some of my favorites.

A Little Goes a Long Way

Essential oils are 50 to 100 times stronger than the herb from which they came, so you only need a few drops to do the trick.

- For a nice, invigorating bath: Use 14 drops of peppermint, 8 drops of calendula, 4 drops of sage, and 4 drops of rosemary.
- For a relaxing bath: Use 9 drops each of lavender, roses, and chamomile, and 3 drops of comfrey.

BATH IN A BAG

You can also enjoy a botanical bath with my time-saving method: Just toss a dozen or so herbal tea bags into an empty tub, and then add a couple of inches of hot water to steep them. Wait 5 to 10 minutes before filling the tub with warm (not hot) water, and step in. My favorite herbal teas for a relaxing bath are chamomile, lavender, and rosemary.

R_X for Insomnia: Make an Herbal Pillow

If you're like me, when you're ready to hit the sack, you don't want to be bothered with counting imaginary sheep or hoping that Mr. Sandman will stop by and escort you off to Snooze Land. Instead, why not be lulled to sleep with an herbal sleep pillow?

For centuries, folks have relied upon these little pillows tucked inside of big ones to help them rest and relax. Medieval historians claim that doctors secretively slipped dried hops inside the pillows of crazy King George III to calm him down enough so that he could enjoy a peaceful slumber each night.

The best part about sleep pillows is that you can make them yourself in no time at all. And not only do they aid in your quest for zzzzs, but they also make nifty, thoughtful gifts for friends and family. Here's what you do:

Step 1. Check your sewing scraps for extra cotton, flannel, or velvet fabric. Cut an 8 x 8-inch square and fold it in half.

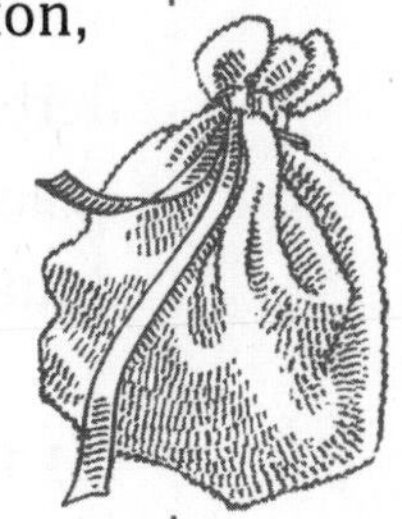

Step 2. Be sure that the fabric is turned inside out first, and then stitch two sides shut. Turn the pillow right side out. (If you don't want to bother with these first two steps, you can just use a store-bought muslin bag with drawstrings instead.)

Step 3. In a small bowl, use a wooden spoon to mix equal amounts of these dried herbs: chamomile, hops, lavender, and rose. The amount depends on how many pillows you want to make. As a bonus, add dried mugwort; it's a real dream-maker!

Step 4. Stuff the blended dried herbs into the fabric pillow and sew it up. (If you're using a muslin bag, just pull the drawstrings close.)

Step 5. Tuck the herbal pillow into your regular pillow — or place it right on top, so that your head touches it. Just like you do for your regular pillows, fluff your herbal pillow a bit to release its sleepy aromas right before you get ready to sleep. Sweet dreams!

Turn Back the Clock with Botanicals

Face it, we all want young, healthy-looking faces. That's where herbs can be terrific allies. Women (and yes, men, too) benefit from keeping skin pores cleaned and unclogged. You can do this yourself with a weekly herbal steam facial and herbal facial mask. The real beauty of this is that you will save time and money by doing it at home.

Get Steamed

Facial steams rehydrate all skin types, making you look years younger in the process. Naturally, the herbs you use will depend upon whether you have normal, dry, or oily skin. But here are the basics:

Step 1. Boil 3 to 4 cups of water in a pan, and then carefully pour it into a large glass bowl. Add 1 cup of dried herbs. For normal to dry skin, use calendula flowers, chamomile leaves, and fennel seeds. For oily skin, use rosemary, witch hazel, and yarrow.

Step 2. Lean over the steaming bowl (about a foot or so away so you don't accidentally burn your face) and drape a large bath towel over your head to trap in this hot moisture. Let the herbal steamer unleash the sweat from your pores for 5 to 10 minutes. Remove the towel and blot your face dry with a clean towel.

Mask Yourself

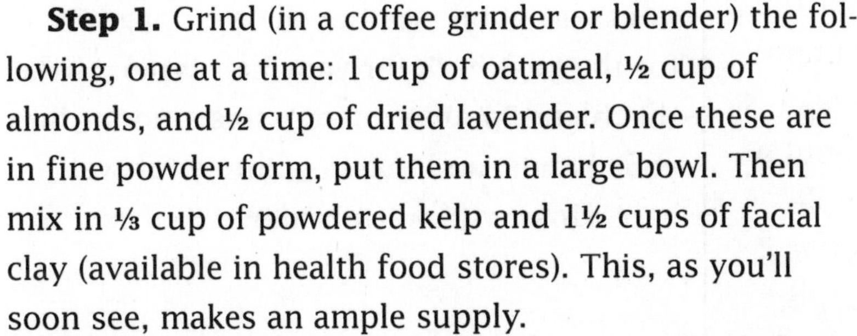

With your steam-cleaned face, you're now ready for an herbal mask for even deeper cleaning. Masks peel away dead skin cells on the surface, giving way to healthy, younger skin cells. These masks can also bolster a tired complexion by stimulating circulation to the area. Making a mask is an easy task. Here's all you need to do:

Step 1. Grind (in a coffee grinder or blender) the following, one at a time: 1 cup of oatmeal, ½ cup of almonds, and ½ cup of dried lavender. Once these are in fine powder form, put them in a large bowl. Then mix in ⅓ cup of powdered kelp and 1½ cups of facial clay (available in health food stores). This, as you'll soon see, makes an ample supply.

Step 2. To make one mask, all you need is a bit of the powder mix. Scoop about ¼ cup into a small bowl, and add just enough lukewarm water to form a paste. Then add 1 teaspoon of honey (to soften your skin) and blend thoroughly.

Step 3. With your fingertips, dab on the paste all over your forehead, cheeks, nose, and chin, being careful to avoid getting any of it too close to your eyes.

Leave the mask on 10 to 20 minutes, and then rinse with warm water. Blot dry with a towel. It's that easy!

Herbs for Healthier Hair

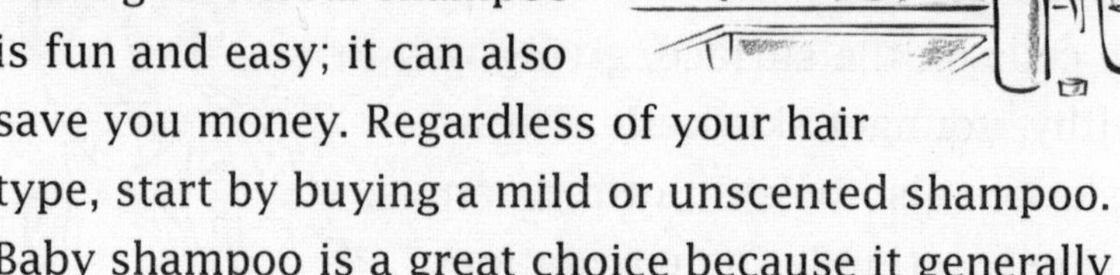

Making an herbal shampoo is fun and easy; it can also save you money. Regardless of your hair type, start by buying a mild or unscented shampoo. Baby shampoo is a great choice because it generally contains fewer ingredients than the adult varieties. Now dilute the store-bought shampoo by half with water. Add 20 drops of essential oil (see the chart on page 75 for the best herb for your hair type). Shake this blend, pour a quarter-size amount into your hands, and massage into your wet hair. Rinse with warm water.

Make It Neutral!

Check the label of the store-bought shampoo. If it contains an alkaline base, add about a tablespoon of apple cider vinegar to the herbal shampoo mix. The vinegar smell will disappear in about an hour or so.

Beauty Basics

Do you think you need to spend lots of money at a fancy spa to get beautiful skin? Think again! Between your herb garden and your kitchen fixin's, you probably have all you need for wonder-working, homemade skin-care products.

Try to keep these beauty basics on hand:

- **Almond oil.** This light oil works for all skin types.
- **Aloe vera.** The juice from this plant is a must ingredient in many lotions and creams.
- **Borax.** Also known as sodium borate, this natural mineral cleanser softens water and skin.

- **Castor oil.** This one's great for dry and aging skin, because of its emollient powers.
- **Coconut oil.** This rich oil moisturizes dry skin.
- **Cosmetic clay.** The main ingredient in facial masks.
- **Grapeseed oil.** This light, fast-absorbing oil is ideal for blemished or oily skin.
- **Honey.** The sweetest ingredient gives herbal creams and pastes some body and also kills bacteria.
- **Lanolin.** This protective oil found in sheep wool makes a nifty moisturizer.
- **Oatmeal.** Not just a breakfast cereal, this grain is also a fortifying cleanser.
- **Rose water.** Mildly astringent, this makes a great toner for dry skin.
- **Witch hazel extract.** As an astringent and bacteria fighter, it puts a curse on acne and dry skin.

Mother Nature's Mane Attractions

Naturally, certain herbs work best with certain types of hair. Dry hair needs moisturizing herbs to restore body and shine. Oily hair needs herbs that curb the "greasy kid stuff" look. Even "normal" hair can benefit with certain luster-enhancing herbs. Nagged by dandruff? Give flakes the brush-off with specific herbs. Here's my all-star hair-care lineup:

Type of hair	Best herbal shampoos
Dry	Calendula, rosewood, sandalwood
Oily	Basil, lemongrass, mints, sage
Normal	Chamomile, lavender, rosemary
Dandruff	Geranium, myrrh, sage

Skin-Softening Massage Oils

There's nothing I hate more than dry, itchy skin. But herbs can keep your skin radiating with a good, healthy glow all year long, through the dry, cold winter and into the hot, humid summer. Here's my favorite basic recipe that works for both dry and oily skins. The only difference is the type of herbs used.

Put a handful of dried herbs into a 1-pint glass mason jar. Then fill the jar to nearly the top with vegetable oil. Twist the lid on tight. Stash the jar somewhere in a warm place, maybe near your stove. Every morning, give the jar a vigorous up-and-at-'em shake. Do this for a couple of weeks. Then open the jar and strain out the herbs using a fine-mesh sieve. Finally, add a few drops of your chosen essential oil herbs and mix well. You now have your very own customized massage oil to rub into your skin each day.

Make Your Skin Grin

Whether you've got dry or oily skin, here's a bunch of herbs that'll bring your skin a healthy glow.

- **For dry skin:** almond, apricot or grapeseed oil; dried leaves or flowers of calendula, chamomile, comfrey, lavender, and roses plus a few drops of lavender essential oil.
- **For oily skin:** almond or apricot oil; dried leaves or flowers of calendula, comfrey, lavender, raspberry, rosemary, and sage plus a few drops of rosemary essential oil.

Herbal Housekeeping

Although we often associate herbs with cooking and healing, once again they demonstrate their versatility by helping you keep your home looking good and smelling squeaky clean. High-ranking members of my clean team include lavender, lemon, and rosemary, as well as distilled white vinegar, baking soda, and isopropyl alcohol.

Creating your own herbal housekeeping formulas is rewarding and easy as 1-2-3. Here are some really swell botanical ways to really clean up around the house.

Make Peace with Grease

Got stubborn grease caked on your stainless-steel sink or tile floor? Fight back naturally. In a medium-size bowl, blend:

1½ cups of baking soda
1 tbsp. of lavender essential oil
1 tsp. of rosemary essential oil
1 tsp. of peppermint essential oil

Sprinkle a little of this mix onto a sponge dampened with warm water, and watch the grease disappear. While you're at it, sprinkle ½ cup of this mix into your toilet bowl, and then set its bubbling action into high gear with a bathroom scrubber.

The Herbal Clean Team

Herbs can be oil-powerful against greasy grubbiness and grime.

- **Eucalyptus oil:** disinfectant
- **Lemon oil:** degreaser
- **Lavender oil:** disinfectant
- **Tea tree oil:** germ-killer

Clean Glass in a Flash

Let the sunshine pour in through clean, streak-free windows by using vinegar, water, and eucalyptus and sage essential oils. All you need is a spray bottle big enough to hold:

3 cups of distilled water
⅓ cup of white vinegar
5 drops each of eucalyptus and sage essential oils

Tighten the lid and shake well before you take aim at the window pane. Polish with a clean, dry cloth. This mix will last for 6 months. Now there's a bargain!

Bug Off!

If you're on the go like me, you know that nothing puts a damper on outdoor activities faster than a bunch of pesky fleas, ticks, or mosquitoes. These little pests seem to come out of nowhere whenever it's time for a hike, a little picnic, or just puttering around in the backyard.

Sure, you can douse yourself with one of those fancy, store-bought spray-on repellents. But you pay the price for convenience by allowing chemicals to seep into your skin and enter your bloodstream. I've got some much safer, surefire ways to give bugs the boot: blooming botanicals.

Use Common Scents

To lessen the chance that you're going to be a main dish on some swarm's dinner menu, try one of my time-tested insect repellent herbs:

- **Basil** *(Ocimum basilicum).* Caught off-guard by an incoming squadron of mosquitoes while down on your knees, tending your herb garden? Now's not the time to start praying! Just grab a few basil leaves and rub them on your exposed arms and legs. Then watch the squadron disappear. Even though basil has a well-deserved reputation as a culinary spice, it has been used for hundreds of years in India and Africa as an insect repellent.
- **Citronella** *(Cymbopogon nardus).* To tame the buzzing horde in your backyard, I heartily recommend keeping a supply of citronella candles burning on your patio or deck. You can also buy this lemon-scented plant as an essential oil from a health food store. Since pure essential oils can irritate your skin, I always tell folks to mix a few drops of citronella with vegetable oil. You can apply this diluted concoction directly to your skin. You may need to reapply it every hour, but you'll smell citrus-y great!
- **Lavender** *(Lavandula angustifolia).* Heed the Boy Scout motto: Be Prepared! Before your next hike or camping trip, mix 1 teaspoon of lavender essential oil with 1 tablespoon of vegetable oil in a small

glass bottle with a tight-fitting lid. The faster you dab a drop or two on the bite or sting, the quicker this sweet-smelling herb can work its magic by easing the itch and reducing the swelling.

- **Pennyroyal** *(Hedeoma pulegioides)*. Here's an herb that really delivers a powerful punch of protection. Pennyroyal has been used since the ancient Roman days against fleas. In fact, its scientific name, *pulegium,* means flea. The great news is that it also keeps mosquitoes and ticks at bay.

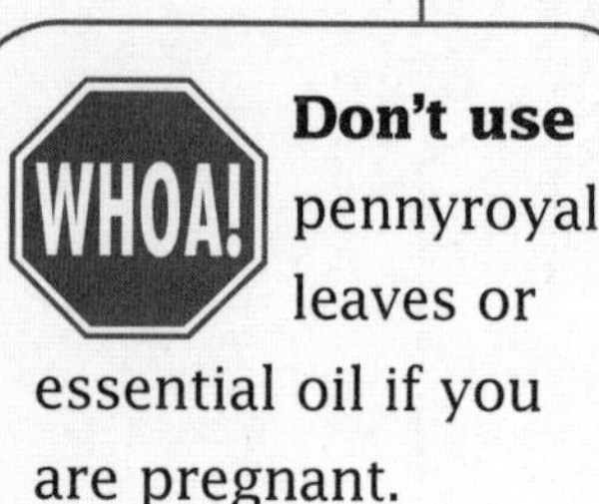

Don't use pennyroyal leaves or essential oil if you are pregnant.

Pennyroyal contains pulegone, which is a mighty insect repellent. To use it, just pick a bunch of leaves and rub them on your skin and clothing. That's all it takes to say bye-bye to bugs! Or, you can pick up a bottle of pennyroyal essential oil at your local health food store. Then the next time you're ready to commune with Mother Nature, simply rub a few drops on the tops of your shoes, socks, and pant legs. (Just don't apply it directly on your skin, because the oil itself can cause irritation.) Don't worry — the oil won't leave a stain.

- **Peppermint** *(Mentha* x *piperita)*. Just 1 drop of peppermint essential oil directly on the sting or bite provides instant and long-lasting relief from the itch and swelling. Peppermint gets your blood pumping to the bite site, where it soon takes the bug's venom away from the skin's surface and reduces the swelling and itching.

Ditch the Itch — Fight the Bite!

Buzzzz. Yowch! You didn't see that bee, but it sure saw you. Or maybe those thirsty little bloodsucking mosquitoes showed no mercy. In any case, you can soothe the ouch and stop the swelling with some plantain or chickweed. That's right, these common lawn weeds work medicinal miracles! Simply rub fresh leaves together in your hands until they are juicy. (You can also stick some leaves in your mouth and chew them into a moist mix first, if you know the lawn is free of pesticides.) Then put this wet poultice smack dab on the bite. Leave it on for 30 minutes or so.

Bug-Be-Gone Spray

As you know, I like to make my own tonics, including this all-natural Bug-Be-Gone Spray. It's a whole lot safer — and cheaper — than those store-bought ones. In a hand-held spray bottle, mix together:

1 tsp. of citronella essential oil
1 tsp. of pennyroyal essential oil
1 tsp. of lavender essential oil
1 tsp. of rose geranium essential oil
1 cup of isopropyl alcohol
1 cup of water

Shake well and then spray lightly on your clothing, arms, and legs, being careful to avoid your eyes or open cuts. Reapply this woodsy-smelling spray every hour or so. Keep the spray bottle sealed up, and you'll have a dynamite bug repellent that'll last for up to 2 years!

Craft a Bug-Free Zone

On hot summer days, I like to sit on my porch with a nice cold glass of lemonade and watch the butterflies dance around my flowers. The last thing I need right then and there is to be bugged by bugs. I've found that some well-placed pots of pennyroyal make my porch bug-free! Evidently, the scent from the sap or oil in these plants sends those little suckers scurrying. During the height of bug season, I even cut some leaves from these plants and hang them in bunches near the doors and windows of my house to create a bug-proof barrier.

If you like variety in your Bug-Free Zone, plant basil, citronella, and peppermint. Those pesky pests will disappear!

Sometimes it seems like herbs have so many uses that I half expect them to be able to make me a cup of morning coffee! But seriously, folks, as I've told you in this chapter, we are truly fortunate to have herbs around and available for use. So whether you're sipping, cooking, or swallowing herbs in whatever form, your body will be filled from head to toe with gratitude and goodness.

CHAPTER

6

Unleash the Power of a Healing Garden

Folks, welcome to Jerry's herb garden! But this is no ordinary garden. No sirree, I'm here to give you the lowdown on how to sow, grow, and let the healing nature of herbs flow through your body. We'll cover everything from aloe to yarrow in this section. And for you trivia and history buffs, we've got plenty of dandy tidbits as well. So read on in good health! (For general information on storing herbs, please refer to chapter 3.)

Aloe Vera

(Aloe barbadensis)

Herbal ID

From its outward appearance, this plant looks like a punk rocker with too much gel in his spiky hair. Although aloe's thick and spiny, leathery leaves rigidly jut out helter-skelter, don't let this tough exterior fool you. The tapering, succulent leaves act as protective outer coverings for the soothing gel inside.

That's Historical!

I tell you, this is one ancient plant! The Bible mentions aloe in the Garden of Eden. Alexander the Great supposedly went to war over aloe. Why, rumor even has it that Cleopatra, Queen of the Nile, credited aloe as her beauty secret! Fast-forward to modern times, and you'll discover that the U.S. Navy once stockpiled aloe for use against radiation burns in case of an atomic attack.

Nicknamed Paradise wood, aloe is a perennial that has truly adapted to centuries of change!

Medicinal Uses: Relieve Burns and Frostbite

Think of aloe as your pal-o — especially after you've spent too much time in the sun and you've got a whale of a sunburn (ouch!). Aloe to the rescue! Its transparent gel delivers blessed relief for sunburn pain as well as minor skin irritations, cuts and scrapes, and poison ivy.

Aloe is jam-packed full of special enzymes and antibacterial and antifungal ingredients that ease swelling, reduce redness, and keep the area from getting infected. Plus, it doesn't hold heat the way oily ointments or salves can. In the winter, aloe can help against frostbite as well. And don't forget: Aloe is a favorite ingredient in many hair-care products and skin lotions because of its natural moisturizing qualities.

Best Medicinal Forms

The easiest way to use aloe as a medicine is to snap off a lower leaf near the center stalk. Remove any spines and then split the leaf in half lengthwise. Scrape out the gel and apply it directly to sunburn, minor wounds, or dry skin. The fresher the gel, the faster the healing. That's why I keep a plant or two within easy reach in my kitchen for quick relief in case I accidentally burn myself. Aloe works well on first-degree kinds of burns, often preventing scar tissue from forming.

A word to the wise, however: For severe burns that form blisters, you should see a doctor immediately for help.

You can also make an ointment out of aloe by collecting gel from a few leaves. Put the gel in a small saucepan and simmer on low heat until it cooks down to a thick paste. Store the paste in clean glass jars with lids — in a cool place — and use as needed.

FAST FACT

True or false? Aloe is a member of the cactus family.

False. Don't let its spiky exterior fool you; aloe actually belongs to the tree lily family.

Growing Tips

Aloe grows best outdoors in Zones 9 and 10 (the hot coastal areas, including the southern regions of Florida, Texas, and California). In all other zones, you should stick to growing aloe indoors as a houseplant. This perennial will grow 2 to 3 feet tall, and it will sport yellow or orange tubular flowers. Don't bother sniffing its flowers, because aloe is essentially aroma-less.

Whether you're planting aloe indoors or out, make sure you have well-drained, fertile soil. Outdoors, give yourself a good 1 to 2 feet between plants because aloe really needs a lot of elbowroom. As far as the heat of summer goes, aloe thrives in full sun, but it will also tolerate partial shade.

For indoor use, place your aloe plant in a container slightly bigger than the plant itself, with soil or planting mix that has good drainage. Aloe isn't a big drinker, so allow the soil to dry out between waterings. There have been times when mine have been without water for a few weeks, and they were still as hardy as the day is long!

Harvesting Tips

Jumpin' jiminy! — aloe reproduces like rabbits, forming little offshoots near the base of the plant. To keep your houseplant about the same size (and to prevent your outdoor garden from being overrun by baby aloes), remove an offshoot by shaking the mother plant out of the pot and gently pulling the young sucker away.

For outdoor aloe plants, use a trowel to make this separation. Make sure that each removed offshoot still has some roots attached to it so that you can immediately plant it in your garden (for you tropical-climate folks) or in a suitable container (for you four-seasons folks). Then you can give this new generation of aloe plants away as gifts to friends!

Cool-Aid for Sunburns

Fend off minor sunburn pain with this fail-safe concoction. In a small bowl, mix together:

4 oz. of aloe gel

2 capsules of vitamin E (just use a knife tip to open and squeeze out the oil)

½ tsp. of lavender oil

1 tsp. of apple cider vinegar

Carefully dab this mixture directly on the sunburned area. Add as much as you need to keep your skin feeling cool, clean, and comfortable.

STORAGE TIPS

Aloe is what we professionals call a ready-when-you-need-it medicinal botanical. You can make and store an ointment (as I explained earlier) — but better yet, just snap off a leaf or two the next time you get a minor burn, cut, or poison ivy and apply the fresh gel to the affected area. Easy as pie.

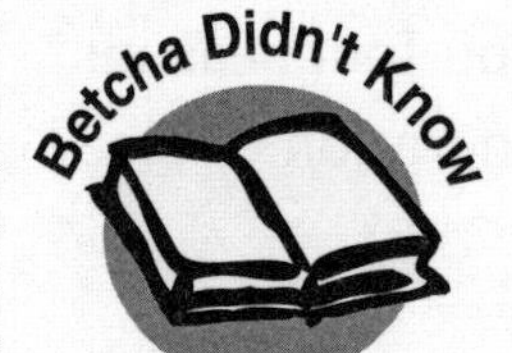

Can you win the state lottery by owning an aloe plant? Maybe, maybe not. Ever since my childhood days, I've heard tales about how aloe plants supposedly protect their owners from household accidents and provide them with good luck. I don't know about that, but caring for an aloe plant is a whole lot better than carrying around a smelly old rabbit's foot!

Angelica

(Angelica archangelica)

HERBAL ID

Angelica's stem is grooved, round, and hollow. If you look closely at its top branches, you'll see they have a slightly blue tint. Leaves grow from dilated sheaths that surround the stem. During blooming season (June to August), this herb proudly displays greenish white, honey-smelling flowers that grow in umbrella-shaped clusters. At its base, the roots are brown to reddish brown and emit an odor that is at first sweet, then bitter and sharp.

THAT'S HISTORICAL!

Monk's the word. Or at least legend has it that back in the 1600s, a Benedictine monk prayed to God for a cure for the great plague affecting people at that time, and lo and behold, his prayers were answered! The Archangel Michael appeared in the monk's dream and told him to use angelica to cure the plague. Maybe that's why *angelica* is Latin for "inspiration." Through the ages, it has also been called Herb of the Angel and Root of the Holy Ghost.

This is one herb with a distinctive birthday: May 8. It usually blooms on that day in honor of St. Michael. Figuring out its birthplace, however, is another matter entirely. Most evidence suggests that angelica first bloomed centuries ago in Syria, but no one is certain. What is known is that 15th-century herbalists would fasten tiny bags of angelica around the necks of children to ward off evil spells.

MEDICINAL USES: AID YOUR DIGESTION

Angelica's leaves and roots contain essential oils and bitter-tasting compounds that can spark an appetite, help digestion, and relieve embarrassing gas. You can also rely on angelica tea when you're fighting a cold, the flu, menstrual cramps, heartburn, and even rheumatic pain.

Heavenly Mash

For a special after-dinner drink with close friends, try making this recipe about 5 days ahead of your feast — that'll give the flavors time to mingle. Here's the rundown on what you'll need:

2 oz. of chopped angelica stems (washed and dried)

2 pints of brandy

1 tbsp. of bitter almonds (skinned and ground)

1 pint of sugar syrup (just boil 2 cups of sugar in a cup of water for 5 minutes and voilà — you've created sugar syrup!)

Steep the angelica stems in a covered container with the brandy for about 5 days. On the day of the dinner party, add the almonds and strain. Finally, add the sugar syrup and mix together. Filter and put this mix into a bottle. Then sip (in moderation, of course) to your success!

BEST MEDICINAL FORMS

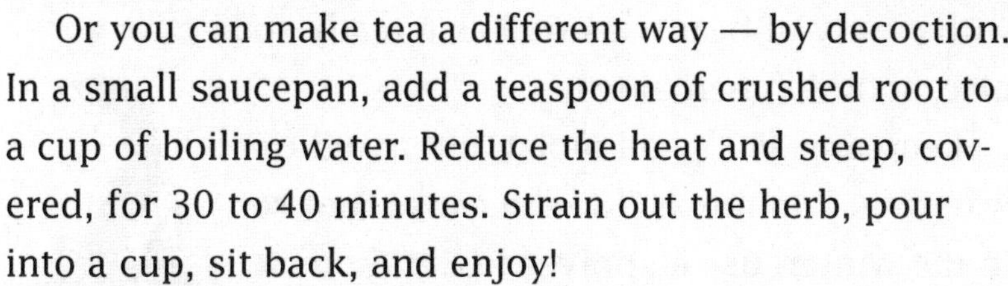

Angelica's leaves can be brewed into a dandy tea (it tastes a bit like celery) by putting a teaspoon of the dried herb (or 3 teaspoons of fresh crushed leaves) in a cup of boiling water. Steep for about 10 minutes, strain out the herbs, and pour into your favorite teacup.

Or you can make tea a different way — by decoction. In a small saucepan, add a teaspoon of crushed root to a cup of boiling water. Reduce the heat and steep, covered, for 30 to 40 minutes. Strain out the herb, pour into a cup, sit back, and enjoy!

For quick medicinal relief, place 20 to 40 drops of standardized angelica extract into a tall glass of water, then drink up. For most conditions, two glasses a day should do the trick. Extracts (also known as tinctures) are readily available at your local health food store.

GROWING TIPS

Whether starting from seed or buying an angelica plant from a garden store, you need to make sure the soil awaiting this herb is crumbly (not packed), moist, and rich. The other necessary conditions are good drainage and partial shade. Spacewise, angelica likes to be about 3 feet away from its nearest botanical neighbor in the garden bed. Height-wise, angelica is like an NBA center compared to most other herbs — when mature, it towers up to 8 feet high!

> ***FAST FACT***
>
> **Even though angelica** resembles celery in aroma, it actually belongs to the carrot family!

Angelica grows in Zones 4 to 9, preferring a cool climate and a slightly acidic soil that's been enriched with compost. The best time for the first planting of angelica is in July to August.

If you want to grow angelica indoors, keep in mind that this herb will thrive but may not reach the stature of its outdoor relatives; for some reason, containers seem to keep them stumpy. But it can still provide you with plenty of beauty as well as a ready source for a nice, soothing herbal tea.

Keep angelica's soil moist, but avoid overwatering. Too much H_2O can cause root rot. In the winter, use a sprayer to lightly mist the leaves each morning to combat dryness in the air. (You'll know it's time to break out the mister when you scuff across the kitchen floor and get a shock as you reach down to pet the family cat!)

HARVESTING TIPS

You need to practice a little patience with angelica. Although it's a biennial, it doesn't usually flower until its third summer. Then, after it flowers and seeds, the main plant usually dies. So in its second year, you should look for any side shoots that you can propagate and bring to bloom. The seeds must be fresh and planted during the fall, within a few weeks of ripening (otherwise, their ability to germinate diminishes).

A BLAST FROM THE PAST

During the late 1700s, American colonists would eat 2-year-old angelica shoots as a vegetable. They also boiled the stalks and rolled them in sugar for a sweet treat!

The good news is: Once you've established a plant and it has self-sown its seeds, you've got a garden friend for life! You'll get best results by harvesting angelica after the morning dew has evaporated. In late summer, cut stems at a node a few inches above ground level. Then strip the leaves from the cut stems. Using a spade, dig roots in dry weather in the early fall after the first year of growth.

Whatever you do, don't drink lots of angelica day after day. Taking this herb for prolonged periods of time can cause a slight skin rash or make some folks more sensitive to the sun's rays.

STORAGE TIPS

Make sure you store this herb (dried leaves or liquid extracts) out of light, heat, and air. These "bad boys" can sap angelica of its healing properties.

A Welcome Angel When You Itch

When the bug bites become unbearable, you can get relief from this true angel of herbs. You can use this treatment for bug bites, as well as for itchiness caused by scratchy clothes or allergies. Here's how:

2 tsp. of dried angelica leaves

2 cups of water

Put the angelica leaves in a small bowl. Bring the water to a boil, then pour it over the angelica leaves and let them sit for at least 15 minutes. When the liquid is cool enough, dab it onto your itchy spots. Stay out of the sun for a few hours after you've used this treatment. Angelica makes some people sensitive to sunlight.

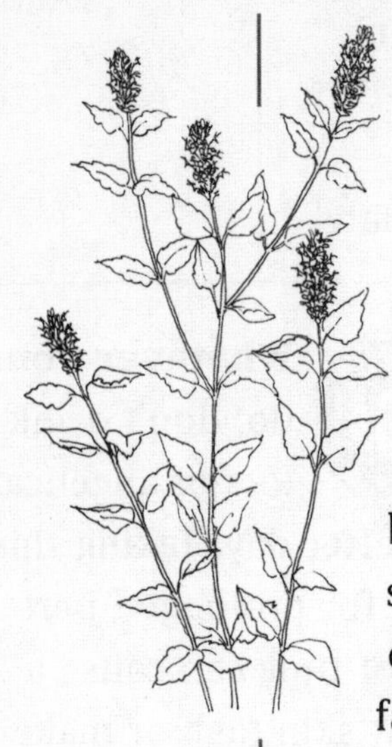

Anise Hyssop

(Agastache foeniculum)

Herbal ID

This shrubby plant features toothed, oval, green leaves on square stems and tiny, purplish blue spikes of edible flowers that bloom in late summer and fall. Its licorice scent reminds me of one of my favorite childhood candies: those old-fashioned, hard black candies that were sprinkled with powdered sugar.

That's Historical!

Native to North America, anise hyssop is also known as licorice mint or lavender mint. In Victorian days, it was second only to lovely lavender in popularity. Native American Indians, notably the Cheyenne and Chippewa tribes, drank anise hyssop tea to relieve chest pains and respiratory ailments. Cheyenne women also used it in their perfumes!

Medicinal Uses: Soothe Tummies and Throats

Folks have relied on anise hyssop for centuries to fight indigestion and to clear up sore throats and congestion.

Best Medicinal Forms

Probably the best way to reap its medicinal benefits is by using anise hyssop leaves and flowers in an herbal tea. Its blend of mint and sweet anise flavors makes it mmm-mmm good. Who says medicine has to taste bad? Not me!

GROWING TIPS

This fragrant herb, which is highly attractive to hummingbirds, grows best in Zones 4 to 9. Make sure you plant anise hyssop in the back row of your garden, because it grows up to 4 feet tall. (Just organize your

Sweetening the Pot

Why spoil a steaming cup of tea with boring old granulated sugar, when you can jazz it up instead? Just make a beeline for some anise-flavored honey. This herbal sweetener is ideal for cold or hot teas; it can also pinch-hit for baking recipes that call for sugar (yep, even chocolate-chip cookies!). To keep a sweet supply on hand, just follow me:

1 tbsp. of fresh anise hyssop (washed and dried) OR 1½ tsp. of dried anise hyssop OR ½ tsp. of anise hyssop seeds

2 cups of honey

Put the anise hyssop in a saucepan and add the honey. Heat on low until the mix is warm (overheating harms the honey, honey!). Then pour the mix into glass jars and tighten the lids. Store for about a week at room temperature.

OK, now you're in the homestretch! Reheat the mix and strain out any loose herbs. Return the honey to the original jars and batten down the hatches. Try a spoonful of this wonderful herbal mix in your next cup of tea, and you'll never go back to plain old sugar again!

garden according to height, like you did for those classroom photos — shorties in front and tall ones in the back, so everyone can be seen!)

Give this perennial plenty of sun, spacing plants about 2 feet apart. Use a standard potting mix, and keep the soil moist and fertilized regularly. If you want to use containers, go with 14-inch pots (but keep them outdoors). Make sure you pinch back plants in the early summer to encourage branching. After the first bloom, you'll guarantee a beautiful second flowering if you cut back the plant by half.

JERRY'S TOP 10 REASONS TO GROW ANISE HYSSOP

1. Bees and butterflies love it.
2. Its spiky stalks are gorgeous — even in winter!
3. Its name reminds me of a favorite aunt, Janice.
4. It smells absolutely fabulous.
5. It's simple to grow, since it self-seeds.
6. Mmmmm, it tastes terrific in fresh-baked bread!
7. It wins botanical beauty contests hands-down with its lavender-blue flowers.
8. It's one of my all-time favorite herbal teas.
9. It stands stately and tall in the back row of any garden.
10. Anise hyssop syrup (made with 5 chopped leaves, a cup of sugar, and a cup of water) on ice cream is a match made in heaven!

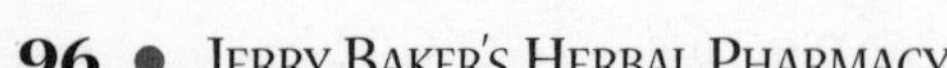

Anise hyssop produces large amounts of seeds, so pinch off any flowers after they bloom. By doing so, you'll extend the bloom season and save on weeding time. The seeds require light for germination and thrive in moist soil at 60°F.

One of the best reasons for growing this hardy herb is that it is rarely bugged by bugs — or diseases.

HARVESTING TIPS

Starting about midsummer, snip off leaves as needed, making sure that you start from the bottom of the plant. It's best to leave at least a third of the plant to grow until the late fall; then you can harvest all of the aboveground parts. Recycle anything you don't use by tossing the clippings onto your compost pile.

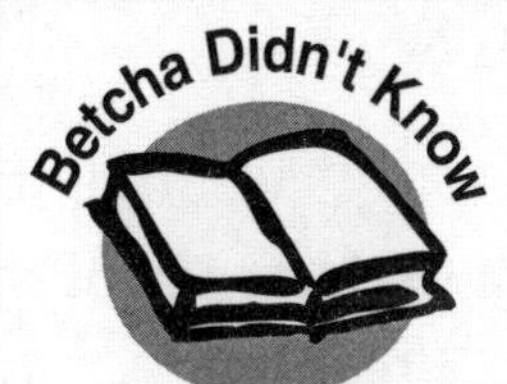

You can get rid of foul-smelling cigar odors as well as damp and musty smells with anise hyssop. It's easy: Just put some vinegar in a shallow bowl and let some of the herb's fragrant leaves float on top. By the next day, those nasty odors will be gone!

STORAGE TIPS

This herb's flowers are very popular with the dried floral arrangement crowd. For quick drying, find a warm, dark, airy place; then hang leafy stems upside down in bunches, or strip fresh leaves off the stems first. When the leaves are thoroughly dried (you'll know because they crumble easily), you can make potpourri. Or you can store them in airtight containers in a cool, dry place until you're ready to use them.

Basil

(Ocimum basilicum)

Herbal ID

This bushy, tender annual features smooth, bright green leaves and spikes of white, pink, or purple florets that bloom from midsummer to fall. Basil emits a strong, fresh fragrance with undertones of mint and pepper. It usually grows 1 to 2 feet tall.

That's Historical!

Basil's roots (I couldn't help myself) can be traced back to India, where it is prized as a sacred plant that brings happiness to households. Folks there would also bury a sprig of holy basil with the dead to offer protection from evil spirits in the next world.

The Italians, on the other hand, had a whole different idea when it came to basil: They swore it was a love potion! In Italy, when a lady was ready for her suitor to arrive, she would place a pot of basil on her balcony, slip into something more comfortable, and sing "Amore . . . !"

In America, we're a bit more practical; we've used basil as a mainstay in the kitchen since colonial times.

A BLAST FROM THE PAST

To this day, members of the Greek Orthodox Church regard basil as a holy plant. Legend has it that this herb was growing at the door of Christ's tomb.

MEDICINAL USES: BANISH BELLYACHES

Basil is nice as a spice, but it works wonders outside the kitchen, too! It is an antispasmodic and general bellyache cure-all. It fights infections, repels insects, stops everyday headaches, and even sharpens your mental alertness.

Let's say you're working in your garden and all of a sudden, a squadron of bloodthirsty mosquitoes heads your way. Beat them to the punch by rubbing fresh basil leaves on your exposed skin — and watch those winged vampires vamoose!

Hey, basil even works on warts! It contains a lot of antiviral compounds that make warts disappear faster than you can say, "Watch me pull a rabbit out of my hat!" Here's a folk remedy my Grandma Putt taught me: Just crush up a few basil leaves, place them right on the wart, and cover the area with a bandage. Change this dressing every day, and the wart should disappear within a week or so.

Betcha Didn't Know

The word *basil* is actually derived from two words. One is the Greek word *basileus,* or "king." The other comes from the word *basilisk,* a legendary reptile that could kill with just one evil glance. Talk about lethal lizards!

Basil's antiviral ingredients also help your body fight cold and flu infections as well as nagging coughs. This pungent herb will help open your pores so you can sweat and snap a fever. I put a tablespoon of basil (fresh or dried) into a cup of boiling water and let it simmer, covered, for about 10 minutes. Then I let it cool a bit and drink up.

For those times when you feel groggy and thick-headed and need a pick-me-up, try this: Dab a few drops of basil essential oil onto a cloth handkerchief and gently inhale. I tell you, it works better than a super-caffeinated cup of coffee!

BEST MEDICINAL FORMS

Basil is great-tasting medicine, whether you're making it into pesto, adding it to a cup of tea, or simply using it to adorn a salad. You can also reap its medicinal benefits by buying basil as an essential oil.

Dazzle with Basil

For a colorful and sweet-smelling potpourri, blend various dried basils in a basket. My favorite varieties are sweet, lemon, and licorice basils. Here's how to make your own pleasing potpourri:

1 quart of sweet basil leaves and flowering spikes

2 cups each of dark opal basil leaves and spikes, rosebuds, rose petals, and rose geranium leaves

1 cup of lavender blossoms

1 oz. of orrisroot

1 oz. of sweet flag powder

Make sure all of the plant materials have been thoroughly dried. Then carefully mix all of the dried leaves, flowering spikes, and lavendar blossoms by tossing them gently like you would a tossed salad. Add the orrisroot and sweet flag powder; then remix. Put the potpourri in a favorite basket, or store it in an airtight container away from sunlight until you're ready to use it.

A word of warning: Essential oils should only be used topically (on the skin) or in a bath (basil is a terrific stimulating herb). Never ingest them!

GROWING TIPS

What garden is complete without basil? Not mine! Just be sure to treat it with a lot of TLC: Tender Loving Cultivation. This annual is very sensitive to frost, so wait for your garden soil to warm up before you plant basil seeds. Even better, start basil seeds indoors about a month before the last threat of frost in your area. Baby it by using a soil rich in organic matter and an extra dose of compost.

Green Thumb Tip

Always plant basil next to tomatoes in your garden — they make terrific neighbors. Basil will help boost the vigor of your tomato plants and repel insects because of its strong, lingering fragrance.

Plant seeds about ⅛ inch deep, and press the soil gently over the seeds. Then sprinkle on some water and cover the containers with clear plastic wrap to trap the moisture. Keep them in a warm spot — like on top of the refrigerator — because basil seeds germinate best at around 75°F.

When the seedlings poke their little heads through the soil, remove the plastic wrap and place the container on your brightest windowsill. Water as needed, being careful to keep the soil moist but not saturated.

Jerry's Words of Wisdom

"Basil is boffo — you can never have enough. Plant plenty for pesto and to protect against pests!"

Freezer Paste??

I've discovered another way to freeze herbs: Make them into a paste! Here's how. First, puree them with oil until they're like a pesto. The herb flavor blends with the oil, and the oil protects the mix from being freezer damaged. Then pack the paste into airtight, freezer-proof containers.

Use the paste like dried herbs, but be careful because the flavor is a lot stronger! This method works well with basil, chervil, chives, dill, lemon balm, parsley, sorrel, and tarragon.

If you want to sow basil seeds outdoors, I've got two words of advice: Be patient! Wait until you're sure all threat of frost has come and gone — basil needs a toasty bed! Plant basil in full sun, keeping about a foot or more of space between the plants. Water plants weekly, especially during the long, hot summer. Your efforts will be rewarded with small spikes of white flowers.

HARVESTING TIPS

It's best to harvest basil only when the leaves are dry. Regular harvesting will ensure bushy growth; I pinch off the flower buds as soon as I see them. I also cut off the top 2 or 3 layers of leaves when the plants are about 8 inches tall. Cut the stems between 2 leaves (at internodes), and hang the harvested leaves and stems in a cool, dry place to air-dry.

STORAGE TIPS

Here's a great way to make sure you've got that distinctive fresh-basil flavor on hand any time of year: Try freezing fresh leaves in olive oil in ice-cube trays.

Presto Pesto!

No cook worth his or her salt should be without basil. Here's an easy way to make one of my favorites, basil pesto:

2 cups of fresh basil leaves, removed from the stem

½ cup of fresh parsley leaves

½ cup of olive oil

2 garlic cloves, peeled

¼ cup of roasted pine nuts

¼ cup of fresh Parmesan cheese

In a food processor or blender, puree the basil, parsley, olive oil, and garlic. Then add the nuts and Parmesan cheese and process briefly, until the pesto reaches the desired consistency. This recipe makes 2 very pungent cups of palate-pleasing pesto.

Bay

(Laurus nobilis)

HERBAL ID

This fragrant perennial tree or shrub sports pointed, shiny, dark green, oval-shaped leaves. Its tiny, yellow-green flowers bloom during the summer. Outdoors, bay trees stre-e-e-etch to 12 feet or more in height. Indoors, in a container, they have a lot less room to wiggle, so they rarely exceed 6 feet.

THAT'S HISTORICAL!

When rummaging through some old folk-remedy books, I discovered why bay has won me over: Its name means "victory" or "achievement." So that's why the Greeks and Romans crowned emperors, accomplished athletes, and esteemed statesmen with laurels made of bay leaves! Hey, mythology buffs: Remember that grove of bay trees lining Apollo's temple? He thought it would keep lightning "at bay."

And Delphic priestesses placed bay leaves between their lips when making prophecies. Talk about eating your words!

MEDICINAL USES: ZAP BUGS

Savvy chefs always keep a supply of bay leaves handy to add some zip to soups, meats, and vegetables. But this versatile herb goes above and beyond the call of duty in the kitchen. Herbalists respect bay as an astringent and digestive helper. It also contains chemical compounds that kill bacteria and fungi.

Plus there's even more for what aches you, literally. **Head:** Don't reach for Bayer — reach for bay instead. It contains parthenolides, which are compounds that make the pain subside. **Teeth:** Want fewer faceoffs with the dentist's drill? Buy a toothpaste with bay in it; it's a proven fighter of tooth decay. **Belly:** To ease the pain of a minor bellyache, make a cup of tea using fresh or dried bay leaves.

BEST MEDICINAL FORMS

This is one of the easiest herbs to use. Leaves — fresh or dried — contain such great healing properties, you'll want a bayloader to stockpile them!

GROWING TIPS

Bay is easy to please — just give it plenty of room to roam. In the garden, leave 5 to 6 feet of space between it and its blooming neighbor. Sow from seed in late spring, or buy plants from a local nursery. If you can't find a spot in your yard that gets full sun, don't bay at the moon; this herb will still thrive in the shade.

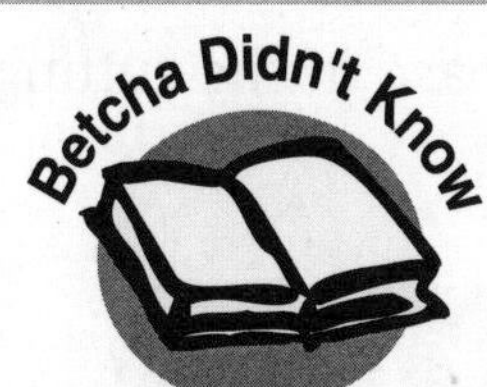

You can keep those winged warriors that inhabit the dark recesses of your pantry at bay by dropping a few bay leaves in your stored cereal, flour, and other grains.

Bay prefers mild climates and soil that is rich, loose, and slightly acidic. It grows best in Zones 8 to 11, especially in places where summers are warm by day and cool at night and winters do not dip below 10ºF. Bay-lovers living in northern zones should protect plants by moving them indoors for the winter.

You can save bay from scale insects by wiping down the leaves and stems with insecticidal soap or rubbing alcohol; neither will have any effect on its culinary taste.

Bay is the proverbial tortoise among herbal garden hares. It grows v-e-r-y slowly, so just be patient. Add to your inside bay inventory by pruning fresh green growth.

I live by the old saying "Make bay while the sun shines." The best time to propagate plants is usually late spring, when there are lots of new tips to choose from. Cut 3- to 4-inch-long shoots of half-ripened stems, right below a leaf joint. Pluck off the lower leaves. Since bay is a slow grower, dip the base of the cutting in a rooting hormone before

Tummy Care Tea

Does your stomach do somersaults (like mine) after eating stuffed peppers? Help it settle down with one of my favorite herbal tea blends:

1 tsp. of dried bay leaves
1 tsp. of ground ginger
1 tsp. of dried mint leaves

Mix the ingredients and scoop 1 teaspoonful into a cup of boiling water. Let it steep 5–10 minutes. Strain out the herbs, and add honey to taste.

placing it in a small pot containing a moist, light, soilless mix like vermiculite or perlite. Encase the cutting in a plastic bag, which will act like a homemade mini-humidifier. Keep the cutting out of direct sunlight. After a week or so, remove the bag; after a month, roots should have formed, and you can transplant the ba(y)by to a sunny place in your garden.

Bug-Free Windows

Here's an easy way to keep mosquitoes, flies, and other insects from staging a "we-want-in" convention at your windows:

¼ cup of vinegar

3 cups of water

8 tbsp. of essential oil of bay

Put the vinegar, water, and bay oil in a spray bottle. Tighten the nozzle and shake well. Clean your windowpanes as you usually do, and see 'em sparkle!

HARVESTING TIPS

It's easy — just pinch off a few leaves whenever the need arises, and rinse them clean. You can work them into recipes immediately, or lay them flat to dry.

STORAGE TIPS

Bay leaves can be frozen at harvesttime. Wash and then dry them thoroughly (test for "doneness" by seeing if they crumble easily in your hand). Then place them in a sealed plastic bag. Record the date and contents right on the bag, and stick it in the freezer.

Bee Balm

(*Monarda* species)

Herbal ID

This upright, bushy plant grows 3 to 5 feet tall, with dark green, oval, pointed leaves that are 2 to 3 inches long. In midsummer, bee balm struts its stuff with edible flowers in white, pink, magenta, scarlet, and purple. Take a whiff and you'll catch a scent that's both citrusy and minty. As a matter of fact, bee balm is a full-fledged member of the extended mint family.

That's Historical!

I'm not certain why, but long ago, bee balm was thought to be a symbol of virtue. Goodness — its reputation has stuck! It's also got a few aliases, including lemon bee balm, wild bergamot, Oswego tea, Indian nettle, prairie bee balm, and spotted bee balm.

Our forefathers in colonial days were so mad at the British taxing them here, there, and everywhere that they rebelled by boycotting black tea. (Remember how they tossed all of that tea into Boston Harbor?) The colonists found, shall we say, a less taxing tea in bee balm leaves. They took to sipping this "freedom" brew, grown right here on good old American soil.

Medicinal Uses: Repel bugs and Tame Tummies

Bee balm leaves contain a compound called thymol, which helps ease nausea, vomiting, and even that embarrassing flatulence. It's also used as a pleasant-smelling antiseptic. If you're under attack by gnats and mosquitoes, just rub fresh bee balm leaves on your exposed skin — it's one of Mother Nature's best bug repellents.

Best Medicinal Forms

If you're feeling like an overinflated dirigible, try a soothing cup of bee balm tea to ease gassy buildup. Combine a teaspoon of dried bee balm leaves with a teaspoon of China tea (black or green) leaves. Put a teaspoon of this mixture into a cup of boiling water and let it steep 5 to 10 minutes. Strain out the leaves and sip the tea, sweetening it (and perhaps your mood) with a teaspoon of honey.

Growing Tips

This hardy perennial can withstand temperatures of minus 30°F. Brrrr! In fact, it loves the outdoors; it just isn't too keen on being cooped up inside.

Bee balm grows well in partial shade in Zones 3 to 9, especially in the hot southern states, but it can also tolerate full sun. Just use a standard potting mix, and keep the soil moist. Add about a ½ inch layer of compost each spring, and you should be all set.

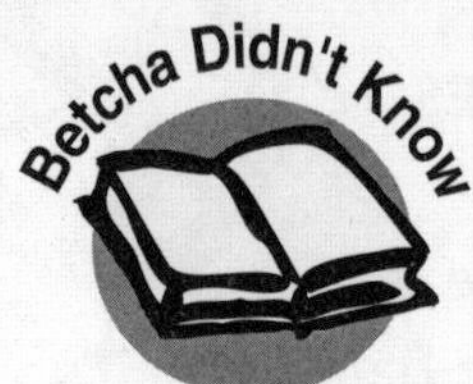

Bee balm loves to "buddy up" to peppers and tomatoes in the garden. So if you want your veggies to be the talk of the neighborhood, plant some bee balm near them. And, as its name implies, bee balm entices bees (as well as hummingbirds and butterflies) to make a beeline for your garden.

Don't say I didn't warn you — bee balm can be a garden hog! Unsupervised, it can literally take over other plants. So try to limit your stash to six plants, and give each one plenty of space — about 2 square feet.

To get a head start on your garden, you can start bee balm from seed indoors. In March or April, sow the seeds in moist starting soil in flats or pots, someplace where they'll get good airflow and plenty of light. Keep the temperature at 75°F. It's safe to transplant your seedlings about a week before the scheduled frost-free date for your area. Pick a cloudy day for transplanting, or hold off until late afternoon when the sunlight isn't as intense — your seedlings will thank you.

Can't get enough bee balm? Get as many plants as you want by dividing the roots in the spring.

HARVESTING TIPS

You can harvest bee balm leaves or flowers almost anytime, but the ideal time is after any dew has evaporated, just before the plants bloom in the early summer and again in early September. You can ensure an encore performance of bee balm next year by cutting back the plants to 6 inches after blooming in the fall and providing some seasonal protection from Old Man Winter.

If you've got a hankerin' for bee balm in a salad, simply snip individual leaves or fresh flowers as needed. For a dried floral arrangement or potpourri, cut the stems a foot or so below the blossoms. Allow the leaves to thoroughly dry in a dehydrator or on screens, and they're ready to use.

Pass the Pest Test

Does the faint bzzz, bzzz, bzzzing of mosquitoes hovering on your window screens drive you buggy? Here's bee balm to the rescue! First, wash the screens with a mild soap. Then spray on my bee balm infusion:

3 cups of water

2 cups of dried bee balm flowers and leaves

A 1-quart glass jar with a lid

Bring the water to a boil in a saucepan. Crumble the dried herbs and place them in the glass jar. Pour the boiling water over the herbs in the jar, bringing the water level to about an inch from the top. Stir the herbs with a wooden spoon to make sure they're well soaked. Put the lid on the jar and let the potion steep for about 15 minutes. Then strain out the herbs and pour the liquid into a spray bottle.

Now you're ready to take up the battle against unwanted pests. Just be sure to spray the screens from the inside out so you don't make a mess on the floor.

Blackberry

(*Rubus* species)

Herbal ID

This global grower answers to plenty of pet names including dewberry and brambleberry. Some species of blackberry are native to the United States, but others make their home in Europe.

Tender perennials, blackberries have slender, prickly branches. In the early summer months, the plant displays white, roselike flowers. Later in the summer, it's loaded with big, juicy, black fruits that can be eaten right from the bush or made into one of my favorites: wine or brandy. Height-wise, most blackberry bushes grow from 3 to 6 feet tall.

That's Historical!

Got a howling big toe? Ancient Greek physicians prescribed blackberry leaves and roots to get rid of gout.

Medicinal Uses: Calm Internal Distress

This is a very safe and gentle herbal remedy to treat a host of whatever-ails-you conditions. Blackberry contains plenty of tannins, but don't expect them to darken your skin. Without getting into the sordid details, let's just say that tannins provide an astringent effect that helps your intestines bind stools to reduce wateriness.

Besides diarrhea, blackberry helps relieve nausea and indigestion, stops bleeding caused by cuts, and heals minor burns. Blackberry also helps soothe tonsillitis and sore throats.

BEST MEDICINAL FORMS

The real medicine in blackberry is found in the bark, roots, and leaves. To relieve the runs, add 2 teaspoons of dried blackberry herb to a cup of boiling water. Let the mixture steep for 10 to 15 minutes, then strain out the herbs and sip. Drink up to 3 cups a day. The tea tastes tangy and delivers a delightfully cool, refreshing aftertaste.

You can also buy tinctures of blackberry from your health food store. The daily dose is 2 to 5 ml in a glass of water. Drink up to 3 glasses daily.

GROWING TIPS

Blackberry grows best in dry, sandy soil where it gets plenty of direct sun. That said, it can also tolerate partial shade. Space plants 3 to 5 feet apart along rows that are 6 feet apart. Keep the plants well pruned for two reasons: to ensure a good yield of berries and to avoid runaway blackberry plants in your garden. (Believe me, I know from firsthand experience.)

The first-year stems are sterile, but flowers will show up on the wood of second-year growth, so be patient. *Note:* For you folks living in northern states, you should protect blackberry leaves in cold weather.

HARVESTING TIPS

It's best to remove all old canes after the fruit has been harvested. Just snap them off at ground level in late fall or early spring, before the new growth appears.

Berry Nice Tea

To relieve indigestion or stop those annoying sniffles, try one of my favorite recipes:

1 tsp. of dried blackberry leaves
1 tsp. of dried rose hips
1 tsp. of dried alfalfa leaves
1 tsp. of dried hibiscus leaves
1 cup of water

Crumble all of the herbs together in a cup. In a small saucepan, bring the water to a boil; then add 1 teaspoon of the herb mixture. Reduce the heat and let simmer for about 15 minutes. Strain out the herbs and pour the tea into a cup. After a few sips, your tummy should start to feel better (and if it's a cold you have, you'll feel like less of a drip!).

Borage

(Borago officinalis)

Herbal ID

Borage, an annual, grows 2 to 3 feet tall. It features floppy stems, fuzzy silverish green leaves, and star-shaped, edible flowers that match the cool blue of a cloudless sky. Borage flowers and leaves taste like salty cucumbers. Although it originates across the ocean, this herb has adapted to and grows quite nicely in Yankee soil.

That's Historical!

Back in the days of Aristotle, Greeks used borage leaves to enliven their wines. Early American settlers used borage to remedy snakebites. Today, this leafy herb is making a comeback in modern gardens. It's not all of the way back, though, so you may have to hunt around a bit to find this herb. Seed catalogs are probably your best bet.

Medicinal Uses: Fight Fevers

Borage has been used for ages to fight fevers, reduce swelling, and soothe sore throats. It also acts as a "firmer-upper" for those times when mild diarrhea strikes. Some nursing moms use borage to help stimulate the flow of breast milk.

✓ Quickie Quiz

Q: What do borage and the Cowardly Lion from *The Wizard of Oz* have in common?

A: Both of them are known as symbols of courage and bravery.

Borage packs its own supply of potassium and calcium, which everyone needs to keep fluids flowing and bones growing. The seeds contain a fatty acid called gamma linolenic acid (GLA). GLA helps regulate hormones and lowers blood pressure.

What's Cookin', Good Lookin'?

For a general healthy pick-me-up, add fresh borage leaves to soups, stews, and sauces.

BEST MEDICINAL FORMS

The leaves, roots, and seeds of this herb are the storehouses of its best medicinal ingredients. You can buy borage in tincture form (also called an extract) at your health food store or use dried leaves for a healthy cup of tea.

To ease diarrhea, clear up a sore throat, or fight off a fever, add 4 ml of borage tincture to a glass of water.

Pick-Me-Up Tea

If you're feeling bone-tired and dragging, just head for the kitchen and whip up this easy shot of energy:

1 pint of water

2 tsp. of dried borage leaves

Boil the water in a saucepan and add the borage leaves. Put a lid on the pan, reduce the heat, and simmer for about 10 minutes. Be careful not to let this boil because you'll burn off the herbal benefits of borage. Then strain the tea and pour it into your favorite mug. To sweeten the deal, add some honey to taste.

Drink up to 3 glasses a day. Or you can add 2 teaspoons of the dried herb to a cup of hot water. Let it steep for about 5 minutes before drinking. Drink up to 3 cups a day for effective relief.

Remember: Everything is better if done in moderation. Eating or drinking borage now and then is perfectly safe. But if you eat or drink a lot of it every day for a long period of time, it can be toxic. Avoid borage if you have liver problems.

GROWING TIPS

I start borage seeds indoors, in 2-inch pots or peat pots, about 6 weeks before the last spring frost. The seeds do dandily if you plant them in a standard potting mix and keep the soil fairly moist and fertilized. Once you're certain the last frost has passed, it's safe to move borage outdoors.

Borage grows best in Zones 3 to 9. Find a spot in your garden that gets at least 4 to 6 hours of sunlight each day. And make sure you give each plant about 1½ to 2 feet of space. This is a very fast grower, so keep an eye on it, keep the scissors handy, and give it a haircut regularly.

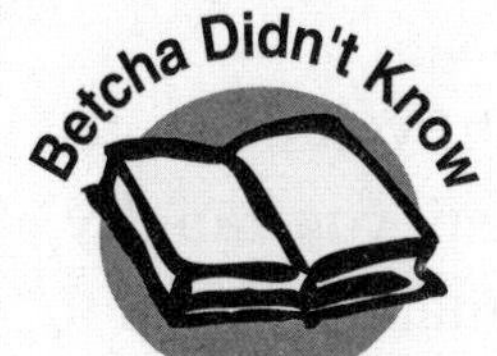

If you really want to impress your friends, try tossing a few borage leaves on the hot coals at your next barbecue. The nitrate in the leaves triggers sparks and pops, creating a mini-display of fireworks!

Borage can be one of your garden's best bloomin' friends. It strengthens the pest and disease resistance of neighboring plants, especially strawberries and tomatoes (tomato hornworms absolutely despise borage). This herb also attracts pollination-minded bees to your garden.

We all have our weaknesses, and borage is no exception — its lower leaves tend to rot. You can prevent this, however, by mulching with light materials like straw to keep foliage off the soil.

Plant borage seeds in late summer, and watch a rosette of leaves develop. Come next May or June, the plant should be showing off a full-flower bloom.

Keep Your Cool

For a neat treat, fill an ice-cube tray with water and add a borage leaf to each cube section. The next time you're ready for a glass of iced tea, pop a borage cube into your glass to liven it up a bit and deliver an extra cooling taste!

HARVESTING TIPS

It's best to gather the leaves before borage starts to flower, which is usually in early summer. Wait until any dew or rain has dried up, then snip off the best leaves, one at a time.

STORAGE TIPS

Borage leaves are best used fresh, but if you don't get to harvest them before the flowers open, you can dry them and store them in an airtight container for up to 2 years.

Calendula

(Calendula officinalis)

Herbal ID

This average-size annual reaches 18 inches in height at its peak. It has 2- to 6-inch-long leaves that are dark green in color with widely spaced teeth. Its sunny orange and yellow flowers usually appear from June to October. With a snip-snip here and snip-snip there, you've got a great collection of cut flowers for any vase.

With calendula, you can sniff all you want; it doesn't give off much of a fragrance.

During a botanical roll call, calendula also answers to the names pot marigold, Marybud, summer's bride, holygold, and gold-bloom. So keep them in mind when you visit your local garden center.

That's Historical!

Let me call you sweetheart, calendula. During medieval times, if a fair damsel couldn't decide which knight in shining armor to select as her suitor, she would turn to calendula for answers. Before heading for bed, she would mix calendula with honey and white wine. Then she'd rub it on her body and fall asleep. She may have stuck to her bed linens, but apparently the image of her future husband also stuck — in her head!

In the Wild, Wild West of the 1800s and on battlefields during the Civil War, cowboys and soldiers used calendula to help heal their bullet wounds.

MEDICINAL USES: HEAL INJURIES

The natural medicine in this plant hangs out in its petals and flower heads. This herb is used to stop swelling, ease spasms, stop bleeding, and fight germ warfare (namely bacteria, viruses, and fungi). It can boost immunity, too.

Not only does calendula treat hard-to-heal conditions like skin ulcers and herpes, but it can also leave your face with a clean, healthy glow and stop athlete's foot from attacking your toes!

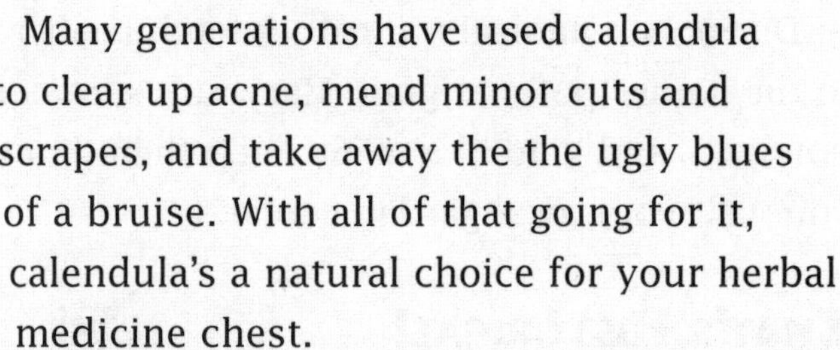

Many generations have used calendula to clear up acne, mend minor cuts and scrapes, and take away the the ugly blues of a bruise. With all of that going for it, calendula's a natural choice for your herbal medicine chest.

For women, calendula can be especially appealing. It helps prevent painful periods and also helps balance female hormones to ensure regular menstrual cycles.

Folks in science labs have traced some of calendula's healing power to ingredients called terpenes; the herb is also high in phosphorus and vitamin C. Calendula gets your white blood cells all pumped up so they can boot out unwanted foreign invaders and help speed healing.

This is one herb that has virtually no irritating properties or toxicities. So I give it two thumbs up and my "Safe Herb Seal of Approval!"

BEST MEDICINAL FORMS

This herb works well inside or outside of your body. For minor cuts and burns, healing begins as soon as you apply calendula as a lotion, poultice, or compress on the tender spot.

For those times when your belly is churning faster than a roller coaster, nothing puts the brakes on indigestion like a cup of hot calendula tea. Bright yellow in color with a taste that's slightly bitter and saffronlike, this tea provides fast, effective relief. To make some of this brew, just add 2 teaspoons of dried calendula florets and leaves to a cup of boiling water. Let it simmer for a good 15 minutes. Drink up to 3 cups a day.

You can also keep a bottle of calendula tincture on hand for emergencies. The typical dose is 1 to 4 ml of tincture in a glass of water, taken up to 3 times a day.

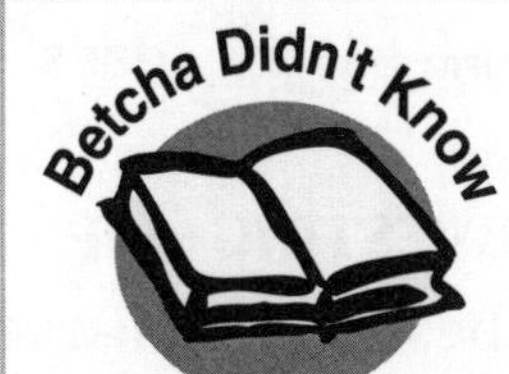

Calendula can help you get back in the swing of things, especially if you've got bunions. Just spread some calendula salve on the tender bunion a couple of times a day for a week. You'll notice a lot less aching in your strides and a lot more bounce in your step!

GROWING TIPS

Calendula is temperamental — but in a good way. This annual can flourish in the winter in southern climates. It will also demonstrate its flower power in the spring and summer in northern climates. In either locale, plant it in an area that gets full sun and where the soil is well drained and not super-rich in nutrients. I like to use it around my vegetable garden as a border. Just make sure to give it about a foot between plants.

> **✓ Quickie Quiz**
>
> How much high school Latin do you remember? (Hey, I only had to take it three times.) The name *calendula* comes from the Latin word *calends,* which means "the first day of the month." Ancient Romans probably named this plant *calendula* because of the long amount of time it stays in bloom.

Calendula is an easy-growing herb that thrives even when conditions are less than good. Even if you barely pay attention to it, it will reward you with plenty of brightly colored blooms. But if you see signs of leaf spot, stem rot, or mildew, rinse off the plants with a hose and pinch off any damaged leaves.

To give calendula a head start in the spring, plant seeds in containers indoors. After the final frost, they're ready to be transplanted outdoors. It doesn't take these seeds very long to pop out of the soil — generally only 10 days — so be prepared.

HARVESTING TIPS

The best time to harvest calendula is during the afternoon when the morning dew is long gone and the blooms are just opening. Here's the really neat part: The more blooms you pick, the more you'll have to pick because the plant is motivated to bloom again!

I like to dry the petals by laying them separately between sheets of brown paper in the shade. Don't let the petals touch each other, or they may discolor or fade. Once they are dry, you can just store them in a glass container in a cool spot away from direct sunlight.

STORAGE TIPS

Besides storing dried petals, you can keep whole, fresh calendula flowers in any kind of bottled salad vinegar. Just add a small handful to the vinegar. Besides having a jazzed-up flavor, your vinegar will be pretty as a picture!

Be Satiny Smooth, Even in Wintertime

The sharp, chilling winter winds can leave your skin feeling as dry as twice-used sandpaper. Make your skin feel smooth and silky with this herbal bath recipe:

½ cup of dried calendula petals

1 muslin bag or cheesecloth with a drawstring

Dried milk powder or oatmeal

Carefully put the flower petals inside the cheesecloth; then fill your bathtub with warm (not hot) water. Pour a little dried milk powder or a few teaspoons of oatmeal under the faucet. Add the bag of calendula petals and let it float around like a rubber duckie. Hop in, and soak yourself in the bath while the herbal oils get to work rejuvenating your dry skin!

Caraway

(Carum carvi)

Herbal ID

A biennial, caraway usually only produces leaves during its first year of life and then flowers during its second — and final — year. But I've found that sometimes it behaves more like an annual, bearing leaves and flowers during the same growing season! This herb is one of the shorter ones, growing no more than 2 feet tall. It has feathery leaves and lacy clusters of whitish and pinkish flowers during the spring and early summer months. A pungent plant, caraway produces spicy seeds, and its leaves taste a bit like dill.

That's Historical!

Caraway doesn't come up in most traditional wedding vows. But why not? According to folklore, caraway ensures that lovers stay together and never part. That might explain why it denotes "faithfulness." Caraway was also thought to have bewitching effects on witches — powerful enough to ward off a whole broom squadron! In colonial times, caraway seeds were carried in small pouches to prayer meetings as a way to curb the appetite and keep people's stomachs from growling during silent prayers! Why didn't I think of that?

MEDICINAL USES: COMFORT TUMMIES

These seeds are well equipped to take your car(es)away. They'll keep tummies tame, promote the onset of menstruation, relieve cramps, and help boost milk production in nursing moms. You can use caraway safely to ease the discomfort of gas, diarrhea, bronchitis, and even laryngitis.

BEST MEDICINAL FORMS

Long before over-the-counter medications ever existed, caraway was used in poultices to ease colds. Folks would just apply the poultice to the chest area to draw out congestion.

For upset stomachs, you can make a mild infusion of caraway in water or milk. Just grind or crush a teaspoon of seeds, then cover with a cup of boiling water and steep to taste.

When Your Appetite Fails

I'm usually rarin' to go when mealtime comes around, but sometimes I just don't feel all that hungry. When that happens, I like to sip about a tablespoon of caraway-flavored wine 10 or 15 minutes before dinner. Here's how to make it:

1 tbsp. of ground caraway seeds

1 quart of white wine

Put the ground caraway seeds into the white wine and let the mixture sit for about a week. Strain the wine through a very fine sieve.

As a tincture, the standard dosage is 4 ml of caraway dropped into a glass of water. You can safely drink up to 3 glasses a day.

GROWING TIPS

Caraway thrives in well-drained, sandy soil and sunny locations, but it will tolerate partial shade in southern climates. I like to work a half-inch layer of compost

Dining Delights

Caraway seeds — whether eaten raw, boiled, or baked — are not only delicious, they're nutritious, too! They make delightful seasonings in apple pie, cabbage, bread, and even boiled potatoes. For a real taste-temptin' treat, try this caraway cheese bread recipe:

4 cups of flour
2 cups of milk
½ cup of sugar
2 eggs
2 tsp. of baking powder
2 tsp. of salt
½ cup of vegetable oil
2 cups of grated cheddar cheese
⅔ cups of bacon bits
2 tsp. of caraway seeds

Using an electric mixer, combine all of the ingredients but the cheese, bacon bits, and caraway seeds in a large mixing bowl. Beat for about 30 seconds. Stir in the three remaining ingredients, and blend thoroughly. Pour the batter into 2 greased 9 x 5 x 3-inch loaf pans. Bake at 350ºF for about 50 minutes. Allow the pans to cool completely before slicing the bread.

into the soil before planting mine. Because caraway grows from a long taproot, it can be tricky to transplant, so I recommend sowing seeds directly in the ground; the best time is in early spring (or mid-fall, if you want an early crop the following spring). Plant the seeds about ¼ inch deep in the soil, and space them about 8 inches apart. A thin layer of compost on top doesn't hurt, either.

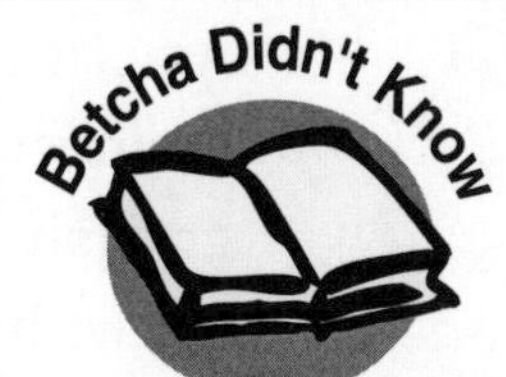

Caraway, among all herbs, has earned its senior citizen card. Get this: Caraway seeds have been found in meals that were left behind in caves during the Stone Age!

HARVESTING TIPS

For a fresh supply of caraway for cooking, pluck tender young leaves as needed when the plant is at least 5 inches tall. Caraway seeds usually ripen around August or September. Cut the seed heads when you notice the seeds darkening in color — but before they start to drop off. Hang them over a screen to collect the seeds, then let the seeds dry in a warm, shady spot with good airflow.

STORAGE TIPS

When you're ready to use dried caraway seeds in cookies, breads, or other foods, soften them up first in boiling water.

Catnip (Catmint)

(Nepeta cataria)

Herbal ID

Like its feline namesake, this perennial has been prowling the gardens of North America and Europe for centuries. A member of the mint family, it has pointy, grayish, scalloped leaves and white flowers with purple spots that bloom from June to September. While its strong-smelling leaves entice felines, its fuzzy-looking blooms are irresistible to honeybees.

That's Historical!

Long before British explorers discovered tea in China, catnip tea was the beverage of choice in England — paws up! It was thought to symbolize happiness, love, and beauty.

Botanically speaking, catnip got its name *(Nepeta)* from the Roman town of Nepeti, where the stuff grew wild.

Medicinal Uses: A Potent Relaxer

Catnip leaves and flowering tops contain acetic acid, tannins, terpenes, and volatile oils — as well as vitamins A, B, and C. These elements work together purrfectly to relieve muscle spasms, help battle colds and flu, nip fevers, ease diarrhea and gas, and relieve symptoms of bronchitis.

Among our furry feline friends, catnip is definitely the cat's meow! Crumble some dried leaves on the floor and watch your cat go bonkers rolling around in it. Even though your cat seems to lose it, there's no cause for alarm. Catnip is not a psychedelic or euphoria-producing drug; it just puts them in a naturally safe and feel-frisky mood. Pretty a-mews-ing!

For two-legged folks, catnip has just the opposite effect. Its essential oils can actually end those toss-and-turn nights. Drinking a cup of catnip tea, in fact, may induce a blissful catnap!

BEST MEDICINAL FORMS

Think of the two Ts: teas and tinctures. They are the best ways to take catnip when you're not feeling up to snuff. To make a tea, just steep 1 to 2 teaspoons of dried catnip leaves in a cup of boiling water for 10 to 15 minutes. You can drink up to 3 cups a day.

For nagging coughs and muscle spasms, try putting 2 to 4 ml of catnip tincture in a glass of water or juice. Give it a stir, and then drink to your good health.

GROWING TIPS

Catnip grows about 3 feet tall in moist, rich soil in Zones 3 to 10. To make this herb feel purrfectly at home, find a spot in your garden that gets sun or partial shade. Give each plant about 12 inches of space to grow. Catnip tends to look scraggly, so cutting back the plants after they flower will keep them looking neat.

Cat alert! Felines from all over will flock to your garden, lured by the catnip scent. So protect your young seedlings until they're big enough to resist overexcited cats, which will roll in them and try to eat them. Keep this old gardening proverb in mind: "If you set it, the cats will eat it; if you sow it, the cats don't know it."

Here are three of my cat-proof strategies.

Option 1: Try planting plastic forks (tines up) in and around your catnip bed. The fork tines will poke at cats when they try to flop and roll in the bed, which should be enough to keep them out.

Option 2: Keep kitties at paw's length by covering your catnip transplants with a chicken-wire cage for a few weeks after transplanting.

Option 3: If all else fails, plant a little catnip in a separate spot in your yard, and make it a cat garden. Then the felines can roll around to their hearts' content without destroying the catnip crop in your people garden.

Catnip grows easily, and without much of a fuss. Its seeds germinate best when they are shallowly planted. Once started, it will self-seed and grow year after year.

In reasonable amounts, catnip is very safe. But it's one of those herbs that you should take only as needed, not every day like a multivitamin. So if your condition does not improve within 2 weeks, stop taking catnip and check with your doctor. And just to err on the side of caution, herbalists and doctors say it's best to stay clear of catnip if you're pregnant or plan on being pregnant in the near future.

HARVESTING TIPS

The best time to collect catnip leaves for drying is from June until September. I always try to dry the leaves on their stems before the plants bloom, because that's when they're most potent. Just strip the leaves from the stems to store them. To keep them at their freshest, hold off on crumbling the leaves until you're ready to use them. Catnip's flowering tops can also be dried — for use in floral arrangements.

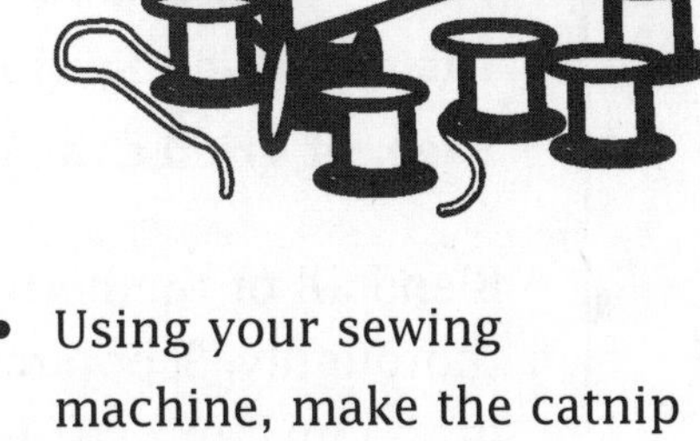

MAKE YOUR CATS MEOW!

For a special gift for that favorite feline of yours, quit mousing around and make your own catnip toy instead of buying one from the store. Here's how to make a homemade mouse that has real scents-appeal for cats:

- Harvest the catnip as soon as the flower buds just start to open.
- Dry the leaves on their stems, then rub them off.
- Get a tough fabric with a firm weave that can tolerate claws and teeth.
- Using your sewing machine, make the catnip toy about 3" by 2".
- Stuff fresh dried catnip leaves into the fabric, making sure to sift out any sharp twigs, and sew it shut.
- Call your cat, give the toy a toss, and, as they said in ancient Rome, "Let the games begin!"

STORAGE TIPS

Dry catnip leaves by air-drying or microwave-drying and store in an airtight glass cantainer. But don't freeze dried catnip leaves; cold puts a real chill on their medicinal properties.

Sweet Dream Tea

If you don't want to count sheep or take a sleeping pill, you can easily fall into a peaceful slumber with this special soothing recipe:

1 tsp. of dried catnip leaves

1 tsp. of dried mint leaves

1 tsp. of dried marjoram leaves

1 tsp. of dried chamomile leaves

Blend all of the herbs together thoroughly. Scoop out 1–2 teaspoons of the mix and stir it into a cup of boiling water. Let it steep for about 10 minutes. Strain out the herbs, and then sip yourself into dreamland!

Cayenne

(Capsicum annuum var. *annuum)*

Herbal ID

Viva la cayenne! Let me tell you, this is one hot annual. This shrubby plant grows 3 feet wide and features slightly curved fruits that turn red, orange, or yellow when ripe. The redder the fruit, the higher the vitamin content. The ripe fruit is a multi-seeded pod with a leathery outside.

Cayenne is also known by these spicy nicknames: chili pepper, hot pepper, and capsicum pepper. But its Greek name, *kopto,* captures its meaning in two words: "I bite." Just one chomp into a cayenne pepper and you'll know in a flash why it earned this name!

That's Historical!

Originally hailing from South America, cayenne is now widely cultivated across the globe for both food and medicine. It's often said that Christopher Columbus introduced cayenne pepper to Europe after his voyages to America.

Herbalists in the 17th century first thought this plant emitted dangerous vapors. (It's easy to see why, since anyone taking a strong whiff will suffer watery, reddened eyes.) Later on, they realized that it was safe to use.

MEDICINAL USES: RELIEVE PAIN

Holy-moly — mouth on fire! The medicinal part of cayenne is the fruit. This pepper heats things up not only in your mouth, but in the rest of your body, too. Cayenne hastens blood flow, speeds circulation, strengthens the heart, and is used as a general tonic for stomach upsets and colds.

I call cayenne Mother Nature's pick-me-up herb. When I feel a bit sluggish, or my muscles are feeling oh-so-achy from a long day of gardening, cayenne comes to the rescue, rejuvenating me and my muscles in a hurry!

Chock-full of vitamins A, C, and E, cayenne rates as a natural antioxidant. It also contains a real powerful substance known as capsaicin that helps relieve pain. A lot of folks with arthritis have found that cayenne gives them temporary relief from aching joints.

Jerry's Words of Wisdom

"Keep the neighborhood dogs and cats from dining on your trash by sprinkling a little cayenne pepper in, on, and around the garbage cans."

MEDICINAL FORMS

You'll find cayenne works its medicinal magic in all of its forms: fresh or dried, powder, tincture, cream, and ointment.

When you need to tend to sore muscles or arthritic joints, dab a little cayenne cream on the skin. The best creams contain 0.025 to 0.075 percent capsaicin. Use up to 3 times a day. *Warning:* Make sure you keep this powerful stuff far away from your eyes and nose — or you'll really be smarting!

When partnered with myrrh, cayenne makes for a terrific mouthwash that not only kills germs, but leaves your breath feeling spicy fresh. Just dilute 5 to 10 drops each of cayenne and myrrh tincture in a half glass of warm water.

Cayenne adds the right zest to Buffalo wings, but it can cause an eye-watering sting if it accidentally gets in your peepers. If it does, immediately flush your eyes with lots of cold water.

For you folks living in the north, you'll never have to worry about icy feet again! Just do what I do on bitterly cold days: Sprinkle a little ground cayenne pepper in your socks, slip on your boots, and your toes will stay toasty warm all day.

To make tea, mix a tablespoon of cayenne in a cup of boiling water, and let it simmer for about 10 minutes before drinking. Or you can keep a bottle of cayenne tincture in your medicine cabinet and take 1 ml in a glass of water up to 3 times a day as needed.

GROWING TIPS

Cayenne thrives in very hot climates like the tropics and subtropics. But it also does quite well in colder places during summer months, or indoors year-round as a houseplant. As long as there is plenty of sun, cayenne will grow in Zones 5 to 11.

Give cayenne moist, well-fertilized soil that is neutral to slightly acid. In colder climates, start the plant by sowing seeds indoors in late spring. Wait until the final frost to plant outdoors. Plant 12 to 18 inches apart, and make sure the soil is well mulched, especially if your summers are dry. As summer turns into fall, there's no need to worry — cayenne can usually withstand a light frost.

Cayenne isn't invincible, but it is one tough hombre, standing up to most common plant pests and diseases.

Harvesting Tips

When the fruit is fully ripe, cut the peppers from the plant — but leave at least ½ inch of stem. Plop the picked fruits right onto screens — or string them together using a needle and fishing line; then hang them up to dry in a warm place that is out of direct sunlight.

Storage Tips

Dried peppers can be stored whole, or you can grind them into flakes using a blender or food processor (just make sure you wait until all the pepper dust has settled before opening it, unless you want a good cry!).

Cold Hands—Take Courage!

I love crispy cold winter days, but my hands don't! Here's an old-time remedy that really works:

2 tsp. of cornstarch **1 tsp. of cayenne**

Mix the cornstarch and cayenne together, then sprinkle a little of the mixture into your mittens. The cayenne will increase the circulation in your fingers and warm your whole hand. Be sure to wash your hands after you remove your mittens. If cayenne gets into your eyes, it will cause them to sting.

Chamomile, German

(Matricaria recutita)

Herbal ID

A member of the daisy family, chamomile is kin to both calendula and echinacea. It grows about 18 inches tall and features delicate, fern-like leaves and daisyish flowers with silver-white petals and yellow centers.

That's Historical!

Chamomile has been healing folks around the world for over 2,000 years. Ancient Greeks called this herb ground apple because of the sweet scent it gives off when bruised or walked on. (That's certainly better than being known as a road apple!) Anglo-Saxons thought highly of this plant, including it among the nine sacred herbs believed to have been given to the world by the god Woden.

Medicinal Uses: Terrific Tension Tamer

Chamomile flowers contain a lot of chemicals that help the body. Sometimes they work as a team; other times they go solo.

Let's say you've got an upset stomach. One of chamomile's chemicals, called alpha-bisabolol, comes to the rescue. For sore muscles, another chemical called azulene is an anti-inflammatory.

Chamomile is a distant cousin to ragweed and chrysanthemums. So if you start to tear up and sniffle at the mention of these plants, you may want to avoid using chamomile just to be on the safe side.

Chamomile works wonders on muscle spasms and protects against ulcers. It also helps us wind down and relax naturally after a hectic day. Some herbalists say that it may be the herb most widely used for relaxation.

Chamomile is also like having a dentist right in your home — minus the drilling! Help keep your gums healthy by getting into this daily habit: Infuse 2 teaspoons of chamomile in a cup of boiling water and let it steep for a good 10 minutes. Drink a cup after every meal and let chamomile do what it does best: kill germs and reduce your risk for gingivitis.

And let's not forget our furry friends. If you tuck a few dried chamomile flowers into your dog's or cat's pillow, it'll help keep fleas from coming home to roost.

A BLAST FROM THE PAST

One of my favorite books from childhood was *The Tale of Peter Rabbit,* by Beatrix Potter. As you may recall, Peter's mum was a pretty smart bunny: She gave Peter spoonfuls of chamomile tea to calm down his tummy and help him relax after a fitful day in Mr. McGregor's garden!

BEST MEDICINAL FORMS

Sip and heal. Chamomile is most effective in a cup of hot water. Find yourself a comfy, quiet spot and enjoy the tea, especially when your stomach is doing flip-flops, you feel a little anxious, or you're just having trouble falling asleep.

To make tea, add a heaping tablespoon of whole dried chamomile flowers to a cup of hot water. Let it steep for 5 to 10 minutes (any longer and it may taste bitter); then strain. A little dab'll do you — just one dried flower delivers more flavor than a store-bought tea bag! You can safely drink up to 4 cups of tea a day.

If you've got a minor eye infection or pink eye, chamomile makes a wonderful — and safe — natural eyewash. Dissolve about 10 drops of tincture in warm water. Dip a washcloth in it, wring it out, and then lay it across your closed eye for 5 to 10 minutes.

Chamomile tincture is also good for upset, irritable bowels. Other forms include ointment (for insect bites), inhalation (for hay fever), and capsules (for indigestion and heartburn).

GROWING TIPS

This is one of the best herbs for beginning gardeners because it's a cinch to grow. Just scratch its tiny seeds lightly into the top layer of soil — don't even bother covering them. Within a couple of weeks, you'll spot some feathery seedlings poking up through the soil.

This perennial ground cover grows best in Zones 3 to 8; blooming time is usually early June. The best part is that chamomile self-sows so easily that you'll only need to buy it once. Plant it in moist, well-drained soil, in sun or partial shade. Each chamomile plant needs only about 6 inches of space, but watch out — it can give your garden the creeps (as in creeping ground cover, not the B-movie horror kind of creeps). In fact, if you're having trouble keeping grass growing in a particular area

Bail Out Dry Nails

Do your fingernails dry and crack easily? Sounds like they need an oil and lube job. So once a day, rub chamomile-infused olive oil into your nails to soothe and moisturize them.

of your lawn, chamomile makes a great substitute. Also, it's a fairly hardy plant that isn't easily bugged by garden pests or diseases.

HARVESTING TIPS

To stock up on a winter's supply of chamomile, you'll need to harvest and dry the flowers in June, before they're likely to mold. Keep about a third of the plant growing at midseason harvest, and gather the entire plant in the fall before the first frost.

HOTEL ZZZZZS

Before your next family vacation or business trip finds you staying in a noisy hotel, pack a container of chamomile leaves and a chamomile dream pillow in your suitcase. It's really easy to make a dream pillow. Take two same-size washcloths, and with their good sides together, sew around three edges. Turn them rightside out. Fill the pouch loosely with about 2 cups of dried chamomile flowers. Then stitch the open end shut. Stick this little pillow on top of your hotel pillow, and soon you'll be sleeping like a baby.

Chicory

(Cichorium intybus)

Herbal ID

This perennial herb features a long taproot that's yellow on the outside, white on the inside, and contains a bitter, milky juice. Between midsummer and mid-fall, chicory will dazzle you with its light blue and violet-blue, shaggy flowers. Often found along roadsides and in hedges, it grows 3 to 5 feet tall.

That's Historical!

Chicory's roots stretch back all the way to ancient Egypt, some 5,000 years ago. That's one old herb! Doctors from King Tut's era apparently discovered that chicory helped to put the brakes on a runaway heartbeat.

In merry old England, chicory broth was a favorite drink of Queen Elizabeth I. In more modern times, Thomas Jefferson imported chicory seeds from Italy for his Monticello farm. His career blossomed right alongside the chicory!

Medicinal Uses: Flush Fluids

Chicory's medicine is concentrated down in its roots. This herb is packed with so many valuable nutrients and minerals that it could rival a bottle of the best multivitamins. Headlining the list are vitamins A, B, and C; calcium, potassium, phosphorus, and iron; plus a bunch of chemicals that kill bacteria and reduce swelling. Put them all together and you've got a mega-medicinal herb tough enough to fight stomachaches and flush your body of excess fluid, yet tender enough to act as a safe, natural laxative.

It's even got a bonus for folks with diabetes: Scientists have proved beyond a shadow of a doubt that fresh chicory root contains inulin, a dietary fiber that's safe for diabetics.

My Grandma Putt used chicory roots as a tonic and mild stimulant to treat sinus woes, jaundice, and even gallstones.

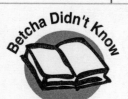

Betcha Didn't Know

Goldfinches love to perch on spent chicory blooms and feast on the seeds. The yellow shade of these winged wonders paired with the vibrant blue of chicory's flowers makes for a beautiful sight in any garden!

BEST MEDICINAL FORMS

Chicory is used as a coffee substitute, food, and herbal medicine. If you're a coffee lover looking to cut back on all those caffeine-fueled cups of joe, try subbing roasted chicory roots as your hot drink. Not only is chicory caffeine-free, but it's smoother tasting than coffee. And it's healthier for you: Chicory doesn't sap your energy like coffee does.

Plus, it's easy to make. First, rinse chicory roots well. Cut them into half-inch slices, and then place them on an ungreased cookie sheet. Let them bake at 200°F until the pieces of root get very dry and brown in color. Take them out of the oven and let them cool completely before storing in tightly closed glass jars.

When you're ready for coffee, throw some roasted chicory root into the coffee blender and voilà: healthy herbal coffee!

If you want to try my gourmet version, blend equal parts of ground chicory root with milk thistle seed and dandelion root. Stir a tablespoon of this mix into a mug of boiling water for a real energy boost. If all of this seems like too much work, bags of chicory "coffee" are available at most health food stores. Check them out for a delightful change of pace.

Chicory leaves also make tasty additions to salads, stir-fries, and pasta dishes.

GROWING TIPS

Hot, hot, hot! Chicory craves a sizzling sun and does well in average to poor, well-drained, lime-rich soil. Sow the seeds in the early spring, and once they're up, thin the seedlings to about a foot apart. I recommend mixing compost into the soil before seeding to keep the chicory healthy. Zones 3 to 9 offer the best climates for growing chicory.

As one of your taller herbs, chicory should be in the back row of the garden so you can have a full, unobstructed view of all your herbs. Its deep taproots grow best in deeply worked soil, but chicory can also thrive in heavy clay soils. So the moral is, don't worry too much about the soil.

This fast grower tends to shed a lot of seeds. So pay attention because once they muscle into an area and develop deep taproots, it can be difficult to thin out a chicory jungle!

Pests and plant diseases generally steer clear of chicory, especially if you avoid planting it in areas that tend to be wet most of the time.

HARVESTING TIPS

Once the plants measure 6 inches tall, you can harvest fresh leaf tips as needed throughout the summer. Make sure you leave at least a couple of inches of stem above ground level for future growth.

STORAGE TIPS

Chicory is terrific fresh or dried, but it freezes poorly.

TICK-TOCK THE CHICORY CLOCK

A famous Swedish botanist named Linnaeus discovered that the bright blue blossoms of chicory open and close each morning and night with clocklike regularity. He was so impressed by its on-time performance that he included chicory in a floral clock that marked the hours with blooms. Talk about a clock that never needs a new battery!

Chives

(Allium schoenoprasum)

Herbal ID

One whiff of this herb will clue you in: Chives belong to the onion family. This lean, green perennial features small bulbs and grass-like, hollow-spear leaves that grow in clumps up to 18 inches tall. In early summer, chives produce tiny, round, lavender and pink flowers.

That's Historical!

Chives originated in Europe and Asia. In ancient Rome, Gypsies were said to use chives for fortune-telling. Others relied on chives to scare away evil spirits. No matter how you slice them, down through the ages they've maintained their reputation for being one of the most useful herbs around.

Medicinal Uses: Stimulate Your Appetite

Chives can help keep a lid on high blood pressure, just like their botanical cousin the onion. Chives also stimulate the appetite and help with digestion. Plus, they're stuffed with healthy amounts of iron and vitamin C. What more could you ask for?

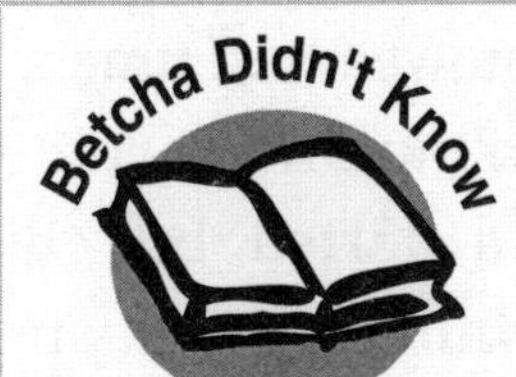

Marco Polo, the travel-by-elephant Italian, introduced chives to Europeans after discovering them during his journeys to China.

BEST MEDICINAL FORMS

Fresh is best, so bon appétit! You can have your medicine and eat it too by sprinkling chives on salads, baked potatoes, or my personal favorite: scrambled eggs.

GROWING TIPS

Start chive plants from bulbs, or from seed in Zones 3 to 10. I like growing them in clumps rather than straight rows. In early spring, you can divide chives into clusters of 5 to 10 bulbs for each new start. Every couple of years, you'll need to divide the old clumps to keep them from becoming overcrowded.

Chives thrive in full sun and average soil that is evenly moist and fertilized regularly. This herb is a big drinker, so make sure you give it plenty of H_2O. Also, give each plant about 10 inches of elbowroom. A little mulch around each plant helps keep grasses and weeds from taking over.

Maintenance alert! Cut and throw away the spent flowers to keep the chive plants from dropping large amounts of seed in your garden. Pinching off flowers after they bloom — also known as deadheading — helps save you weeding time.

I don't know exactly when the feud started, but chives are definitely not on speaking terms with peas. (You won't see chives sporting a bumper sticker that reads GIVE PEAS A CHANCE.) So keep the roots from wrestling by planting these two garden adversaries far apart.

HARVESTING TIPS

The nice thing about chives is that they're ready when you are. Snip the fresh leaves as needed throughout the entire growing season for a fresh oniony dip, for soups, salads, omelets, casseroles, or other favorite dishes. In late fall, before Jack Frost starts nipping at the bulbs, transplant a few clumps into containers. Leave them outdoors for about 8 weeks after the first frost, to give them time to adjust to their new containers. Then bring the pots indoors and put them on a sunny windowsill. Pick a spot that gets at least 5 hours of direct sunlight each day. You'll be rewarded with fresh, tasty chives all winter long!

Viva la Chive Vinegar

To liven up your garden greens salads, try my simple recipe for chive vinegar. The acid in the vinegar draws out the essential oils in chives to deliver a full, clean bouquet of flavors. Just follow these four steps:

Step 1. Chop up about a cup of chives and chives blossoms.

Step 2. Heat 2 cups of white wine vinegar or cider vinegar in a saucepan on the stove until it's warm. Do not let it reach a boil.

Step 3. Bruise the chives by rubbing them between your fingers as you drop them into a glass jar. Pour the warm vinegar into the jar and seal it shut.

Step 4. Let this vinegar-chive mix steep for a couple of weeks. Then open it up, strain out the herbs, and reseal. *Et voilà!* You have a hardy supply of herbal seasoning looking lovely with lavender hues.

When harvesting, cut chives only when they are dry, meaning dew- or rain-free (otherwise, they get slimy very quickly). Here's how to do it: Take a knife and slice through the greens about an inch above ground level.

Stems and flowers can be dried easily for later use. Over time, chives usually keep their size and color but may lose some of their distinctive, pungent odor.

STORAGE TIPS

Rinse freshly cut chives under a faucet to clean away any dirt or pesky bugs. Give them a gentle shake, put them in a plastic baggie, and store in the crisper drawer of your refrigerator. You can also preserve chives in the freezer, but not in baggies. Instead, puree chives with water in a blender. Then freeze them in ice-cube trays for on-call use, especially during the winter months.

Home-dried chives lose their flavor quickly, so I prefer keeping a fresh supply in the winter on the windowsills or buying freeze-dried chives. Somehow, the commercially prepared chives seem to keep their flavor much better than homemade ones.

HALT THE SALT!

If you want to reduce the amount of salt in your diet, you can try salting herbs the way my Grandma Putt used to do. It's an old-fashioned way of culinary herb preservation that works delightfully well with chives. First, harvest your chives, then wash and let them dry completely. In a glass jar, pack alternate layers of fresh chives and salt. For best results, make sure that the first and final layers of salt are thicker than the middle layers. Put the lid on the jar and place it on a cool, dry shelf in your kitchen, within arm's reach of the stove. Then, instead of using the salt shaker when recipes call for salt, reach for the chive shaker. You'll cut your salt intake by half without sacrificing any flavor!

Jerry's Words of Wisdom

"I'm not going to tell you that herbs or any other cool-temperature plants that require a lot of sunlight can be brought back to health in a warm kitchen, especially if they are in a west or northwest window. But if the temperature in the window goes below 45°F at night and does not rise above 60°F during the day, then herbs will probably thrive."

Cilantro

(Coriandrum sativum)

Herbal ID

Cilantro is a bright green, leafy annual that feels right at home in the kitchen (as do its seeds, which are called coriander). The leaves are parsleylike, and the tiny flowers are pinkish white and edible. This herb offers a refreshing, unique taste that, for some folks, takes time to acquire. With repeated sampling, though, its aroma grows on you and makes you long for more!

That's Historical!

It's hard to pinpoint it exactly, but my best research says cilantro originated in the Middle East. Its popularity soon spread to Asia and Europe — particularly Thailand, China, Spain, and Portugal — and now it's gaining fame here in the United States.

Medicinal Uses: Freshen Your Breath

Although you may know cilantro as the herb that makes salsa, well . . . salsa's seeds are just the thing when your stomach is upset, or when you're feeling tense. Chewing the seeds also freshens your breath.

Growing Tips

Pay heed: This is one herb you need to seed. Sure, you can buy mature cilantro plants from mail-order sources or the local garden center, but by that time, the plant's life is just about over. Cilantro plants flower, or "bolt," quickly once they're planted in the ground, a time-saver if it's coriander you're after.

Sow the seeds just under the surface of the soil. Use standard potting mix, and keep the soil moist and fertilized regularly. I like to use a nutrient-rich fish fertilizer. You can plant the seeds right in the garden or in 12-inch pots. For the garden scene, space them about 18 inches apart in full sun or part shade. In about 2 weeks, germination will take place. To maintain a steady supply of lush cilantro all season long, it's best to plant a new batch of seeds every few weeks.

Cilantro is a tender herb that can't take chilly weather. Fortunately, it grows easily indoors during the cold winter months. I like to keep pots of cilantro in a cool spot that gets plenty of bright light. If you start seeds in the fall for a winter's supply, don't expect them to bloom. These indoor plants won't flower like their outdoor summer cousins, but their leaves and roots will still be tasty.

Supermarket Shopping Savvy

For the best cilantro in the produce section, select the sprigs with roots attached. The roots help the herb last longer and provide a highly prized taste of their own. Stay clear of any batches with yellow or brown leaves or slimy-looking spots.

DASTARDLY DISEASES

You can easily earn a PhD (Plant-helping Doctorate) in gardening by being on the lookout for early signs of diseases that can strike cilantro, particularly powdery mildew and leaf spot. To avoid both, plant cilantro where it will have plenty of air swirling around it.

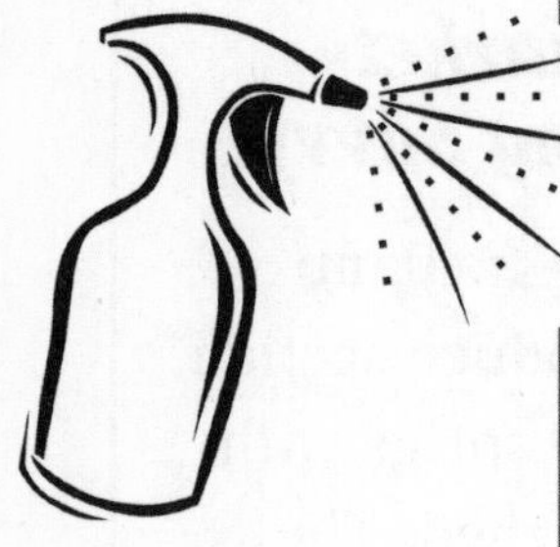

If powdery mildew infects your cilantro plants, you can rescue them by mist-spraying chamomile tea on the leaves. Or dissolve 1 teaspoon of baking soda in 2 quarts of water and spray it on the leaves. Either way, treat daily until the mildew vanishes.

HARVESTING TIPS

Like any annual, cilantro's sole aim in life is to reproduce itself. If you let your plant go to seed, it will die and go to that great garden in the sky. But if you pinch off the flower stems as they appear and don't let the plant create seeds, it will keep on growing throughout the season.

You can snip off leaves anytime you need for salads, pastas, and other favorite dishes. But when you're ready to harvest the seeds, wait until about 45 days after planting. Make sure they are fully ripe: A telltale sign is brown seeds that smell super spicy.

STORAGE TIPS

A fresh, steady supply of cilantro is certainly the best. Whether you collect the cilantro from your garden or buy it from your grocery store's produce section, you can prolong its freshness by first washing the leaves. Then wrap the clean cilantro in damp paper towels and place it inside a plastic bag. Seal it and store in the crisper drawer of your refrigerator. Or you can keep a bouquet of flowers in a vase of water on the windowsill. Just change the water daily to keep it fresh.

Alas, forget about freezing cilantro leaves; the chill kills its flavor. But you can try two creative storage methods with butter and oil. Cilantro makes a wonderful butter. Just soften unsalted butter (or margarine), and mix in chopped cilantro and lemon juice. For each batch, aim for 4 parts butter, 2 parts cilantro, and ½ part lemon juice. Store it in the refrigerator or freezer.

Say Sí! Sí! to Salsa

Salsa without cilantro is like, well, Fred without Ginger, or Batman without Robin. Treat your guests to this great homemade salsa sauce they'll never forget:

⅓ cup of fresh cilantro, chopped finely

8 tomatillos, husked, rinsed, and chopped (or you can use canned tomatillos)

½ cup of green chilies, chopped

2 serrano chilies, minced and seeded

½ cup of chopped onion

1 tsp. of minced garlic

Blend all of the ingredients in a food processor or blender until they're nearly as smooth as pudding. Refrigerate this zesty mix for at least an hour before serving. Then pour it into a bowl, and dig in with tortilla chips! This recipe makes about 1½ cups of fresh salsa.

Clover, Red

(*Trifolium pratense*)

Herbal ID

Red clover answers to the names wild clover and purple clover, too. All belong to the legume family. Clover features trifoliate leaves that spring up from the roots of lanky, reddish stems. In the heat of the summer, pinkish purple flowers emerge with blooming splendor. These flowers provide a delicate, sweet taste.

That's Historical!

Ancient Chinese cultures revered clover as a plant that was blessed with medicinal value. They used it to stop coughs, act as a natural diuretic, and fight cancer. Long before modern science, the Chinese realized that in order for tumors to grow, they need a steady supply of blood to survive. It turns out that clover contains a compound called genistein that starves tumors by preventing new blood vessels from forming.

Holy cow! Long ago in Europe, red clover was used as a fodder crop for cattle. In addition, many Christians thought the triple-leaf clover could shoo away witches and sorcerers, so they adorned their churches with them.

Medicinal Uses: Clean Skin and Fight Coughs

Clover makes an excellent natural skin cleanser. The good part: Clover is free of any artificial ingredients that can irritate sensitive skin. In addition, its flowers can stop a cough in its hacking tracks for folks with whooping cough and bronchitis.

It seems that clover is chock-full of compounds called isoflavones that some studies suggest help prevent certain kinds of cancer (including breast and prostate). It also contains phytoestrogens, noted for their abilities to balance hormones and relieve menstrual and fertility problems. Clover also sports a lot of key vitamins and minerals, including vitamins B and C, plus calcium, magnesium, and potassium.

Folks who smoke cigarettes can help kick the habit by chewing on fresh clover flowers instead. Clover satisfies the oral needs of smokers, and it is nicotine-free!

BEST MEDICINAL FORMS

An herb of many talents, clover is available in many healthful forms. When picked from the garden (make sure it's free of pesticide sprays), its leaves can be crushed in the palm of your hand and put directly on insect bites and stings for almost instant relief from itch and pain.

As a tea, I recommend you put 3 teaspoons of dried clover flowers in a cup of boiling water, and let it steep with a lid on for 10 minutes. Then strain out the herbs and sip. For coughs, 3 cups a day does just dandy! Clover tea is also a liver ally, helping to keep this important organ cleansed and working properly.

In tincture and capsule forms, clover helps relieve a

couple of skin conditions: eczema and psoriasis. The daily dose is 2 to 4 ml in tinctures, and 2 to 4 g in capsules, up to 3 times a day.

There are also some more unusual ways to take clover. For generations, some of my kinfolk have taken spoonfuls of clover syrup to quiet dry, persistent coughs. Others have raved about how clover compresses ease their arthritic aches and pains. A clover eyewash clears up conjunctivitis naturally if you add 5 to 10 drops of clover tincture in a full eyecup and rinse each eye. Last, but certainly not least, folks tell me that you can relieve vaginal itching by douching regularly with a clover infusion.

WHOA! **If you buy a** tincture or other pre-packaged clover product, make sure you get the nonfermented version. Fermented clover is not safe, and therefore it should be avoided. Because red clover is a blood thinner, you should not use it if you are going to have surgery. Avoid red clover if you are pregnant.

Growing Tips

Most meadows throughout the United States, Canada, and Europe are literally covered with clover. Although it is technically a short-lived perennial, a lot of gardeners regard clover as an annual or a biennial. It barely reaches 2 feet high and needs lots of sun.

Clover is an easy-to-grow herb that doesn't need much fussing. For best results, sow the seeds over a wide area in the spring. You can also sow a crop in the fall for the following spring. A lot of farmers use clover as a cover crop because it returns nitrogen to the soil. Also, clover isn't very picky — it thrives in common garden soil and even in rock gardens!

Harvesting Tips

It's ideal to harvest the flowers when they are in full bloom. In late summer, check the plants daily for new blooms. Also, it's best to air-dry the blossoms rather than oven-dry them. I like to dry the blossoms on a screen in a warm, dry, shady spot.

Storage Tips

Store the air-dried blossoms in an airtight glass container in a cool, dry place.

Arthritis, Move Over with Clover

Now, clover won't cure your arthritis, but if you start the day with a cup of clover tea, it will go a long way toward easing some of your aches and pains.

1 tsp. of dried red clover blossoms, crushed

1 tsp. of dried alfalfa leaves, crushed

Add these herbs to a cup of boiling water. Steep for 5 minutes. Strain out the herbs and sip. Add a teaspoon of honey if you want to sweeten it up a bit.

Dandelion

(Taraxacum officinale)

Herbal ID

Dandelion is one of the most recognizable (and cursed) plants ever to set foot in a lawn or garden. It can shoot up to 12 inches in height, seemingly overnight. It produces spatula-like leaves and sun-yellow flowers that can bloom year-round in some warm climates. As a full-grown adult, the flower turns into a seedy puffball that disperses seeds here, there, and everywhere with the slightest breeze.

That's Historical!

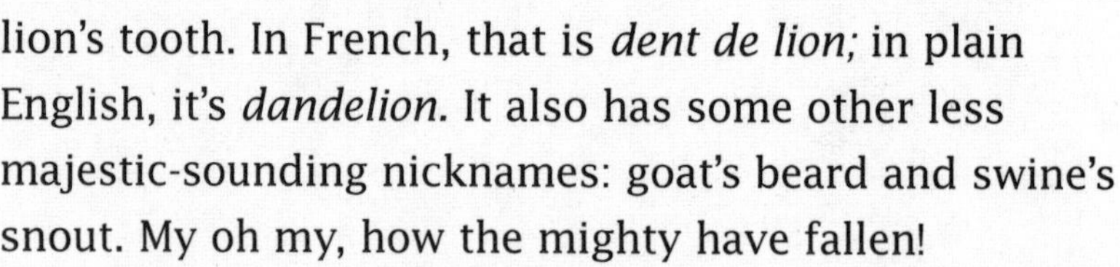

If a dandelion could talk to other plants, it might thump its leaves against its long stalks and declare, "I'm king of this garden!" That's because its name was derived by a 15th-century surgeon who thought the plant's leaves looked a lot like a lion's tooth. In French, that is *dent de lion;* in plain English, it's *dandelion.* It also has some other less majestic-sounding nicknames: goat's beard and swine's snout. My oh my, how the mighty have fallen!

As far back as a thousand years ago in China, dandelion was used to treat breast cancer. Other ancient cultures valued this "weed" as a blood purifier.

MEDICINAL USES: PUMP UP ON POTASSIUM

Dandelion roots and leaves are used for a bunch of health reasons. The leaves are one of Mother Nature's best sources of potassium — a real important mineral your body loses with frequent urination. It also packs a healthy dose of vitamins A, B, C, and D, as well as iron and manganese.

Dandelion roots help keep the liver in shape by acting like a cleansing tonic. They also stimulate the digestive juices.

In general, folks in quest of the perfect manicured lawn despise the dandelion. But herbalists and doctors value its role as a health ally. It's been used to treat jaundice, muscular rheumatism, flatulence, ulcers, constipation, indigestion, heartburn, acne, and gallstones. The bitter compounds in its leaves and root act like a mild laxative and digestion stimulator as well as a powerful tonic.

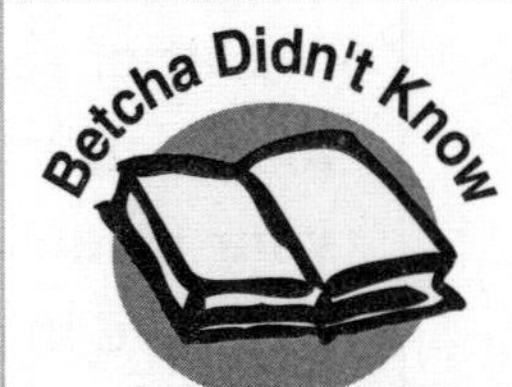

Dandelion roots that have been dried, roasted, and ground make one dandy coffee substitute. A handful of its leaves also contain as much calcium as a glass of milk.

BEST MEDICINAL FORMS

The easiest — and tastiest — way to take dandelion is by munching on a bowlful of freshly picked (and washed) young leaves. Yum yum! They'll act as natural cleansing agents in your body. Actually, all parts of the dandelion are edible, except for the stem. But a word of warning: Stay away from older leaves; they're bitter tasting.

If you are pregnant or planning on being so in the near future, my doctor friends say err on the side of caution, and don't take dandelion as a medicine. Otherwise, it is safe to take for short periods of time to cure what ails you. Also, pick dandelions only from places you know are free of pesticides and other harmful chemical sprays.

There are two ways to drink dandelion: as a tea and as a puree juice. To make a tea, combine a couple of teaspoons of dandelion root and a cup of water in a saucepan. Let it boil, and then simmer for 15 minutes. Drink up to 3 cups a day. Sweeten with honey if you can't stand the bitterness. For the juice, puree some leaves in a blender with water and pour into a glass. Drink up to 3 glasses a day of this if you're fighting constipation.

Out of season, keep a bottle of dandelion tincture or capsules handy in your medicine cabinet. Both forms are effective in restoring lost potassium and keeping your liver healthy. If you're over 40 and have trouble digesting foods, take 5 to 10 drops of dandelion root tincture or 1 capsule right before mealtime. The bitters will help your body absorb nutrients and encourage digestion.

Dandelion may also help get rid of warts. Simply squeeze the stem and root till a white sap oozes out. Spread that goo smack dab on the wart every day for a week or so.

GROWING TIPS

Are you kidding me? Dandelions don't need any help to grow and thrive. In fact, they'll make their home wherever they feel like it: meadows, fields, ditches, and lawns — even the most meticulously kept gardens! That's because their stakelike, milky roots drill deep into the ground — any ground. Dandelions grow easily in wet or dry, rich or poor soil; in sun, partial shade, or full shade.

Dandy Wine

Next to the grape, the dandelion is most highly regarded among wine drinkers. For any home-bottlers out there, here's one of my favorite recipes:

16 cups of dandelion flower heads (freshly picked with stems removed)

2 oranges, sliced

1 lemon, sliced

1 tsp. of gingerroot, crushed

1 gallon of water

4 pounds of sugar

½ oz. of wine yeast

Put the dandelion heads, oranges, lemon, and ginger in a muslin bag. Then place the bag in a pan with the gallon of water and boil for 20 minutes. Strain, then add the sugar to the pot. Add the yeast and let the mix sit for an entire week. Then strain and bottle, capping the bottles loosely for the first few days, and then more tightly. Wait a good 6 months (no one wants to serve wine before its time) before drinking.

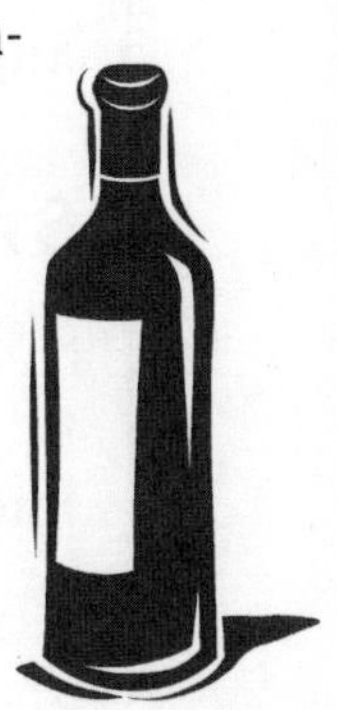

For the beginning gardener still looking for his or her green thumb, this is a can't-fail plant. I guarantee that even if you've never grown anything before, you can grow dandelions. Just plant them in rows, and then watch their yellow heads pop out. The confidence you'll gain will motivate you to plant other herbs.

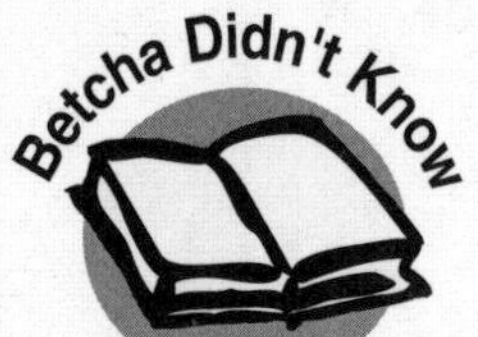

My Grandma Putt was always a bundle of energy at spring-planting time. Then one day she shared her secret with me: her spring tonic. She took 2 teaspoons of dandelion juice (pressed from fresh leaves) and added it to milk. She drank this once a day to really get her motor going in a hurry!

HARVESTING TIPS

Dandelion roots are best collected in fall. Split the roots lengthwise before air-drying or roasting them in a slow oven. Harvest young, fresh leaves for salads and soups.

STORAGE TIPS

Store dandelion leaves and roots in the crisper section of your refrigerator. Do not freeze them: The bitter cold knocks the medicinal bitters right out of the plant.

Dill

(Anethum graveolens)

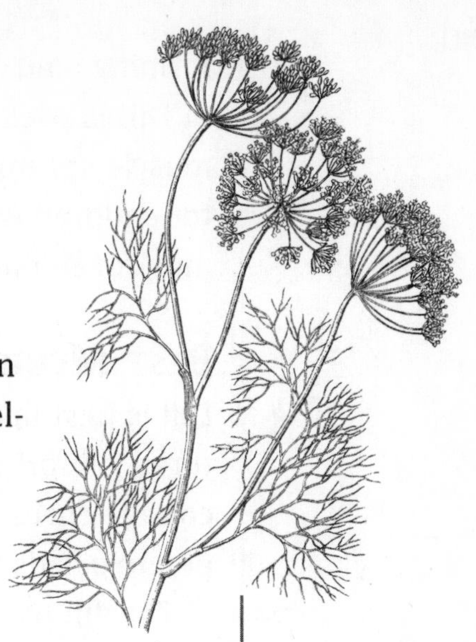

Herbal ID

This annual displays feathery, bluish green foliage, angular hollow stems, and tiny, yellow, edible blossoms. It grows 2 to 4 feet tall. In an herb garden, dill makes a soft, delicate backdrop for the smaller herbs. The seeds are pungent, while the leaves are fragrant but mild.

That's Historical!

Ancient Romans and Greeks were said to burn dill seeds as incense. In fact, the Romans were so silly over dill that they planted it all over Europe during their travels. The Egyptians would munch on dill seeds to relieve gas. In the Middle Ages, Europeans believed dill would shoo away storms. Colonists settling in the United States chewed on dill seeds during church services because they thought this herb symbolized protection, money, and love. (They also fought off hunger pains during those really long sermons!)

Medicinal Uses: Zap Internal Gas

Dill offers a more appetizing way to soothe upset stomachs than some of those not-so-tasty store-bought medicines. Chewing on dill seeds helps relax the smooth muscles in the stomach and halt gas bubbles from forming; and, as a bonus, it freshens your breath!

Dill is packed with aromatic volatile oils that tame muscle spasms and aid in digestion. It also works great for children with colic and helps stimulate the flow of milk for nursing moms.

BEST MEDICINAL FORMS

Dill is best taken in teas and tinctures, or sprinkled on fresh salads, cottage cheese, meat, fish, soups, sauces, and even potato salads.

For dill tea, pour a cup of boiling water onto 2 teaspoonfuls of crushed dill seeds. Let it steep about 10 to 15 minutes before drinking. If you're prone to gas, drink a cup of dill tea before meals. In tincture form, take 1 to 2 ml 3 times a day.

Gas-Away Tea

When you want to relieve the bloated, gassy feeling you sometimes get by eating certain foods, try this surefire cure:

1 tsp. of dill seeds, crushed

1 tsp. of dried peppermint

1 cup of boiling water

Mash the dill seeds by putting them in a plastic baggie and hitting them with a rolling pin or wooden mallet. Then put the dill and peppermint in a big mug. Pour in the boiling water. Cover, and let it steep about 15 minutes. Strain out the herbs and then sip slowly. You'll be feeling better in no time at all!

GROWING TIPS

Dill is easy to grow. Sow seed in well-drained, well-worked soil with lots of sun. Average soil and regular fertilizing will keep dill happy. Thin the seedlings, leaving them about 10 inches apart. If possible, find a sheltered spot to plant dill because stiff winds can damage its fragile leaves. Or do what I do: Help them help themselves by planting them in groups to keep them better supported against windy weather.

In most climates, you can make successive plantings from April through July. About every 2 weeks or so, start a new crop. Just keep dill away from fennel. These two herbs look alike, but they definitely don't like each other. So put the dill next to cabbage, where it'll do just fine.

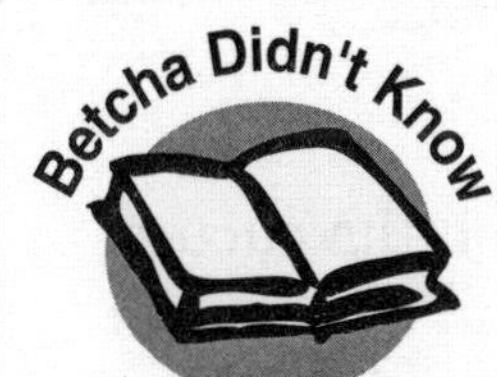

Dill makes a healthy substitute for salt. So sprinkle your food with dill seeds instead of the white stuff. Scientists have discovered that just 1 tablespoon of dill seeds contains 100 mg of calcium — more than you'll find in a small glass of milk!

At the end of the growing season, leave behind a few plants — chances are, they will self-sow for next spring.

HARVESTING TIPS

You must wait until the seeds turn brown. That's the sign that they're ripe and ready to be picked. But don't wait too long — harvest the seeds before they drop from the plant. Cut the stems about 8 inches below the umbels and put them upside down in a paper bag. Then fasten the bag shut with a bread tie, bundling up

Perfect Garlic-Dill Pickles

Pickles aren't pickles without the all-important ingredient: dill. Try this recipe for the next family picnic:

4 lbs. of pickling cucumbers, unwaxed

6 cloves of garlic

6 dill flower heads

6 fresh dill leaves, 6 in. each

6 large, fresh grape leaves

6 small, fresh hot red peppers

1 quart of garlic cider vinegar

1 quart of water

½ cup of noniodized salt

Thoroughly wash the cucumbers, put them in a bowl and cover them with cold water. Cover the bowl, and stick it in the refrigerator for about 12 hours.

In each of 6 pint-size jars, place a garlic clove, a dill flower and leaf, a grape leaf, red pepper, and enough cucumbers to fill it.

In a deep kettle, blend the vinegar with water and salt. Let it boil on high heat until the salt is dissolved. Pour the liquid into each of the jars. Wipe the rims, put on two-piece lids, and fasten with screw bands.

Place the sealed jars on a rack in the kettle. Add enough boiling water to cover the lids by 2 inches. Then cover the kettle and let it boil for 15 more minutes. Carefully remove the jars from the kettle.

Allow the jars to cool before removing the bands, labeling, or storing them. Wait about a month before enjoying these pickles, and refrigerate the jars after opening.

the stems along with the top of the bag. Punch a few holes at the top and hang it up to dry. Once the seeds dry, they'll drop into the bottom of the bag, where they can be collected for long-term storage.

Fresh from the garden, snip foliage from the sides of the stems and add to your favorite recipes.

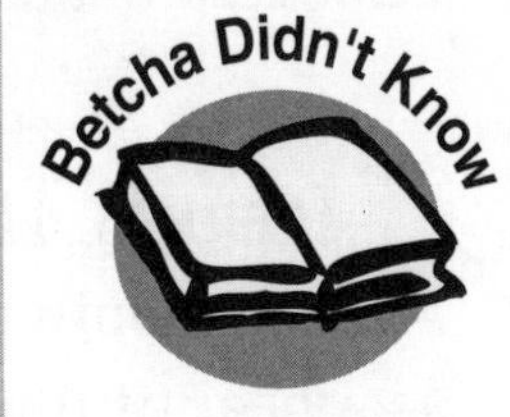

Dried dill blooms can also be turned into beautiful garlands, wreaths for doors, and potpourris.

STORAGE TIPS

You have several storage options with dill: fresh, dried, or frozen. To store air-dried herbs like dill, always leave the foliage intact to retain the flower longer. To freeze dill, just wash it, shake off the excess water, tuck them in labeled containers, and pop them in the freezer. Or you can chop up dill into itty-bitty pieces, put them into ice-cube trays, add water, and freeze for use all winter long!

Echinacea

(Echinacea angustifolia; E. purpurea)

Herbal ID

Native only to North America, echinacea is a beautiful plant that features long, green stalks crowned with purple, daisylike petals and a cone-shaped, seedy top. The individual flower heads are usually 3 to 4 inches across. Dark green leaves grow along the stems. While the flowers and stems are stunning to look at, it is the plant's thick, black root that is used for its remarkable therapeutic properties.

That's Historical!

Many people refer to this herb by its more popular nickname: purple coneflower. My relatives near the Mason-Dixon line call it Missouri snakeroot. Plains Indians along with other Native Americans are believed to be the first to have discovered echinacea's medicinal benefits — and none too soon! Echinacea turned out to be an invaluable remedy for poisonous-snake bites.

Surprisingly, echinacea took a backseat when people turned to antibiotics to cure what ailed them. But echinacea was too good to be forgotten. It was "rediscovered" in the 1970s and has been gaining in popularity ever since.

MEDICINAL USES: ZIP UP YOUR IMMUNE SYSTEM!

Achoo! Echinacea is Mother Nature's answer to the common cold. It also helps fight sore throats, ear infections, bronchitis, minor burns, allergies, viral infections, and even toothaches. The roots contain active ingredients that are surefire fever-beaters, inflammation-reducers, and immune-system boosters.

To maximize its benefits, use echinacea as needed when you start to feel a little under the weather. However, prolonged daily use (for more than 3 months at a time) actually weakens its effectiveness — if you use this herb too often, your body gets used to and starts to ignore it. Better to use echinacea only when you really need it so your immune system won't take it for granted.

BEST MEDICINAL FORMS

Echinacea capsules or tinctures are very effective and widely available. Be sure to follow the directions on the label when you use this herb. You can also try echinacea tea; unfortunately, it has a bittersweet taste, and it lacks the healing punch that capsules and tinctures provide.

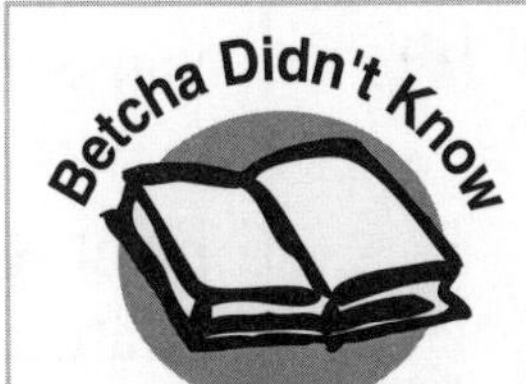

Echinacea is the top-selling medicinal herb in the entire world — and one of the most scientifically studied herbs to boot!

GROWING TIPS

For green-thumb-growing success with this plant, make sure you have fertile, well-drained, moderately moist soil. This perennial likes full sun to light shade and easily tolerates hot, humid temperatures. Sow the seeds when the temperature reaches 70°F. You'll know it's time to plant when it's warm enough outside to make you sweat, but not so hot that all you want to do is take a nap in the shade. I've used that rule my whole life, and so far I've never had a bad batch of echinacea — and I get more than my fair share of naps, too!

When you're sowing echinacea seeds, make sure to space them at least a foot apart. Plants that grow too close together get their roots tangled up the same way that people who live too close together get all caught up in each other's business. In either case, it's not what you would call a real healthy situation.

What I really like about this beautiful, medicinal herb is that echinacea requires little or no maintenance: Simply plant it and then walk away. You don't need to water it unless there's a drought. Even though the plant is tall and thin — often growing to a height of 3 feet or more — its stem is very strong and generally does not need staking for support. In mid- to late June, you'll be rewarded with vibrant purple flowers that should last until October.

You Snooze, You Lose!

Echinacea is widely used to support the body's immune system against bacterial and viral attacks. It's best to start taking the herb as soon as you begin to feel a cold or flu coming on. If you wait too long, you will lose your chance; echinacea will not cure a cold or flu after the illness has taken hold.

HARVESTING TIPS

Wait until your plants are at least 2 years old before harvesting them. It's even better if you can wait until they've been growing for 4 years before digging them up, because more mature plants mean more potent plants. The best time to harvest echinacea is just after the plant has bloomed — usually in early fall. Wash and dry the roots, then chop them up to prepare them for storing.

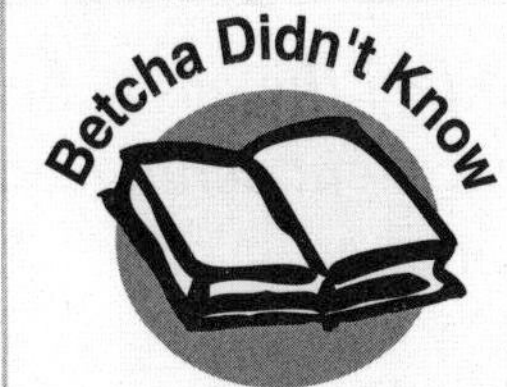

While echinacea is versatile and safe, excessive amounts can make you dizzy or nauseated.

A Homemade Tincture

Why buy from the store when you can make it yourself? is my main motto. I always like to have echinacea tincture on hand to ward off illness before it sets in. Here's how to make this terrific tincture:

¾ cup of vodka or grain alcohol

¾ cup of distilled water

1½ oz. of dried echinacea root

Combine all of the ingredients in a jar. With the lid screwed on tightly, give it a shake. Then store it in a cool, dark place for 2 weeks. You can remove the solid pieces of echinacea root by straining the liquid through a coffee filter, if you so desire.

Arthritis Antidote

If you start to feel the old aches and pains creeping in, try making my excellent echinacea antidote. In a stainless-steel saucepan, mix:

2–3 tsps. of fresh echinacea root
1 cup of water

Bring the mixture to a boil and then let it simmer for 10 minutes. After drinking a cup of this concoction, it will only be a matter of minutes before you are back out in the garden swinging a hoe, your arthritis all but forgotten.

STORAGE TIPS

As with all dried herbs, keep echinacea in a glass jar with a tight-fitting lid. Store the jar in a cool, dark place, like a cellar. Light and heat are known to zap the strength (potency) of the plants, so by storing them in the cellar, you can count on the herbs being fresh as a newborn babe the next time you use them.

Eucalyptus

(Eucalyptus globulus)

Herbal ID

I lost track of the exact count, but there are more than 500 species of eucalyptus in existence. Collectively, these evergreen trees are noted for their silvery leaves and pungent, bitter aromas that smell a lot like Vicks VapoRub (P-U!). Silver-dollar tree and blue gum are among the tallest of the bunch, growing up to 6 feet a year; some have even reached heights of 500 feet! The blue gum is far and away the most famous, and features smooth, bluish gray bark and silvery blue, leatherlike broad leaves.

That's Historical!

Throw another shrimp on the barbie, mate! That's right, eucalyptus hails from the land down under. Aboriginal tribes in Australia have used it for centuries as both a fever remedy and poultice to treat wounds and skin inflammation. They also discovered that the roots stored plenty of drinking water. Legend has it that a director of the Melbourne Botanical Gardens in the 19th century introduced eucalyptus to North America and Europe. Now it is widely cultivated and actually grows wild in California.

Eucalyptus essential oil works wonders when applied to your skin, but don't ingest it — it can hurt you!

Medicinal Uses: Clear Your Sinusus and Chest

This herb's leaves, as well as the oil distilled from them, are what pack the medicinal punch. The chemical ingredients help kill germs, fight upset stomachs, tame fevers, soothe coughs, and clear up congestion. As they say — cool!

Best Medicinal Forms

Eucalyptus is an adaptable, woody perennial that is good for whatever ails you. Depending on your condi-

Shoo, Fly, Shoo!

Instead of spraying a whole slew of store-bought bug sprays that are full of chemicals, why not try my homemade recipe for chasing away flies, fleas, and a host of other insects?

10 drops of eucalyptus essential oil
10 drops of pennyroyal essential oil
10 drops of cedarwood oil
25 drops of citronella essential oil
4 ounces of sweet almond oil

In a glass container with a lid, shake up all the oils together. Scent cotton balls with a few drops of this mix and dab it on countertops, windowsills, and other places that are prone to bug invasions. They absolutely hate the scent!

For the occasional outdoor walk or hike, rub a small amount of this herbal blend between the palms of your hands and apply it to any exposed skin. Just be careful not to get the oil near your eyes. You'll smell great and be able to enjoy the great outdoors without being bugged!

tion, it can be used as a tea, tincture, inhalant, compress, and even a gargle.

As a tea infusion, put 1 to 2 teaspoonfuls of dried or fresh eucalyptus leaves (crumbled or crushed, of course) into a cup of boiling water. Let it steep for 10 minutes. Strain and sip. As a tincture, the daily recommended dose is 1 ml 3 times a day.

To clear up chest congestion due to colds, bronchitis, asthma, and flu, boil water over a few leaves and inhale the steam. For sore throats, laryngitis, or plain old bad breath, dilute 5 drops of eucalyptus essential oil in a glass of water. Stir it up and gargle — but do not swallow it! The cineole compound in eucalyptus is powerful enough to kill odor-causing bacteria, and its aromatic oil delivers a cooling effect on tender, inflamed throats.

For minor arthritic pain or muscle aches caused by too much yard work, combine 20 drops of eucalyptus oil with 20 drops of rosemary oil in a small bottle of almond oil. Using it as a massage oil, gently rub it into sore joints and muscles.

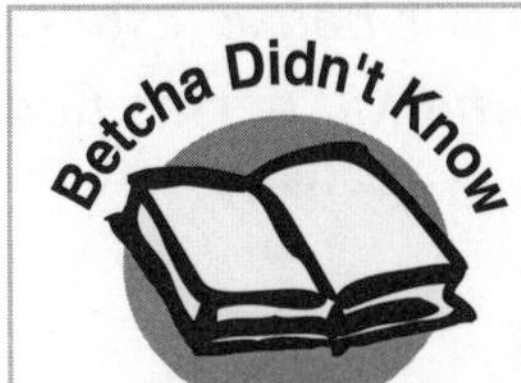

Eucalyptus oil is nature's answer to smelling salts. A drop or two on a handkerchief is usually enough to revive someone who has fainted.

GROWING TIPS

Eucalpytus is fairly hardy, but it can't tolerate temperatures below 20°F. Outdoors, it grows best in Zones 8 and 9 as an annual bedding plant in light-textured, well-drained soils that get lots of sun. Everywhere else, grow it indoors in pots.

All varieties of eucalyptus bloom, but the exact flowering time varies. In general, most plants produce clusters of white, cream, pink, yellow, orange, or red flowers.

HARVESTING TIPS

For those of you interested in crafts, you'll be glad to know that eucalyptus leaves, branches, and seedpods dry quickly and are very easy to use.

STORAGE TIPS

Like their leafy counterparts, essential oils fare best in glass containers stored in cool, dry places.

Clear the Air!

You can keep your house (especially your bathroom) smelling lemony fresh and kill germs floating in the air with my herbal disinfectant spray.

1 cup of water
½ cup of dried eucalyptus leaves
½ cup of isopropyl alcohol
2 tsp. of eucalyptus essential oil

In a small saucepan, boil the cup of water and soak the dried eucalyptus leaves in it. Reduce the heat and let it simmer 15 minutes. Then let it cool. Strain out the herbs and pour the infusion into a glass spray bottle, along with the alcohol and essential oil. Tighten the nozzle lid and shake well. Spray into the air as needed. This elixir will last up to 6 months if stored in a cool, dry place.

Evening Primrose

(Oenothera biennis)

Herbal ID

This perennial features delicate pale yellow, four-petaled flowers. As its name implies, evening primrose blooms at night, usually right around dusk. Through the years, it has also been called scabbish, cure-all, and tree primrose.

That's Historical!

Give credit where credit's due, that's my motto! The first folks to discover the healing powers of evening primrose were Native Americans. They used to boil the seeds and use the liquid to hasten the healing of wounds. Some tribes also ate this wild edible plant. In fact, the Cherokees sipped on evening primrose tea to lose weight, and after a long day on the trail, they'd use the hot root to soothe itchy, sore hemorrhoids. Early American settlers used evening primrose for digestive and bladder problems. To this day, evening primrose is used in Britain to treat multiple sclerosis.

Medicinal Uses: Fight Pain and Swelling

Evening primrose is one herb that both herbalists and mainstream physicians like. Scientists have figured out that oil from its seeds contains a fatty acid that goes by the name of gamma linolenic acid, or GLA for short.

The body uses this hormonelike substance to fight swelling and act as a blood thinner. Evening primrose also contains phenylalanine, one of the best natural sources of pain relief I know.

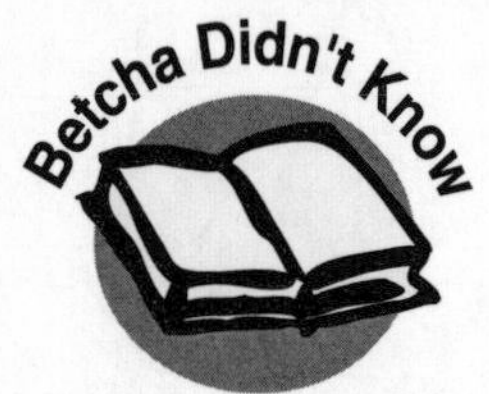

Taking evening primrose oil regularly will help keep your skin from becoming dehydrated — even during the cold, blustery winter! There's even talk that it may put the brakes on the aging process. Wouldn't that be nice?

Like many healthful herbs, this one is really versatile. You can use it to treat a wide range of ailments, including atherosclerosis (hardening of the arteries), attention deficit disorder, diabetes, eczema, headaches, irritable bowel syndrome, premenstrual syndrome, and rheumatoid arthritis. It seems to balance hormones, boost the immune system, keep cells strong, and reduce inflammation. This herb may help even more conditions — we're still discovering all of its therapeutic benefits.

Evening primrose oil is in the spotlight lately for its possible role in dieting. Its stimulating effect on the body can actually help convert fat into energy. Now, wouldn't that be a welcome treatment for losing those unwanted pounds!

BEST MEDICINAL FORMS

Trying to extract oil from evening primrose is too difficult of a job to try at home; I know — I've tried. This is one herb I recommend you buy at a health food or drug store. The best way to take evening primrose oil is in capsule form. The recommended daily dose is 1,000 to 2,000 mg or 3 to 6 capsules.

Your local health food store may also stock it as an oil product. You can apply the oil right on your skin to treat scaling, redness, and itching.

If you want to add more body to dry hair, try taking one to three 250-mg capsules of evening primrose oil up to 3 times a day. That's a great tip for folks who use blow-dryers to style their hair.

GROWING TIPS

This herb prefers dry soil in Zones 4 to 11. If you stack its height against other plants in your garden, it's one of the tallest, so put it toward the back of your garden. And give it lots of sun.

Bothered by Boils?

Boils can be extremely painful and sometimes hard to heal. My Grandma Putt showed me how to put these pretty flowers to use against those nasty nuisances. Here's all you need:

A handful of fresh or dried evening primrose leaves

Gauze

Chop the leaves up as finely as you can, so that they become moist and release their volatile oils. Fold the gauze into several layers to make a pad the right size to cover the boil. Put the chopped-up leaves right over the boil, then cover it with the gauze pad and hold it in place with another strip of gauze. Leave it in place for about ½ hour. You can follow this treatment several times, waiting 2 or 3 hours between treatments.

Good news for you "brown-thumbers" out there — evening primrose is a tough plant that will reward you with flowers year after year as long as you keep them mulched, watered, and trimmed. They like to spread out, so give them plenty of growing room.

You can sow this plant in the fall in mild climates or start it indoors in the spring. Use peat pots and transplant after the final frost — it's your call! If you find yourself too busy with springtime planting, then fall back to planting it later in the year.

Be sure to snip off the faded flowers after they're done blooming, a process known among gardeners as deadheading. What you're doing is giving the plant a breather — it won't have to work as hard to push out new generations of beautiful blooms. By its second birthday, the plant should sport 3- to 6-foot stems with branches that are loaded with buds.

Count your lucky stars. This is one of the safest herbs found in Mother Nature's medicine cabinet.

HARVESTING TIPS

You can harvest evening primrose seeds all winter long. Try grinding them into flour and using them in a low-fat bran muffin mix to help shed a few extra pounds.

The leaves are delicious, too. Snip them as needed during the growing season and add to salads. Some folks I know also boil the roots and serve them as vegetables on dinner plates. The point is that this is an edible plant from top to bottom, so don't let anything go to waste!

Fennel

(Foeniculum vulgare)

Herbal ID

From a distance, fennel looks like a mist of green spider webs, very featherly and delicate. If you didn't know any better, you'd think it was a cousin of dill. It grows in clumps of 8- to 12-inch-wide green leaves attached to stalks that can grow up to 5 feet high. During the heart of summer, clusters of lacy, yellow flowers bloom atop the stalks.

There are actually two main types of fennel: regular fennel, with sweet, licoricey-smelling leaves; and Florence fennel, with large, tender bulbs.

That's Historical!

In the days of Julius Caesar, ancient Romans thought serpents sucked the juice from fennel plants to sharpen their eyesight. Gladiators sported wreaths made of fennel leaves, thinking they gave them added strength. Maybe that's why fennel has been a symbol for heroism.

Ancient Greeks fawned over fennel as a weight-loss aid. Its Greek name, *marathron,* comes from a verb meaning "to grow thin." In Europe during medieval times, hungry churchgoers would chew on fennel seeds during sermons to keep their stomachs from rumbling!

On the other side of the globe, fennel ground into a fine powder poultice has been used in China for hundreds of years to hasten relief from nasty snakebites.

MEDICINAL USES: BOOST YOUR DIGESTION

Herbalists classify fennel as a carminative herb, which soothes the intestines and stomach to reduce gas pains and that bloated feeling. Fennel seeds eaten before meals can also trigger your appetite and increase the stomach acid that helps with digestion.

The seeds contain fever-reducing, antispasm, and expectorant powers that calm coughs due to colds and bronchitis. Fennel also relieves laryngitis and sore throats, and it stimulates milk flow in nursing moms. As an essential oil, fennel relieves the soreness and aches in overused muscles and arthritis.

WHOA! **Fennel as** a medicine should be used only as needed. It's fine to take it occasionally for minor tummy ailments. But my doctor friends tell me that you should not take fennel every single day for more than 6 weeks, unless you're also under medical supervision.

And here's a bonus: A cold compress of fennel seeds reduces the swelling around puffy eyes. Just pour a cup of boiling water over 2 teaspoons of fennel seeds. Cover and let steep for 10 minutes before putting it in the refrigerator overnight. In the morning, strain out the seeds, and your eye-pleasing medicine is ready! Dip a paper towel into the fennel tea. Find a comfortable, quiet place to lie down with your head propped up on a pillow. Shut your eyes and put the moistened paper towel over your eyes. In 10 minutes or so, your eyes will sparkle and look refreshed. This recipe makes enough for five daily treatments.

BEST MEDICINAL FORMS

As one of nature's medicines, fennel offers you many choices. You can chew on fresh seeds, sip a cup of tea, massage your skin with essential oil, or drink a cup of water with a bit of tincture added to it.

To make fennel tea, put 2 teaspoons of fennel seeds (slightly crushed to activate their medicine) in a cup of boiling water. Let stand for about 15 minutes; then strain out the seeds and sip slowly. You can drink up to 3 cups a day for routine stomach woes. To prevent flatulence, drink a cup of fennel tea before sitting down for a meal.

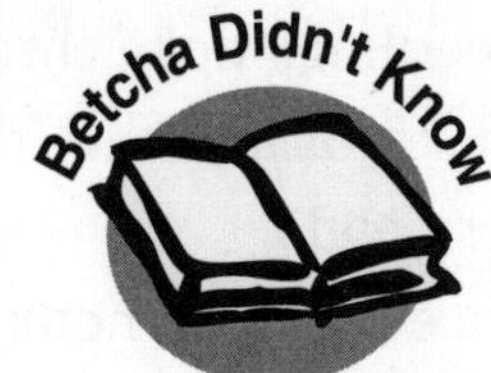

Fennel stalks have an appearance and texture that is a lot like celery, but they and the leaves actually taste like licorice. Here's another "nosy" fact on fennel: It removes the fishy odor from seafood and fish when added during the cooking process.

Fennel essential oil works wonders as a chest rub to clear up congestion. Just dissolve 10 drops of fennel, 10 drops of thyme, and 10 drops of eucalyptus essential oils in 4 ounces of sunflower oil and massage gently into the chest.

As a tincture, the daily recommended dose is 1 to 2 ml 3 times a day in a glass of water or juice.

GROWING TIPS

This perennial sports long taproots and tender stems, hates transplanting, and must be sown right in the ground. It likes balanced soil that's neither too acidic nor too alkaline and appreciates compost and finely raked topsoil. Fennel is hardy in Zones 6 to 9, but you can grow it as an annual in colder areas.

Wait until after all threat of frost has passed before you plant fennel. It prefers sunshine and well-drained soil. Press the seeds gently into the soil, and cover them. Then wet the soil with a fine mist from a watering can or hose. If no rain is forecast, plan on watering daily until the seedlings poke through the soil. When the seedlings stand a foot tall, thin them out and cut away the spent flower heads.

Since it can sometimes cause other plants not to grow well, I tell folks to plant fennel in a spot all by itself.

HARVESTING TIPS

Harvest fennel seeds when the leaves start turning colors (other than green) in the fall. Cut off the seed heads and put them in a paper bag. The leaves and stems can be snipped as needed for fresh salads or frozen for reserves. You can also cut the stems, tie them together, and let them hang upside down over a bag to catch the seeds.

STORAGE TIP

Don't freeze fennel — it loses its medicinal powers!

Jerry's Fennel Spring Tonic

Celebrate the onset of spring each year with this cleansing tonic:

1 tsp. of fennel seeds, crushed or mashed

1 tsp. of alfalfa leaves, dried

1 tsp. of dandelion root, ground

Combine the three herbs in a small bowl. Scoop a teaspoon from the mix and add it to a cup of boiling water. Let steep for 10 minutes; then strain out the herbs and sip. It's just like a kick in the pants to get you going!

Feverfew

(Tanacetum parthenium)

HERBAL ID

In the garden, feverfew may just win the beauty contest among other botanicals. It features eye-catching, lacy leaves and delicate, white petals that are highly reminiscent of small daisies.

Its lobed leaves have a sharp scent that reminds some gardeners of chrysanthemums. This bitter-tasting plant grows up to 2 feet tall.

THAT'S HISTORICAL!

The unusual name of this herb is derived from featherfew, referring to the plant's delicate petals. Centuries ago, it was also known as flirtwort and vetter-voo. Feverfew dates back to ancient Greece, where it was mentioned in medical books as a remedy for inflammation and menstrual-flow woes.

By the 17th century, famous herbalist Nicholas Culpeper noted feverfew's headache powers in his book *Culpeper's Complete Herbal.* He wrote, "Feverfew is very effectual for all pains in the head." He was truly a scientist a-head of his time!

MEDICINAL USES: ZAP HEADACHES FAST

Feverfew acts just like Mother Nature's aspirin. It has a prestigious reputation for being a great herb remedy for migraine headaches, and it costs a whole lot less than prescription medications to boot!

Its benefits, however, go way beyond migraines. Feverfew eases dizziness, tinnitus (also known as ringing in the ears), and arthritis. It also relieves painful menstrual flows.

If you're among the 10 percent of people who get mouth sores from chewing on feverfew leaves, don't fret. You can get the same medicinal benefits by steeping the leaves in boiling water and drinking a tea. Feverfew is bitter-tasting, so you may want to sweeten it up a bit with a teaspoon of honey. It can cause skin rashes for some folks, and pregnant women should not use it at all.

So how does feverfew work? Its chemical ingredients prevent spasms by relaxing blood vessels and stopping swelling.

Feverfew also kick-starts digestion. For those of you who need to have a more scientific explanation, the active ingredient in feverfew is parthenolide, which helps to prevent excessive clumping of blood platelets.

Best Medicinal Forms

Ideally, fresh feverfew is best. As I always say, "Eating a leaf a day keeps the migraine away!" Frozen leaves can also be used. When the leaves themselves are not available, tinctures or freeze-dried capsules work effectively, too. Buy capsules that contain 0.2 percent parthenolide for best results. For capsules, take 250 mg 3 times a day. For tinctures, take 30 drops 3 times a day in a glass of water or juice.

To stop menstrual pain, try drinking a cup of feverfew tea.

GROWING TIPS

Find a spot in your garden that has slightly acidic, well-drained soil and gets full sun. This is ideal, although feverfew will also tolerate partial shade. Treat it as you would a short-lived perennial, and know that it grows best in Zones 5 to 7.

Wait about 2 weeks after the final spring frost, then sow the itty-bitty seeds into well-worked soil, about 12 inches apart. Sprinkle a little soil over them, and keep them slightly moist. In no time at all, you'll have armies of tiny, lace-leafed seedlings that will need to be thinned out. Look for blooms anytime from June to September.

Feverfew is pretty resilient against most garden pests and diseases, so there's not too much you need to worry about on that front.

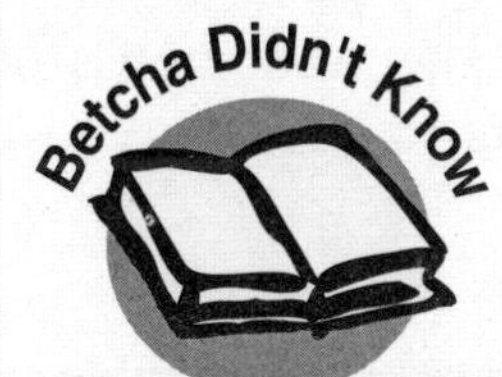

Here's the real buzz on feverfew: Bees hate the odor of its pollen and will steer clear of these plants. So make sure you don't plant feverfew next to plants like raspberries, which depend on bee pollination to make their fruit.

HARVESTING TIPS

After the flowers bloom, cut them off and throw them on the compost pile. If you don't, feverfew will self-seed and soon take over your garden. I like to do my harvesting in the morning, just after the dew has dissipated. Snip off individual leaves one at a time and cut whole stems about an inch above ground level. To air-dry, simply hang the stems upside down.

STORAGE TIPS

Want a supply of feverfew year-round, even in the dead of winter? It's easy! Just place clean, dry feverfew leaves on a cookie sheet, making sure to leave some space between the leaves. Stick them in the freezer for a couple of hours, and then lift them off the cookie sheet. Transfer them to a reclosable plastic bag and then store them in the freezer. When you need a leaf, just pluck one from the bag!

Anti-Migraine Tea

Migraines can be devastating. I know, because my grown children still get them. But they fight the throbs with this easy-to-make tea:

1 tsp. of dried feverfew leaves and flowers

1 tsp. of dried lemon balm flowers

Mix the herbs and scoop a teaspoon into a cup of boiling water. Let it steep 5–10 minutes. Strain out the herbs, and sip away until the head pain is gone.

Garlic

(Allium sativum)

Herbal ID

Garlic is cultivated around the world. Up to 15 cloves can be clustered inside the papery sheath of each bulb. When garlic blooms, the tiny flowers tend to be white and pink in color, but you'll get bigger and better garlic if you cut off the garlic flowers as soon as they appear.

I tell you, garlic tends to get a bad rap in the breath department, but nothing can top the smell of fresh garlic bread as it's being pulled from the oven!

That's Historical!

Tales of garlic's benefits go way back. It's mentioned in some biblical passages, and maybe Moses should have considered adding an 11th Commandment: Thou shall eat garlic! Its medicinal value is unequaled among herbs. Hippocrates, the father of medicine, used garlic on patients with low energy, poor digestion, respiratory problems, and parasites. Greek physician Dioscorides wrote in the first century B.C. that garlic "clears the arteries and opens the mouths of the veins."

For centuries, garlic's abilities have been well touted in folklore on several continents. But it wasn't until 1858, when Louis Pasteur formally proved that garlic kills many kinds of bacteria, that it gained entry into scientific journals. And the rest, as they say, is history!

MEDICINAL USES: FIGHT INFECTIONS

Among herbalists, doctors, and scientists, garlic is the undisputed king of botanical medicine. It helps the body in ways no other herb does. When it comes to health, garlic is a true garden variety. Here's a laundry list of garlic's unmatched qualities: kills bacteria; has antiviral benefits; clears congestion from lungs; aids in digestion; lowers blood cholesterol and blood sugar levels; may reduce risk for heart disease; thins blood to prevent clots; promotes sweating to break fevers; and acts as an antihistamine. And did I mention that it's also very effective in treating acne and skin infections?

Its volatile oils contain a sulfur compound called allicin that releases its medicine — and that unmistakable odor — whenever it's crushed or chewed. Garlic also contains some non-smelly valuable ingredients, which include enzymes, B vitamins, minerals, and flavonoids.

Hundreds of scientific studies confirm many of garlic's attributes of boosting circulation as well as reducing cholesterol and fats in the blood supply. Scientists have learned that garlic's aromatic compounds are easily released in the lungs and respiratory tract, where they're on call to fight bacteria and viruses.

Ward Off Dragon Breath

There's no such thing as a free lunch, and as good as garlic is for you, it does come with a price: bad breath. Fight back naturally with these good-for-you tastebud-pleasers:

- a sprig of fresh green parsley
- a handful of licoricy fennel seeds
- a handful of cardamom seeds
- a giant, fresh red strawberry

BEST MEDICINAL FORMS

Forget that old saying "An apple a day keeps the doctor away." The real medicine in your garden is found in garlic. Eat a fresh clove 3 times a day and your troubles will be over. If you're worried about your breath, substitute odor-controlled garlic oil capsules with enteric coatings (the daily dose is 500 mg). But just to be on the safe side, nibble some fresh parsley or fennel seeds, or swish your mouth with a minty-fresh mouthwash afterward!

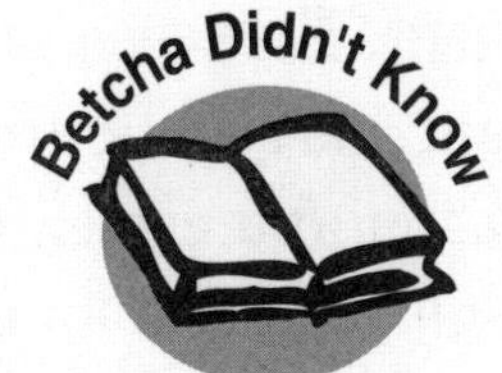

The unofficial garlic capital of the world is Gilroy, California. Local folks celebrate this beautiful bulb with garlic festivals each year. There's even a restaurant in San Francisco that serves only garlic-focused entrées!

Actually, there are a lot of terrific ways to take garlic as a medicine. If you've got warts, corns, or acne, mash a clove of garlic and gently rub it on the trouble spot. To keep your arteries free and clear, try a glass of garlic juice once a day. For folks always on the go, keep a supply of garlic powder capsules on hand, and take 2 g a day to stave off heart problems and keep your blood pressure in line.

My Grandma Putt used to treat my childhood earaches with garlic. She'd place a few drops of warm garlic oil in my ear and let it work its magic. To make the oil, she sliced a garlic clove, added a little olive oil, and heated them for a short time. She strained the mixture before putting it in my ear!

For culinary delights, cooked garlic is wonderful — but it loses a lot of its medicinal punch. So if you're looking to improve your health, stick with the raw form.

GROWING TIPS

You could start garlic from seed, but cloves grow much faster and easier. Whichever way you choose, be sure to give garlic a lot of sun and well-drained soil. It's also up there on my "foolproof herbs" list because it's so easy to grow.

The best times to plant garlic are in the middle of fall or early spring. For early-spring plantings, expect a crop by late summer. For fall plantings, you'll be rewarded the following summer with a

BE A STINKER WITH ATHLETE'S FOOT

Tired of itchy, burning toes caused by athlete's foot or some other irritating fungal infection? Well, put your foot down — in a tub of garlic water. Crush several garlic cloves, and drop them in a tub of warm water with a little rubbing alcohol. Then gently place both feet in the tub, and let them soak for about 10 minutes a day. Garlic has been proven scientifically to stop fungal infections. Of course, the garlic foot bath may cause your loved ones — and even the family dog — to temporarily steer clear of you!

harvest of large bulbs. Garlic roots get established before winter arrives.

To plant garlic, gently pull the little cloves from the bulb and set them about 6 inches apart, about 2 inches down in the soil, pointy end up.

During the summer, keep a close eye on the stalks, and cut the flowers back so you can redirect the plant's energy right to the bulbs. Be careful not to overwater garlic, because if you do, the bulbs will rot.

If you're taking anticoagulant medicine to thin your blood, check with your doctor before eating a lot of garlic. You don't want too much blood-thinning occurring! And just to be on the safe side, if you're a big garlic eater, give your surgeon the "heads up" before going "under the knife."

HARVESTING TIPS

Garlic's multi-clove bulb is best unearthed just about the time the leaves start to turn yellow. Dig up the bulbs when most of the top growth has turned brown.

All-Purpose Varmint Repellent

If you've got critters running rampant and damaging your fruit trees, garlic can help. Try my All-Purpose Varmint Repellent:

2 eggs
2 cloves of garlic
2 tbsp. of hot chili pepper
2 tbsp. of ammonia

Mix all of the ingredients in 2 cups of hot water. Then let it set and "stew" for a few days. When you're ready, paint it on the tree trunks and watch the little varmints scatter!

Gently lift the bulbs, and let them dry in the sun on a sheet of paper for about a week.

STORAGE TIPS

If you leave the garlic cloves intact, they are virtually odorless; but once you crack open that seal, look out! To keep crushed cloves from spreading their pungent aromas to other foods in the refrigerator, put them in a reclosable plastic bag.

If you want to freeze garlic, peel and chop the cloves first. Then stick them in a sealed plastic bag in your freezer. Be sure to label it.

Crooner's Delight

Believe it or not, as Ripley used to say, but garlic is a terrific voice coach. If you're planning to sing or make a public speech, try this tea to keep your vocal cords in tip-top shape!

1 tsp. of minced garlic
2 tbsp. of fresh lemon juice
2 tsp. of honey

Add the garlic and lemon juice to a cup of boiling water. Then stir in the honey until it's dissolved. Do not strain out the garlic. Sip and enjoy; this terrific tea will lubricate your larynx!

Ginger

(Zingiber officinale)

Herbal ID

This tender perennial, which grows in Zones 9 to 11, sports grassy leaves that can grow up to 4 feet tall. In "captivity," ginger rarely blooms, but wild varieties in the woods display conelike spikes of yellow-green flowers. But its real trademark is its roots. Gnarly and knotty, the roots deliver a spicy aroma that can warm and invigorate you.

That's Historical!

Ginger was born in Asia, where the Chinese have used it as a medicine for over 2,500 years. In fact, the *Pen Tsao Ching (The Classic Book of Herbs)* deemed ginger to be one of the best herbs for maintaining good health. An ancient Indian proverb spoke highly of this spice by stating, "Every good quality is contained in ginger." Thousands of years ago, Greek bakers were using ginger to make gingerbread. This nice spice was first introduced into the Americas by Spanish explorers.

Generally, ginger is very safe. However, if you've been diagnosed with an ulcer, go easy on the ginger medicine. Its spiciness could just aggravate the situation.

Medicinal Uses: Eliminate Nausea

Inside ginger's roots, you'll find a pair of valuable essential oils: gingerols and shogaols. They team up to fight nausea, that queasy-uneasy feeling we sometimes get in the pit of our stomachs. That's why it's Mother Nature's No. 1 cure for motion and morning sickness.

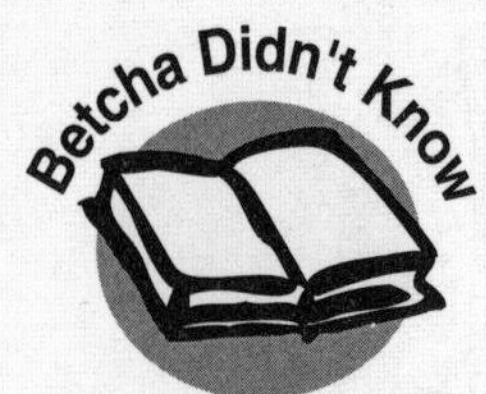

Ginger works better than any of those fancy ingredients used in store-bought motion sickness medications such as Dramamine. Don't just take my word for it — it's been scientifically proved in many studies!

Ginger's ingredients also ease pain from diarrhea and gas, stimulate the appetite, subdue menstrual cramps and migraines, promote sweating to break a fever, and even kill germs.

In the bloodstream, ginger is believed to make platelets less sticky and less prone to clotting. Used externally, ginger provides some much-needed TLC on joints aching from rheumatoid arthritis and muscles smarting from sprains.

Because of its reputation as a germ-killer and antioxidant, ginger is often used to preserve foods, especially in hot and humid climates.

BEST MEDICINAL FORMS

Ginger offers you variety — as a tea, tincture, capsule, or fresh bits of roots. All of these forms will give you a boost medicinally.

Hot ginger tea is terrifically tantalizing. It'll warm you up from the inside out on bitter-cold days. I enjoy putting a teaspoon of fresh, shaved gingerroot into a cup of boiling water and letting it simmer for 5 minutes. Then I remove the root, cup my hands around the warm mug, and sip away to my heart's content.

For ginger in tinctures, remember this motto: A little bit goes a long way. All it takes is 2 to 10 drops per glass of water to warm up your circulation and fight gas, indigestion, and nausea. Capsules work very quickly for folks prone to car or any other kind of motion sickness. Try taking a 250-mg capsule about an hour before you travel to keep your stomach shipshape! You can take up to 3 capsules a day.

For body woes like muscle sprains and achy joints due to rheumatoid arthritis, ginger essential oil provides relief when gently massaged into the skin.

Finally, viva la France! French doctors often help their patients deal with flatulence (P-U!) and fevers by having them eat sugar cubes containing ginger drops.

Good for the Tum-Tum Tea

For those times when it feels like your stomach is taking you on the roller-coaster ride from hell, put on the brakes by sipping some fresh ginger tea. Sure, you can use premade ginger tea bags, but for true effectiveness, fresh is best.

Grate a tablespoon of fresh gingerroot into a cup of boiling water. Let it steep for 15 minutes. Strain out the ginger and sip. If you're prone to upset stomachs, make this a part of your regular routine — drink a cup before breakfast, and another one right after supper.

GROWING TIPS

Ginger demands the hot, humid climates that only the tropics and subtropics can offer. In the Sun Belt states like Florida, it can grow outdoors quite well. Just plant it in an area that gets some shade and give it moist, fertile soil.

If you're a ginger fan but live in Minnesota or some other cold state, no problem. Ginger grows year-round indoors, especially inside greenhouses. Just make sure you plant the roots in pots that contain a blend of com-

Spicy Soda That Sizzles

Treat your friends and family to homemade ginger ale with plenty of fizz:

2 cups of fresh, thinly sliced gingerroot (unpeeled)

2 cups of water

2 cups of granulated sugar

12 ounces of carbonated water or seltzer

Put the ginger and water in a large pot and heat it on the stove over medium heat. Let it simmer for about 30 minutes, and then remove it from the burner. Allow it to steep for an hour. Strain out the ginger, then add the sugar to the water. Return the pot to the burner and boil the mixture until the sugar dissolves. Cool, then put a lid on it and store it in the refrigerator.

Before serving, stir in the carbonated water or seltzer. Pour some into a glass with ice cubes, and you've got yourself a mighty fine brew that will quench even the toughest, low-down thirst!

post, peat, and sand. Then turn up the heat and encourage this plant to sweat! It craves lots of warmth, light, moisture, and humidity.

Ginger may be temperamental when it comes to climates, but it is refreshingly resilient against most garden pests and diseases. So don't worry; be happy!

HARVESTING TIPS

After its first full season, yank (and I mean yank) the ginger plant up out of the ground and remove all of the leaf stalks. Cut or break off enough of the root to meet your health — and kitchen spice — needs; then replant the rest. Wasn't that easy?

STORAGE TIPS

Ginger can be used fresh or dried, but obviously the best taste comes from the freshest form. After harvesting it, store the roots in the refrigerator until you're ready to use them. You can keep them wrapped in paper towels inside a plastic bag for about a month or so. I like to grate some gingerroot right into a tea or other recipes.

If you're drying the roots, keep them in airtight containers until you're ready to use them.

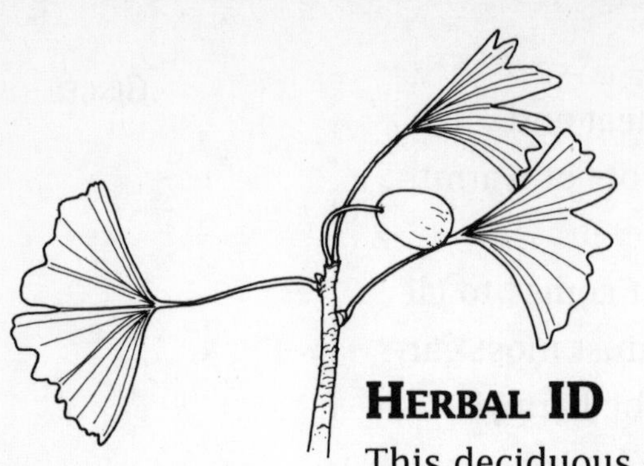

Ginkgo

(Ginkgo biloba)

HERBAL ID

This deciduous conifer loves to reach for the sky and touch the clouds. Some ginkgo trees grow to be 125 feet high and 50 feet wide! Also known as the maidenhair tree, it has fan-shaped leaves that shimmer emerald green under the summer sun and turn to golden yellow in the fall. Its bark is corky and gray in color.

People tend to overdo it with ginkgo because of all its benefits. Sure, it's got a reputation as a brain herb, but more won't make you smarter. Keep your daily amount under 240 mg; otherwise, you may develop diarrhea and induce vomiting.

THAT'S HISTORICAL!

The age-old question is: Just how old is ginkgo? That's a toughie. Suffice it to say, ginkgo trees have been around for millions of years. In fact, they may be the oldest trees on earth!

For over 5,000 years, the Chinese have relied on ginkgo as one of their most trusted herbs, because of its benefits to the brain. And Europeans, who were introduced to ginkgo in the early 1700s, prized the oils extracted from its leaves, claiming it kept them mentally sharp. But North Americans latched on to the trees at the end of the century for their ornamental, not their medicinal, value.

MEDICINAL USES: REVITALIZE YOUR CIRCULATION

This is one herb that really gets around — inside the body, that is! Ginkgo improves circulation and blood flow from head to toe, even in the itty-bitty capillaries of your brain — which is no easy feat! Ginkgo also acts like the fountain of youth in the body, helping to keep your organs and cardiovascular system young and fit as a fiddle!

So what gives ginkgo all of its medicinal power? A couple of big words: ginkgo flavone glycosides and terpene lactones. These two compounds team up for mental clarity (less forgetfulness); improved circulation (lower blood pressure, fewer problems with varicose veins); head-clearing abilities (bye-bye headaches, vertigo, and tinnitus — aka ringing in the ears); and mood elevation (blues begone!)

And there's more! Ingredients called ginkgolides work against allergies — especially helpful for people with asthma.

Ginkgo has been gaining popularity in the United States, but Europeans have long known of its medicinal value. Germany, in fact, has a commission that studies herbs, and ginkgo is sold there by prescription.

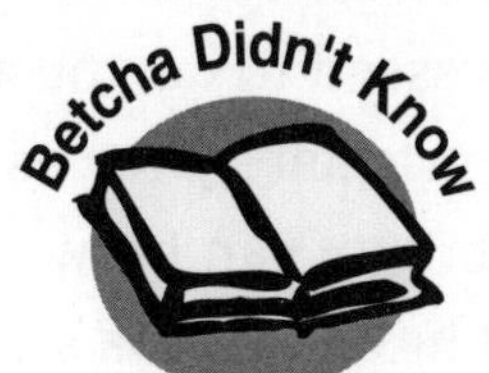

Ginkgo trees are either male or female. So how do you tell them apart? Good question. Only females produce fruit and flower (but only if a male is within range to supply pollen). It's not uncommon for female ginkgo trees to be flowerless for the first 20 to 50 years of life, so it may take decades to determine the gender of your ginkgo! But ginkgo's medicinal value is in the leaves of either male or female trees, so if you've only got one or the other, that's OK!

BEST MEDICINAL FORMS

The heart of ginkgo's medicinal value is contained in its leaves, as well as the seeds and fruit. Unfortunately, they taste yucky right off the branch. Plus, you'd have to eat a wheelbarrow full to make any difference in your health. The volatile oils from the leaves must be squeezed and processed to do you any good health-wise.

Fortunately for us, there are saner ways to take this herb. You can brew a tea using dried ginkgo leaves; all you have to do is sweeten it with honey to mask its bitter taste. Three cups a day is plenty.

Or you can go to your local health food store and buy ginkgo in tincture or capsule form. As a tincture, the standard dose for adults is 30 to 50 drops in a glass of water or juice, up to 3 times a day. As a capsule, the

Mind Matters

Well, I can't promise that you will suddenly remember everything about Einstein's theory of relativity, or be able to rattle off all of the answers on Jeopardy, but you can certainly give your brain a healthy workout by drinking this mind-expanding ginkgo tea every day:

½ tsp. of dried ginkgo leaves
½ tsp. of dried rosemary
½ tsp. of dried gotu kola leaves
1 tsp. of dried peppermint

Mix all of the herbs, then scoop a teaspoon of this blend into a cup of boiling water. Let it steep for about 10 minutes. Strain out the herbs, and sip away!

daily dose is 120 to 240 mg. Make sure you buy products that say "standardized" on the label to ensure you're getting enough ginkgo per dose.

As effective as ginkgo is, as with all herbal remedies, you must be patient. Ginkgo takes awhile to kick in. On average, most folks see noticeable improvement within 6 to 8 weeks of taking ginkgo every day.

GROWING TIPS

Give ginkgo well-drained soil and a place sheltered from strong winds that gets sun and partial shade. It grows best in Zones 3 to 9. Ginkgo in the home garden is virtually maintenance-free. It's rarely bugged by pests or diseases; it just takes its sweet old time to grow.

HARVESTING TIPS

The bizarre world of ginkgo continues. It bears golden fruits that smell like spoiled butter — and taste even worse! The real treat is the nuts inside the fruits, which you can harvest in the fall. Roasted or boiled, they deliver a delicious, almond taste.

Ginseng

(Panax ginseng; P. quinquefolium; Eleutherococcus senticosus)

Herbal ID

Yep, you read it right — there are actually three types of ginseng. Siberian ginseng (known to botanists as *Eleutherococcus senticosus*) is a spiny-stemmed shrub that reaches a height of about 9 feet in 10 years. It's found in northeast Asia. The American type (known as *Panax quinquefolium*) is a perennial that can grow to be 2 feet tall or more, with five oblong, finely etched leaflets at the top of its stem. It has a pleasant-smelling root and bears red berries in the fall. The third type, *Panax ginseng* — known as Korean ginseng — features branched roots that resemble arms and legs and has therefore been dubbed the "man root."

Just to add to the confusion, ginseng also answers to a host of other nicknames: root of life, a dose of immortality, devil's shrub, sang, man's health, and five fingers. With ginseng, you can't tell the players without a scorecard.

North-central Wisconsin, from Minneapolis to Green Bay, is the ginseng capital of the United States, producing up to 95 percent of America's crop. But get this: Most American ginseng is shipped elsewhere, especially to Asia. And most Americans take the Siberian form of ginseng because it is less expensive and easier on the body. *Say what?* I told you this was a confusing herb!

THAT'S HISTORICAL!

Ginseng is one of the oldest herbs known to humankind; it's been used for more than 5,000 years. Why, it was thought of so highly as a cure-all — including its power to restore *chi,* or "life force" — that a Chinese medical manual 2,000 years ago listed it as the most important herb of its time!

More recently, Native Americans used American ginseng to fight off headaches, fevers, exhaustion, earaches, and menstrual irregularities.

A BLAST FROM THE PAST

Although ginseng has a reputation as an aphrodisiac, whether it actually does anything to the libido has yet to be scientifically proved. However, the Ginseng Board of Wisconsin did include a recipe for Sex Muffins (loaded with ginseng) in its annual cookbook! Hmmm, now we know what those folks in Madison, Wisconsin, are doing on those long winter nights!

MEDICINAL USES: BOOST YOUR ENERGY

Worldwide, studies have shown ginseng's ability to boost energy levels and support the immune system. In Asia, it is still used to ease the pain of childbirth and to enhance and increase sexual desire.

Among ginseng's nearly 20 active ingredients are something called ginsenosides. They are super-duper in the versatility department, preventing your memory from getting fuzzy, keeping your liver nice and strong, calming your nervous system and stomach, and acting as tranquilizers and pain relievers.

But you need to make sure you're taking the right ginseng for your health needs. Siberian ginseng, which is the most versatile, is the best one for folks who are new to using herbal medicines. It helps relieve stress and physical fatigue. American ginseng is cooling by nature. It's best used to relieve chronic chest congestion and dry coughs and to tame nighttime sweats. Asian ginseng is warming by nature. This one is noted for boosting energy and mental sharpness; it also treats chronic diarrhea.

Ginseng can raise your blood pressure, so folks taking medicine for high blood pressure should check with their doctors before taking ginseng, just to be on the safe side. Sometimes mixin' and matchin' just isn't heartpleasin'!

BEST MEDICINAL FORMS

You've got a couple of choices: You can chew ginseng root or brew it into a tea. One teaspoon of ground ginseng in a cup of boiling water should do the trick. For convenience, ginseng is also available in health food stores and supermarkets — in capsule, tablet, and tincture forms.

Ginseng won't work its magic overnight, so give it some time to work. Ginseng must be taken every day for several weeks before you start noticing any improvement, but don't take it for more than 3 weeks.

GROWING TIPS

For simplicity's sake, let's stick with American ginseng. Although wild ginseng is found in cool, wooded areas, the bulk of this knee-high perennial is cultivated commercially in Wisconsin. (And you thought this state was famous only for its cheese and the Green Bay Packers!)

Ginseng prefers soil that is rich, loamy, and well drained. Keep it out of direct sunlight by planting it under forest trees or a wooden lath frame built over the planting area. You can also use it for low edgings in your garden.

The best time to sink the roots in soil is fall; plant them about 2 inches deep and 8 inches apart. Then sit back and be patient — the roots (where ginseng's medicine is stored) take a good 5 to 7 years to mature.

HARVESTING TIPS

Good-and-ready ginseng roots are forked and measure about 4 inches long. To keep the forks intact, you have to be extra careful when digging them up. Any dirt that sticks to them should be very gently brushed off, so do away with that urge to scrub-a-dub-dub.

Gin-zing Tea

Need to get your motor running, and you're tired of the same old cup o' joe? Here's how to add a boost to your step with this energi-zing tea:

1 tsp. of ginseng root, ground
1 tsp. of dried borage leaves
1 tsp. of dried mint leaves
10–20 drops of ginkgo biloba tincture

Let the ginseng simmer in a pot (about 5 cups) of water for 30 minutes, but keep a lid on it! Then add the borage and mint and let the blend steep for 15–20 minutes. Finally, add the ginkgo. Strain out the dried herbs, and sip up to 3 cups a day. The tea has a parsleylike taste that can be sweetened with honey.

To dry ginseng, you need a warm and well-ventilated room. Stick the roots on something like a window screen that's set up like a shelf. Basically, you need air circulating all around these guys. Turn them frequently, but tend to them like babies so you don't break their forks! They may take several weeks to dry.

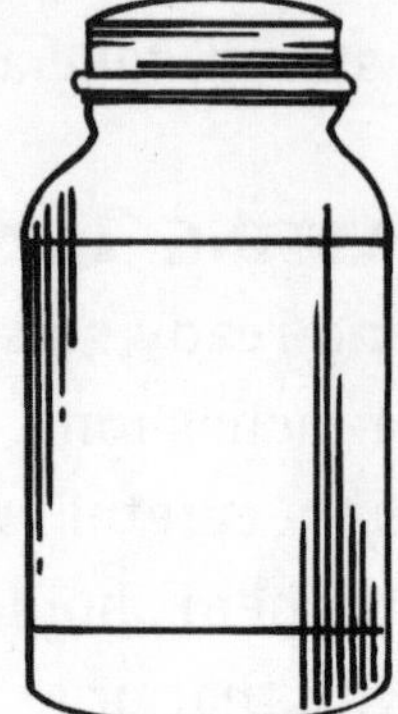

STORAGE TIPS

Store dried ginseng roots in a glass jar with a tight-fitting lid, so no little critters are tempted to nibble on them.

Jerry Baker's Tonic Wine

My Grandma Putt taught me the value of taking home-made tonics for a general all-over feeling of goodness. Here's one of my favorites:

1 oz. of ginseng root, ground
8 almonds
5 dried apricots
2 pints of red wine

Mix all of the ingredients together in a container. Seal with a lid and let stand for about 2 weeks. Then strain out the solids and pour the liquid into a small glass. Drink a glassful a day, and soon you'll feel A-OK!

Hop

(Humulus lupulus)

Herbal ID

Let me hop right to it by telling you what this perennial looks like! It's a twisting climber that has pliable, sturdy stems; delicate, spade-shaped leaves; and conelike flowers.

Hop plants are either male or female. The flowering females tend to be petite, cone-shaped, and yellow-green in color, and contain a substance called lupulin, which delivers the herb's medicine. The blooming guys, on the other hand, grow in loose bunches.

That's Historical!

Way back in the 14th century, some clever soul discovered that hops made a tastier beer than the mead or ale beverages that were previously concocted from fermented honey. In fact, for all of you folks who speak Spanish, here's a quicky lingo quiz: What does *flores de Cerveza* mean? Translated, it means "flowers of beer," which is a nickname for the hop plant.

Hundreds of years ago, the kings of England were said to have stuffed their pillows with hops so they could sleep peacefully — and without tossing and turning from headaches, which they surely had after a long day of ruling. Other folks believed that hops helped stop quarreling. During their glory years, the ancient

Romans used to eat young hop shoots like asparagus; some folks still enjoy this treat.

This is a safe herb generally, with no known problems if used with other medications. But don't use hops as a medicine if you're under a doctor's care for depression.

Medicinal Uses: Stimulate a Flagging Appetite

Certainly there is more to hops than a lot of brew — ha-ha! As much as hops are valued as flavoring agents for beer, they are also vital members of Mother Nature's botanical health brigade.

With hops, the rule is the (more) bitter, the better. Some herbalists think that the bitter ingredients in hops, known as humulone and lulupone, may trigger appetites.

Hops also contain volatile oils. The berries and fruits seem to perform many health roles: germ-fighters, muscle-tamers, sleep-inducers, and mind-calmers. There is even the possibility that hops may help flush toxins from the body, as well.

Best Medicinal Forms

Belly up to the bar — a good beer sometimes sounds like good medicine! But to really get the biggest health bang out of your hops buck, it's better to stick with teas, tinctures, and capsules.

To make hops tea, put 2 teaspoons of dried fruits (or hops flowers) in a cup and pour boiling water over them. Let steep a good 15 minutes before drinking. For times when I have trouble sleeping, I don't count sheep. I just make a cup of this tea, hop into bed, and catch some zzzzzs!

Or you can buy hops in tincture form at your local health food or drugstore. The recommended daily dose is 1 to 4 ml in a glass of water or juice, taken up to 3 times a day.

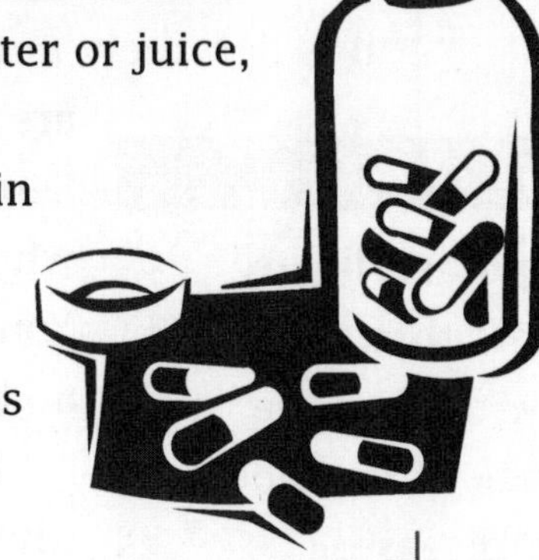

The dried fruits of hops also come in capsule and tablet forms, which are quick and convenient. The daily dose is 500 to 1,000 mg, taken up to 3 times a day.

GROWING TIPS

Before you grow hops, make sure you've got plenty of headroom, because they can easily grow up to be 20 feet high in a single season!

Hops belong to the cool-climate clan of herbs. They do really well in moderate climates (especially Zones 3 to 7) where winter temperatures can dip to below 10°F. Hops don't do as well in subtropical and tropical climates.

For hops that are tops, sow seeds in rich, loamy soil that's neutral to slightly acidic. Make sure the area gets full sun or partial shade, and keep it well watered. I tell my gardening friends to space the seedlings about 2 feet apart.

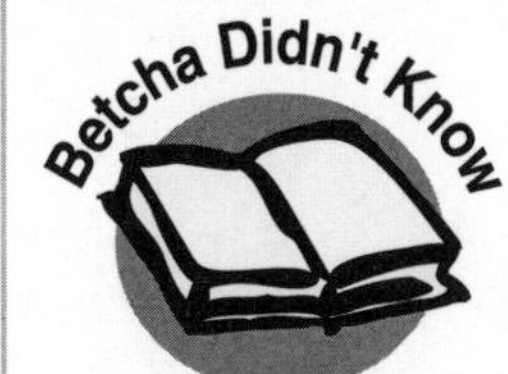

Legend says that a pillow stuffed with hops will help relieve an achy tooth and let you get a good night's rest.

Before the plants poke their heads up through the soil, stick sturdy poles in the ground at the base of the plantings. Come July, you can train the twining stems by hand.

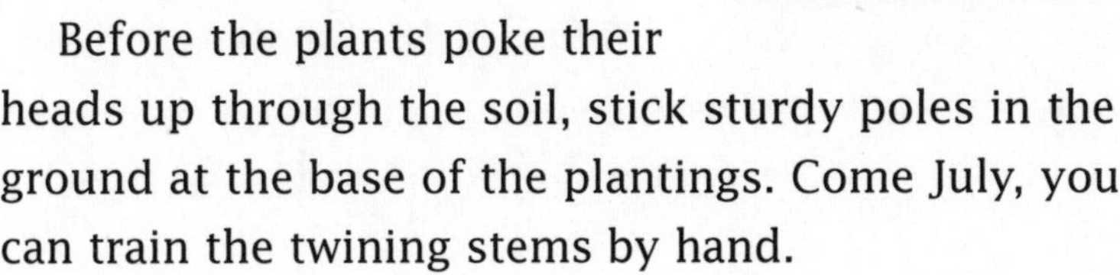

Harvesting Tips

In a nutshell: Your nose knows. If the fruit smells bad, it is definitely not fresh. Collect the cones before they are fully ripe, usually during August and September. You can tell they're ready when they're brown to amber in color. You can dry the cones in the shade or in an oven set at 125 to 150°F.

FAST FACT

Hops are hardy plants that are able to withstand the attack of most pests and diseases.

If you're going to take cuttings or divide the hop plants, spring is the time to do it. After the frost turns the stems brown, cut plants back to the ground.

Storage Tips

It's best to use hops without delay, because they quickly lose their punch. In fact, the hop plant releases its trademark peppery, bitter odor at room temperature because it's evaporating. So whatever you do, don't freeze hops.

Horehound

(Marrubium vulgare)

Herbal ID

This hardy perennial features a spindle-like root; bushy, downy stems; and clumps of woolly, gray-green, heart-shaped leaves. During peak gardening season — usually June to September — this herb produces tiny, creamy white flowers along the upper stems. Horehound also is known as marrubium and hoarhound.

That's Historical!

Egyptian priests referred to horehound as the seed of Horus, bull's blood, and eye of the star. You Bible students may recall that horehound is mentioned in early writings as one of the five bitter herbs consumed by Jews during Passover. The Palestinians believed horehound delivered a wish for good health. The ancient Greeks used horehound as an antidote for rabid-dog bites. And back in the late 16th century, author John Gerard wrote of horehound as being an antidote for "those [who] drunk poyson or have been bitten of serpents." As you can see, it was used for a little bit of everything.

Medicinal Uses: Cancel Coughs

Nowadays, the plant's dried leaves are used medicinally as an expectorant and muscle-spasm stopper. It is especially valued in treating bronchitis and whooping cough because it helps relax the smooth muscles while clearing the lungs of mucus. Not surprisingly, horehound can help someone with asthma breathe a little easier, and a person with hoarseness or a frog in the throat speak more clearly — works great for singers and speech-givers.

Externally, horehound works wonders on minor cuts and scrapes.

BEST MEDICINAL FORMS

Think of the two Ts — teas and tinctures — when you want to use horehound. In a tea, a little goes a long

Really Sweet Deal

Horehound is a main ingredient in many cough drops and hard candies. Here's a recipe I got from my Grandma Putt that I still use today:

Put 1–2 cups of fresh horehound leaves in a pot with 4 cups of water. Slowly bring it to a boil; then let it simmer for 15 minutes. Strain out the horehound. Remove the pot from the stove; add 3 cups of brown sugar and 3 cups of granulated sugar. Stir with a wooden spoon until the sugar is all dissolved.

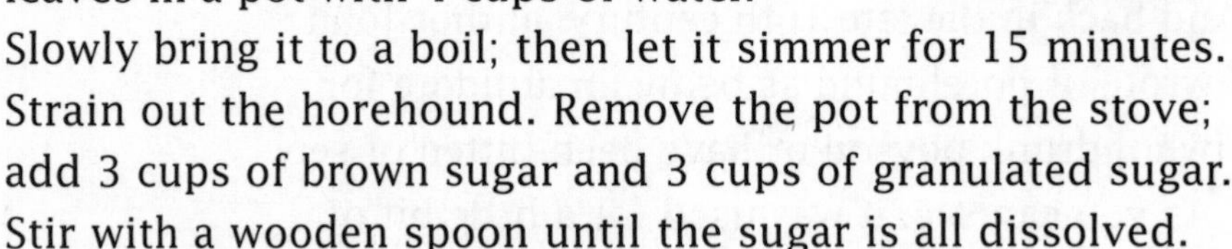

Bring the syrup to a boil again, and then remove it from the heat. Pour your herbal batter into a 9- by 13-inch greased baking pan.

As soon as the candy hardens, break it into bite-size pieces and wrap each in waxed paper. Talk about your sweet deals — children just love 'em.

way. All you need is a half teaspoon of dried horehound in a cup of boiling water. Let it steep 10 to 15 minutes before straining and drinking. You may want to sweeten it up with a teaspoon of honey. You can drink up to 3 cups a day of this bittersweet, musky herb.

For those times you're in a hurry, or away from the stove, you may want to try a tincture of horehound. Drop 1 to 2 ml of horehound into a glass of water or juice to help clear your throat and lungs. You can safely take this amount up to 3 times a day.

GROWING TIPS

Because horehound rarely grows more than 3 feet high, it's best placed toward the front end of your garden. Its favorite soil is sandy, well drained, and not overly rich. You might even add some sand and coarsely ground limestone to the potting mix — it can only help!

Horehound is partial to the mild climates of Zones 4 to 9. It loves the sun and is fairly hardy in the bug- and disease-resistance departments; but it can fall prey to winterkill, especially if the soil stays moist.

For best results, sow the seeds directly into the soil. In a few weeks, you should see some signs of life. Space the plants about 12 inches apart, and keep them pinched back to prevent them from bullying other plants. Horehound self-seeds enthusiastically, and if you let it go, it will soon overrun your garden.

If you want a bumper tomato crop, grow horehound nearby; it makes a great companion

A BLAST FROM THE PAST

In Old English, it's said that horehound got its name from the term *har hune,* which means "downy plant."

plant. When you're working in your garden, keep an eye and ear open since horehound also attracts bees.

HARVESTING TIPS

The best time to harvest horehound leaves is between June and September, on a clear, dry, sunny morning, before the blossoms have developed. Dry them in a shady spot, making sure the temperature never dips below freezing.

In the plant's first year, cut the foliage sparingly. After that, it's a good idea to divide the plants every few years to control growth and maintain their vigor.

STORAGE TIPS

Just chop the freshly harvested leaves and store them — as usual — in airtight containers, away from heat and sunlight, until you're ready to use them. Horehound does not freeze well, so don't bother.

Hound Away a Cough

If you're looking for a natural way to silence a nagging cough due to a cold, bronchitis, or even whooping cough, make this concoction part of your daily morning regimen:

1 tsp. of dried horehound leaves

1 tsp. of gingerroot, ground

1 tsp. of dried coltsfoot leaves

Blend all three herbs and scoop a teaspoonful of the mix into a cup of boiling water. Let it steep for about 10 minutes; then strain out the herbs. Add a teaspoon of honey, if you like, and sip the cough into silence!

Horseradish

(Amoracia rusticana)

Herbal ID

This plant produces clumps of broad, green leaves that sprout from 3-foot stems. Look for small, white flowers during blooming season.

Deep down in the ground, horseradish plants produce thick, fleshy roots that are brown on the outside, white on the inside.

That's Historical!

Hold your horses! While horseradish most likely came from the soils of Eastern Europe, it is now cultivated around the world. Centuries ago, Europeans used it as both a medicine and a condiment.

Medicinal Uses: Decongest Your Head and Chest

It's not been scientifically proved, but many herbalists believe that horseradish helps the body — particularly as a natural antibiotic. That's why it is often used to help relieve colds and sore throats, as well as indigestion and heartburn.

I like to think of horseradish as one of nature's decongestants. Need proof? Try adding a couple of teaspoons of peeled, grated horseradish root to a favorite sandwich, and your nose will be running (and you'll be dashing for a tissue) in no time at all!

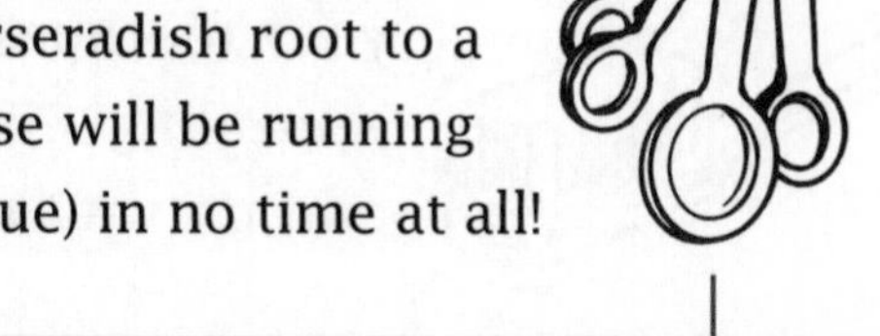

Some herbalists believe horseradish can stimulate an appetite and act as a diuretic. For some folks, dabbing a little horseradish tincture on pimples seems to help draw out the infection and restore a clear complexion.

Be careful handling fresh horseradish. Before you rub your eyes, itch your nose, or scratch your face, wash your hands thoroughly with soap and water!

Also, for those of you with sensitive skin, horseradish may cause a slight rash or mild blister. Finally, be forewarned — a little is more than enough: Eating large amounts of the raw root can be toxic.

What we do know is that horseradish, like mustard, contains sulfur, volatile oils, and glycosides that help clear nasal passages, rev up an appetite, and fight germs.

But grating the root can be harder on the eyes than cutting up onions, so make sure you have plenty of air circulating before you tackle this task.

BEST MEDICINAL FORMS

It's the horseradish taproot that packs the medicinal punch. You can clear up congestion by grating a fresh root and eating a half teaspoon of it up to 3 times a day. Out of season, horseradish is available in tincture form from health food and drug stores. The daily dosage is 2 to 3 ml in a glass of water or juice, up to 3 times daily.

Look, Ma, no bacteria! While horseradish won't whiten your smile, adding a dab of the root to your toothpaste (doesn't that sound appealing?) is believed to help kill germs and prevent mouth ulcers.

If you're looking for some natural relief from painful, itchy hemorrhoids, try a homemade horseradish poultice. Apply a thin layer of fresh horseradish to a wet cloth, and place it on the hemorrhoids for 5 to 10 minutes. The ingredients in the horseradish seem to speed up the healing process by improving blood flow to the affected area.

Finally, what about those nagging old aches and pains due to rheumatism? Horseradish to the rescue! My Grandma Putt told me that nibbling on tiny pieces of fresh horseradish every morning worked wonders for her — and she was as spry as a spring chicken well into her golden years!

Pulling In the Reins

For all of you horseradish fans who prefer your own homegrown, garden-variety over supermarket selections, here's a nifty way to preserve this herb-with-a-bite as a seasoning for your favorite soups, sauces, stews, and meats:

2 lbs. of fresh horseradish, peeled and grated

1 cup of malt vinegar (or white wine)

Put the grated horseradish into hot, sterilized mason jars. Fill each jar with the vinegar or wine, to within ¼ inch of the top. Put on lids and rings; then store the jars in the refrigerator until you're ready to use them.

GROWING TIPS

This plant is a great confidence-booster for rookie gardeners — no matter what you do, it's hard to mistreat! Horseradish grows best in full sun, in Zones 5 to 9. A hardy perennial, it likes deeply dug, rich, moist soil that is neutral to slightly acidic.

You don't need a lot of horseradish — in fact, one plant serves a family quite well. Another reason to limit the number of horseradish plants you grow — this one's a real garden hog. Left unchaperoned, it'll muscle out the other plants in your garden quicker than you can say Arnold Schwarzenegger.

Your horseradish will do best if you plant the young roots (about 9 inches long) straight into the soil, so that the crown is about 4 inches below the surface. Space the plants about 18 inches apart. By midsummer, you should see tiny, white blossoms.

Tea with a Kick

If your sinuses feel all blocked up, try grating a teaspoon of fresh horseradish into a glass of water. Add the juice from a quarter of a fresh lemon. Stir and drink up; you should be breathing easier in no time at all!

HARVESTING TIPS

Plenty of folks like to harvest the pungent, fleshy root during late fall or the following spring. During the season, however, just break off what you need. Replant a couple of roots and bring the rest indoors. About every 2 years or so, you'll need to replant the batch. Just make sure you remove all of the old roots before planting the next generation (sounds a lot like *Star Trek!*).

STORAGE TIPS

When stocking up on fresh horseradish, give the roots a good going-over with a scrub brush before storing them in the refrigerator. You can also pack the roots in dry sand, and store them in a cool place like the basement.

Both methods will keep the horseradish fresh for about 3 months. Forget about freezing or cooking horseradish — its medicinal value, as well as its taste, will quickly gallop away!

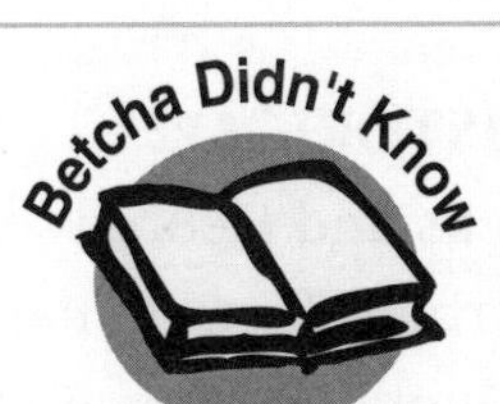

If someone faints due to heat exhaustion and you happen to have some horseradish handy, crush a small piece of it under the person's nose — its pungent aroma is a mighty powerful eye-opener!

Hyssop

(Hyssopus officinalis)

Herbal ID

This perennial, shrublike herb has delicate, woody stems with thin, dark leaves and spikes of blue, mauve, or white edible flowers. It grows up to 3 feet tall. Its fresh young leaves add a nice minty flavor to salads.

That's Historical!

Ancient Greeks and Hebrews valued hyssop as a sacred cleansing herb. In fact, its name means "cleanliness." Benedictine monks were said to have used hyssop in making herbal liqueurs. In Psalms 51:7, David spoke of this herb in a prayer with the words, "Purge me with hyssop and I shall be clean."

Cleanliness is certainly next to godliness, but hyssop also had a different kind of cleanliness among 17th-century Europeans. Long before aerosol sprays were invented, people "cleared the air" of smoke, cooking, and other lingering odors by tossing hyssop on their floors. Then each time they stepped on the plants, a pleasing fragrance was released.

Medicinal Uses: Calm Coughs and Heal Cuts

Both the leaves and flowers of hyssop are used for medicine. Hyssop is a terrific cleansing herb. It possesses the power to clear up congestion, reduce swelling, tame muscle spasms, and improve circulation. That's why it's been used for centuries to calm coughs, bronchitis, colds, and sore throats. When used as a poultice, hyssop can help mend minor cuts speedily, reduce swelling, and take away those dark rainbow colors created by a bruise.

Best Medicinal Forms

Teas and tinctures are the best ways to ingest hyssop. Whether you're trying to harness a nagging cough or soothe a sore throat, try putting a teaspoonful of the dried herb into your favorite cup. Add boiling water and stir. Let simmer 10 to 15 minutes; then strain out the hyssop and drink. You can do this up to 3 times a day.

In tincture form, hyssop works best when you take 1 to 4 ml in a glass of juice or water, up to 3 times daily.

Again, hyssop works quite well as a poultice. You can also use its essential oil on your skin; but remember: Don't ever ingest essential oils!

Growing Tips

Hyssop will do quite nicely in your outdoor garden or indoors. Either way, make sure to give this shrubby perennial plenty of bright light. Stick with

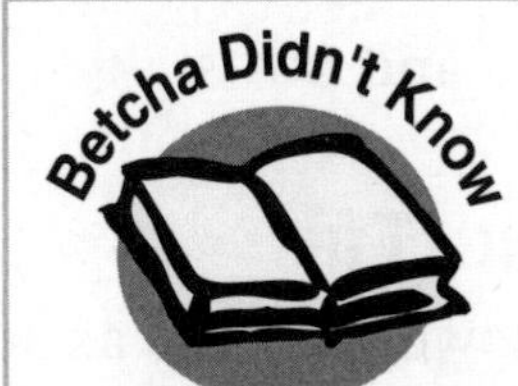

This herb is a member in good standing of the mint family! It's also the flavoring agent found in the liqueur Chartreuse.

a standard potting mix and light soil that is slightly acidic, and allow the soil to dry out a bit between waterings. Also, make sure to give this herb plenty of fertilizer on a regular basis to keep it growing on the right track.

If you're planning to grow hyssop inside, it needs lots of room. So use 12-inch pots or other large containers.

Outdoors, hyssop performs double-duty: first as a medicinal herb, and second as a garden defender against bugs, slugs, and other thugs! It grows best in Zones 3 to 9, with full sun or light shade.

Keep the plants about a foot apart, and plant them in front to show them off. Hyssop plants rarely grow more than 3 feet tall.

Sow the seeds on the surface and just cover them lightly with soil in the early spring. Plan on 2 to 6 weeks until germination. You can divide mature plants in the spring or fall. Just keep in mind that you'll need to replace hyssop about every 5 years or so.

As a bonus, hyssop's nectar seems to be a beacon for hungry hummingbirds and honeybees. Plus, it's a generally healthy plant that tends to be free from diseases and pests.

HARVESTING TIPS

Collect the flowering tops as soon as they open, which is usually around August. Pick a nice morning just after the dew has disappeared. Also, be sure to clip off spent flowers to promote bushier, fuller growth. You can snip off portions of the stalk when you just need a little, or cut whole stems to dry the flowers and leaves. Allow them to hang in bunches upside down to dry naturally, and they'll provide an inviting fragrance.

For indoor plants, you can collect the young shoots as often as you need to for use in salads, soups, meats, poultry, fatty fish, and stews. For medicinal use, harvest only the leaves and flowers.

If you are taking medication for high blood pressure or you're pregnant, check with your doctor before taking hyssop, just to be on the safe side.

HYSSOP: TAKE ME AWAY!

When you feel achy all over and stressed to the max, treat yourself to a nice, relaxing hyssop herbal bath before you head for bed. I guarantee it'll help you get a good night's sleep. Simply gather about 3 cups of fresh hyssop leaves, tuck them inside an 8-inch-square muslin bag, and pull the drawstring to close it. Drop it in the running bathwater (warm, not hot), and add a few teaspoons of oatmeal. Let the bag float as you soak, and soon your troubles will also float — away!

CAN THE AIR FRESHENERS

To get rid of nasty or stale odors around the house, try making your own air-clearing potpourri. It's easy; just follow these steps:

- Blend 1 cup each of hyssop flowers, calamus root, and elecampane root with 2 cups of dried thuja cedar twigs and leaves.
- Scoop a cup of this herbal mix and put it in a pot with 4 cups of water.
- Let simmer until the fragrance makes the whole house smell nice.
- Store the rest of the mix in an airtight container in a cool, dry place so it's ready to knock out the next odoriferous cloud — like the next time you cook fish!

Kava

(Piper methysticum)

HERBAL ID

Native to many Pacific Ocean islands, this plant actually belongs to the pepper family. It has lush, emerald green, heart-shaped leaves. Take a peek at the leaves — they're shiny and smooth on both sides. The plant grows thick and averages 8 feet in height. Some plants, however, soar to 20 feet or more!

THAT'S HISTORICAL!

Among Pacific Islanders, kava has played a vital role in special ceremonies — from weddings to shindigs for royalty or meetings hosted by village elders. Drinking a bit too much kava can send an Islander to the nearest palm tree to grab a relaxing nap.

When 18th-century British missionaries spotted the natives slumped under trees, they mistakenly thought they were drunk! They scurried back to Europe, where scientists dubbed the plant *Piper methysticum,* which is Latin for "intoxicating pepper." But the natives knew better — kava provided them with much-needed, restful sleep, without any hangovers!

Even today, a kava drink is regarded as one of the highest forms of welcome an Islander can bestow upon dignitaries. During visits to the island of Fiji, VIPs including former President Lyndon Johnson, First Lady

Hillary Clinton, and Pope John Paul II have all been served this welcoming beverage.

MEDICINAL USES: ELIMINATE ANXIETY

The spotlight ingredient that delivers the medicinal punch in this herb is known as kava-lactone. It provides pain-relieving, worry-lifting, muscle-relaxing, and mood-mellowing abilities. This herb seems to deliver a "don't worry; be happy" sense of contentment, and it may even sharpen mental acuity and memory.

Kava is viewed among herbalists and natural medicine doctors as the No. 1 anti-anxiety herb. It works great for those times when you may feel edgy and uptight, worrying about the "what ifs" in your life.

Kava's ingredients work gently to naturally relax the nervous system and calm you down. Scientific studies have shown that kava is actually safer (and a whole lot cheaper) than prescription sedatives because it is nonaddictive and free of side effects, if used sparingly. That's good to know in any language!

In addition, kava acts like nature's aspirin by relieving head and body aches. Kava is also a natural choice to treat painful urination, restlessness in the legs, muscle spasms, and insomnia.

Mellow Yellow

People who take a lot of kava for a long time may notice their skin turning yellow. This temporary tinge will fade away when the amount of kava intake is decreased.

BEST MEDICINAL FORMS

A cup of warm kava tea is just the thing to calm your nerves. Grate 1 to 2 teaspoons of dried kava root into a cup of boiling water. Cover, then let steep for a good hour. Strain, and then sip up to 2 cups a day. But be forewarned: Kava is mighty bitter-tasting. If your tongue feels a bit numb, there's no cause for alarm. For most folks, it takes awhile to acquire a taste for kava, so you may want to add some honey; or try tinctures or capsules instead.

When you're in a hurry and need to save time, try taking kava as a tincture. Add 30 to 40 drops to a glass of water or juice and take up to 2 times a day. Kava is also available in capsule form. Just read the label for dosage amount, and make sure it says "standardized" — that's your guarantee that the required amount of medicine from this plant is in every capsule.

GROWING TIPS

Kava is best suited to the rich soil of volcanic islands in the Pacific, where it is regarded as a major cash crop. Like the tropical plant it is, it mingles well with papaya, banana, yams, and sweet potatoes. Obviously, kava is not at home in America's heartland, but you folks down south, take note!

Even though you can't really grow kava outside of the subtropics and tropics, it's still interesting to know how it's grown. In the islands, kava

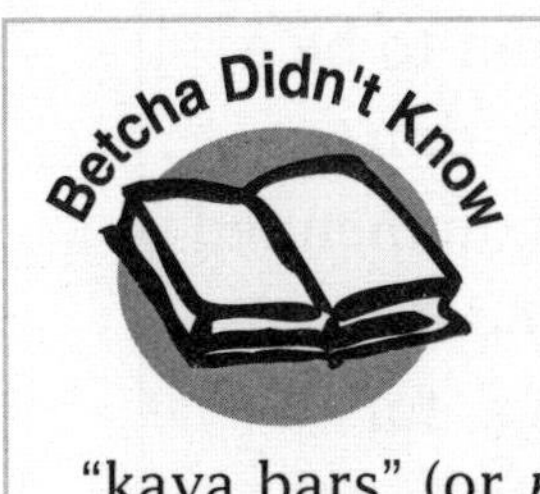

In the Pacific Islands, people flock to nonalcoholic "kava bars" (or *nakamals,* as the locals call them) to help them unwind after a hard day's work.

is planted much like sugarcane. Sections of stalks, often sliced from the young branches of an older bush, are placed in mud trenches and allowed to sprout. Growers make sure the young stalks are kept away from direct sunlight and wind.

Harvesting Tips

Patience is a virtue — and essential when growing kava. This plant requires a good 5 years to mature before it is ready to be harvested as a drink or medicine.

Besides storing kava teas, tinctures, and capsules the usual way — in airtight containers out of direct sunlight and heat — you can store dried kava root the way Islanders do: in jute sacks.

Although kava is generally considered to be a very safe herb, don't exceed the recommended dose. One standardized capsule of kava, for instance, will help you calm down. Two will act like a sedative and put you to sleep!

Lavender

(Lavandula angustifolia)

Herbal ID

While there are 28 known varieties of lavender, I'm going to stick with the one that offers the most medicine. It's a hardy, multibranched shrub that can withstand temperatures below freezing, and features lavender-blue (as well as white and pink), spiky flowers in midsummer.

It has silver-green foliage — on slender stalks that grow over 20 inches tall — delivering a heady, welcoming fragrance.

That's Historical!

Talk about your squeaky-clean reputations! Lavender comes from the Latin word *lavare,* which means "to wash." It may be what led to the term "wash-and-wear."

Back in the late 1500s, Langham said, "[Add] lavender in water, wet thy shirt in it and dry it again and wear it again." Not the most eloquent of quotes, but you get the idea.

Centuries earlier, the Greek physician Dioscorides said lavender was a perfect remedy for feelings of grief and depression. And during Victorian times, uptight leaders recommended lavender to the masses as an antiaphrodisiac to get them out of the mood.

MEDICINAL USES: SHOO AWAY THE BLUES

Lavender is a real "put-you-at-ease" herb. That's because it contains ingredients that work solely and naturally to rid your body of tension that can lead to headaches, tight muscles, and toss-and-turn nights.

Some of my aromatherapist friends tell me that lavender not only relaxes and calms them down, but also shoos away fatigue and blue moods. When used as an essential oil, it can also cool down and help heal tender skin that's been harmed by the sun or minor kitchen burns.

This extremely safe herb also kills all kinds of germs and boosts the immune system.

BEST MEDICINAL FORMS

Lavender is really easy to use as a medicine. You can tap into its powers by using fresh leaves, tinctures, essential oils, and — if you dare — tea.

Instead of taking aspirin or other over-the-counter headache remedies, try using lavender essential oil the next time a real head-pounder gets you on the ropes. Simply dilute 5 drops of lavender essential oil with a tablespoon of almond oil. Dip your fingertips into this oily mix and then, using circular motions, slowly massage the oil into your temples, forehead, and neck. Your headache should vamoose — and without any side effects!

If you're tired of counting sheep or counting backwards from 100 to try to sleep at night, use lavender to lull you into a well-deserved slumber. Put a few drops of lavender essential oil on your pillow or a few drops in running bathwater. Either way, your mind and body will be relaxed, and ready for sleep, thanks to nature's sedative.

Are you feeling adventuresome? Try brewing yourself a cup of lavender tea. Frankly, it's not one of my favorite herbal choices because it tastes a bit like perfume. But if that doesn't scare you off, just put a teaspoon of dried lavender flowers and leaves in a cup of boiling water. Let steep for 10 minutes, strain out the herbs, and enjoy your scented sips!

GROWING TIPS

A garden without lavender is like, well, Laurel without Hardy or Chip without Dale: not complete, in my book! Lavender is wonderful to behold and divine to smell, and it makes a practical addition to any herbal medicine chest.

This perennial needs full sun and light, sandy, well-drained soil that's slightly alkaline to slightly acidic. It's a hardy plant, but it's vulnerable to winterkill if the soil is poorly drained and the summers are hot and humid. It thrives best in Zones 5 to 8.

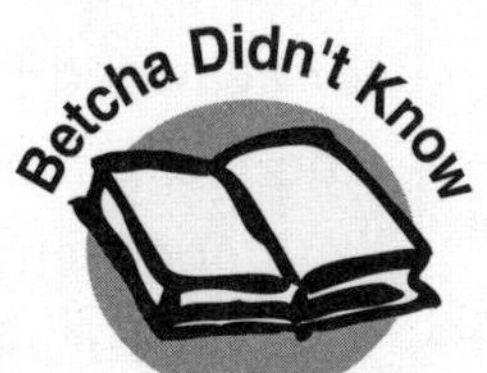

French chemist René-Maurice Gattefosse discovered lavender's healing powers by accident. While working in his perfume lab in the 1920s, he burned his hand. In a panic, he plunged it into the nearest liquid vat, which happened to be filled with lavender oil. He pulled out his hand and voilà: The pain quickly disappeared, and the burn healed without a trace of a scar! Strange, but true!

The best way to grow lavender is by stem cuttings, not by seed sowing. If at all possible, cut a healthy sideshoot off a mature lavender plant (one that's about 3 years old). Stick the cuttings about 4 inches apart in the soil. To best display lavender in outdoor pots, I add a handful of lime to the soil in the fall, after the final blooms.

WHOA! **If you are** looking for a relaxing herb, make sure the package reads *Lavandula angustifolia* and not *Lavandula stoechas.* The latter is a Spanish variety that actually makes a person feel invigorated. It's definitely not something you want to add to a warm bath before heading off to bed!

For indoor lavender, I like a standard potting soil mix with a pH of 7 to 8 in 2-inch pots. You can also put lavender in mixed containers, as long as the other herbs sharing the "turf" can tolerate the same pH. Water with a fine, misty spray, and let the soil dry out between waterings. Once a month, add some liquid fish or seaweed fertilizer to the soil. Place the pot in an area that gets bright light and cool temperatures. With a little TLC, you may even get midwinter blooms!

HARVESTING TIPS

Regular harvesting of the flowers will help your lavender plants produce even more flowers. The more, the merrier, I always say. I harvest 2-inch pieces (leaves and stems) around May and dry them on a rack. Later in the season, I harvest mature flowers and foliage by bundling them up and hanging them upside down like bats to air-dry out of direct sun. It's best to harvest lavender in the morning, after the dew has dried but before the hot afternoon sun shows its bright, beaming face.

Lavender spikes should be cut as soon as the flowers in the head open — but well before they show signs of fading.

In the dead of winter, lavender's springlike scent still wafts about outside — definitely a plus on those blustery cold days!

STORAGE TIPS

To preserve the freshness and potency of essential oil of lavender, keep its lid sealed. Take a whiff every now and then to make sure it still has a strong, fresh scent. Staleness is a sure sign that the bottle has lost some of its medicinal muscle!

As far as dried lavender flowers and leaves are concerned, keep them in resealable bags in a cool, dry place.

Sweet Dreams

Besides a restful night's sleep, how about one filled with wonderful dreams? Here's how to create your own dream machine:

Mix a half cup each of dried lavender, lemon balm, and hops, and dump them into a muslin bag. Pull the drawstring closed and slip the bag into your pillowcase or under your pillow. Lay your head down, and then it's sweet dreams, baby!

Lemon Balm

(Melissa officinalis)

Herbal ID

This hardy perennial, which also goes by the name Melissa, is a weedy mint. There are times when it looks like it's on the brink of death, but then it comes roarin' back, looking fit as a fiddle. Lemon balm grows up to 2 feet tall, with 2-inch oval, scalloped, yellow-green leaves and tiny, white, edible flowers. It's real easy to identify: The lemon-scented leaves are a dead giveaway!

That's Historical!

In medieval times, fair maidens were said to carry lemon balm as good luck charms — to meet and fall in love with their Prince Charmings. Nicholas Culpeper, a 17th-century herbalist, described lemon balm as an herb that "driveth away all troublesome cares and thoughts arising from melancholy." Modern-day translation: Lemon balm improves gloomy moods!

King Charlemagne flexed his royal powers by commanding that every monastery garden contain lemon balm. He believed its beauty and value as a medicine were far too important to be overlooked.

Lemon balm is an extremely safe herb. About the only caution is for folks who have glaucoma. Some studies suggest that lemon balm may elevate pressure in the eyes.

Alchemists in the 18th century made potions out of lemon balm, which they believed would renew youth. Too bad Ponce de León, the explorer who searched in vain for the fountain of youth in America, didn't know about this; it could have saved him the trip!

MEDICINAL USES: SOOTHE COLD SORES

Lemon balm is effective against such ailments as cold sores, migraines, and insomnia. Its leaves contain virus-fighting tannins; it's also loaded with antioxidants, which fortify the immune system in its battle against viruses. Lemon balm's natural and safe head-clearing ingredients make it a terrific choice to challenge migraines and fight fevers.

This multipurpose herb also contains ingredients called terpenes, which are known for their natural sedative abilities. Unlike many over-the-counter and prescription drugs, this is one sedative that's safe enough to take while driving or operating heavy machinery.

BEST MEDICINAL FORMS

Lemon balm makes one of the best-tasting — and best medicinal — teas I've ever found! Try taming a headache by putting 2 teaspoons of dried lemon balm leaves in a cup of boiling water. Let it steep and cool. Strain the herbs, then sip. And if you're engaged in hand-to-mouth combat with a cold sore, dab a little lemon balm tea right on the site. Talk about lip service!

You can also toss a handful of dried leaves into a muslin bag and drop it into a warm bath for added relaxation after a long, stressful day.

A pricey, but very potent, medicinal form of lemon balm is essential oil. A few drops diluted in vegetable oil can be applied to a minor sore, cut, or insect bite to hasten the healing process.

You should also keep a bottle of lemon balm tincture in your medicine cabinet. The recommended dose is 2 to 3 ml in a glass of water or juice. You can drink up to 3 glasses a day to calm nerves, treat herpes, or get rid of a headache.

Betcha Didn't Know

Lemon balm's scientific name, *Melissa,* is derived from the Greek word for "honeybee." That helps explain why our buzzing buddies simply adore this herb. In fact, old-time beekeepers used to rub newly built hives with lemon balm just to attract bees to them!

GROWING TIPS

Lemon balm makes an excellent border plant; just give it a lot of sun (a little shade is OK).

A standard potting mix will work fine, as long as you keep the soil moist and fertilized regularly. I like to start lemon balm from seed; but transplants, divisions, and stem-cutting methods also work well. I've found that although seeds take longer to germinate, they seem to produce the sturdiest plants. When planting, I give each plant about 2 feet of elbowroom. They grow best outdoors in Zones 4 to 9.

Unlike the rest of the mint clan, lemon balm doesn't have a "Wall Street takeover" mentality in the garden. It'll get bushy, but it won't dominate. To grow lemon balm indoors, position your pots where there is bright light and cool temperatures.

Whether you grow lemon balm indoors or out, keep it from going to seed and self-sowing by pinching off any blooms. This will make the plants bushier, too.

HARVESTING TIPS

No need to hurry or be on a tight harvesting schedule with this herb. You can harvest its sprigs any time. By midsummer, when the white buds form, cut the plant back so there's only about 3 inches of stem remaining aboveground. You can use the leaves, fresh or dried, to make extracts. When harvesting, keep this in mind: The leaves lowest on the plant are the highest in essential oils. All fresh leaves can be washed and used in salads. The best way to dry lemon balm leaves is to spread the cut stems on a screen and place the screen in a hot, dry, dark room. It's important to dry the leaves quickly, or they'll turn black. As soon as the leaves are dry, store them in an opaque, airtight container.

The Ultimate Fish Dish

Lemon balm is mmmmm delicious as a pesto sauce dripped over broiled or grilled seafood. My recipe can be completed quick as a wink. Here's all you have to do:

Finely chop about 2 cups of fresh lemon balm leaves. Add ½ cup of olive oil and 3 garlic cloves (peeled and crushed). Mix these ingredients together, and presto — homemade pesto!

Licorice

(Glycyrrhiza glabra)

Herbal ID

Licorice's botanical name was derived from the Greek word *glukus,* which means "sweet" (and *rhiza,* which means "root") — and sweet it is, yet it contains no sugar! You may be surprised to learn that licorice is actually a very nice-looking perennial. It has beautiful blue to white flowers and is native to Asia, Europe, and the Mediterranean. This tender plant is easily identified by its 4-inch fibrous taproot, which appears wrinkled and brown on the outside and sun yellow on the inside. The stem sports three to seven pairs of dark green leaflets. At maturity, licorice may reach a height of 3 feet.

That's Historical!

The best historians can figure is that licorice has been used as a medicine since about 500 B.C. The ancient Chinese referred to licorice as the "great detoxifier" that helped rid the body of poisons. As one of the oldest herbs used as a tonic, it's earned the title "grandfather of herbs."

Long before the invention of toothbrushes, folks used licorice roots to give their teeth a good cleaning. They would just peel off the bark of these long, narrow roots and splay the fibers, giving them a bristlelike effect.

In England during the 1600s, licorice was often boiled with figs and given to folks with coughs and chest pains due to congestion. It cleared them up in a hurry.

MEDICINAL USES: BOOST YOUR ENERGY

This sweet-tasting herb helps the body reduce swelling, soothes arthritic aches and pains, stimulates the adrenal glands for energy, keeps cholesterol levels in check, activates the bowels, and delivers estrogen-like hormone help. There is some evidence to suggest that licorice may also work for allergies, hepatitis, herpes, coughs, and ulcers.

Just a spoonful of licorice helps the medicine go down by masking the yucky taste of other herbs essential to taking care of these conditions. In recipes, licorice goes well with fenugreek, sage, and turmeric.

So just how sweet is licorice? Its medicinal root contains glycyrrhizin, an ingredient 50 times sweeter than sucrose. Glycyrrhizin is one of nature's anti-inflammatory agents and also has some antiviral and estrogen qualities. Licorice also contains flavonoids, known as antioxidants and bodyguards, which are good for the liver. Finally, chemists have determined that licorice offers an excellent natural source of iron.

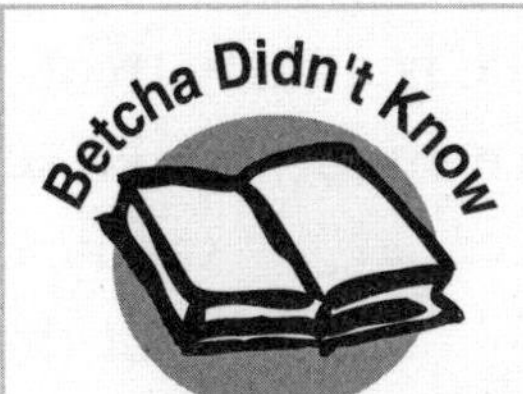

Chewing on a licorice stick is a healthy substitute for folks trying to kick the smoking habit without gaining weight. It's a natural, sugar-free sweetener that seems to satisfy the oral cravings smokers get when going "cold turkey."

BEST MEDICINAL FORMS

Mary Poppins used a spoonful of sugar to help the medicine go down, but she could have used licorice, the medicine that comes in candy form! No, I'm not talking about those licorice candies you buy at the movies. Head for a health food store for the real licorice candy: the hard, sweet-tasting juice sticks.

Licorice root, fresh and dried, is also available in tinctures, teas, capsules, and syrups to treat many conditions. As a tincture, the daily dose is 1 to 3 ml in a glass of water or juice, up to 3 times a day.

To make a cup of licorice tea, put a teaspoonful of the root in a pan with a pint of water. Bring to a boil, then reduce the heat and let simmer 10 to 15 minutes. You can drink up to 3 cups a day. The daily dose for licorice root capsules is 5 to 6 g.

GROWING TIPS

Licorice is a tasty treat. If you want to grow your own licorice supply, make sure you give it soil that is deep, sandy, crumbly, and well tilled. Find a spot that gets direct sun, and propagate the plants by stem or root cuttings in the spring. To make sure the taproots grow straight and tall, get rid of any stones in the soil. During the dog days of summer, licorice plants will show off their flowers. It doesn't like the cold, so if you live north of Zone 9, you'll need to grow it in a pot and bring it indoors for the winter.

If you are taking medication for high blood pressure or a speedy heartbeat, check with your doctor first before using licorice. This herb may tend to worsen those conditions.

Sore Throat, Be Gone!

For those unfortunate times when you get a sore throat on top of a lingering cold or the flu, licorice can help soothe the scratchiness and help you swallow easier. Try this easy-to-make gargle:

Boil a teaspoon of licorice root (fresh, dried, or powdered) in a cup of water. Simmer 10–15 minutes. Let it cool down enough so that you can swish it around in your mouth and gargle Or sip it to soothe your sore throat.

HARVESTING TIPS

Licorice needs plenty of time to mature, so you'll have to wait three fall seasons to harvest it. You should also harvest it before the flowers bloom, or the root will lack the quality needed for medicinal purposes.

When the time is right, dig up the roots, give them a thorough cleaning with the hose, and allow them to dry. To prepare the plants for winter, simply cut the shoots or canes back to soil level in November.

STORAGE TIPS

Dried licorice root can be chopped and stored in an air-tight container for up to a year.

Marigold

(Tagetes patula)

Herbal ID

In the garden world, marigolds win a lot of popularity contests because of their eye-catching, bright orange and yellow flowers. At dusk, the blooms close and nap until dawn. This hardy annual bush also has narrow, pale green leaves and grows no more than 2 feet tall, depending on the variety. Once you get a whiff of the pungent odor of bruised marigold flowers, you'll never forget the smell.

That's Historical!

Through the ages, marigolds have been a jack-of-all-trades — they've been used to treat everything from toothaches to snakebites! Seventeenth-century herbalist Nicholas Culpeper called the marigold a "comforter of the heart and spirits." In fact, its name means "happiness." In medieval times, marigolds were used to fight plagues and pestilence. And during the Civil War, their leaves were used to treat soldiers' battle wounds.

Medicinal Uses: Heal Wounds and Calm Cramps

It may be tricky finding marigolds in health food stores; but don't give up, because this herb offers many marvelous health benefits. The flowers, when brewed into teas or made into tinctures, cover the four antis: They are anti-inflammatory, antiseptic, antiviral, and antispasmodic. Marigolds work wonders on ulcers, minor fevers and infections, sore throats, and wound healing. They also tame painful menstrual cramps.

Scientists have discovered that marigold flowers contain saponins, essential oils, flavonoids, and mucilage — key ingredients to your health. And the flowers are edible — the incredible, edible marigold! They make terrific additions to salads, soups, cookies, and breads.

BEST MEDICINAL FORMS

Talk about flower power! To unleash the medicinal marvels of marigold flowers, put two fresh flower heads into a cup of boiling water and let them infuse for 10 minutes. You can drink up to 3 cups a day. It's even safe enough to give children over 5 years old, as long as you cut the dose in half. An even easier form is to take 1 to 4 ml of marigold tincture up to 3 times daily.

But that's not all! When used on the skin as a compress, lotion, or bath oil, marigolds seem to stop swelling, ease

Eye See

If you have the misfortune of developing a sty in your eye, help is just a blink away! A sty is a small, painful, pus-filled boil that forms at the base of an eyelash, which is caused by a bacterial infection. Marigolds can provide fast relief.

First, wash your hands thoroughly with warm soap and water. Carefully dab (maybe using a cotton swab) some marigold cream on the sty.

Or make a cup of marigold tea. Dampen a compress with this tea (once it's cooled down), and apply the compress to your closed eye for 10 minutes, up to 3 times a day. The sty will soon be history!

the ache of varicose veins, soothe itchy skin rashes (including athlete's foot), and heal minor cuts. It works dandy on dry, wind-cracked skin, and is even safe enough to be used on diaper rash!

GROWING TIPS

If you want to dress up a border, you just can't miss with marigolds. They grow best in Zone 5 or colder, especially if you start seeds indoors about 2 months before the last scheduled spring frost. Barely cover the seeds with soil. You can transplant the seedlings to your garden about a week before the last frost.

Give marigolds lots of sun in the milder northern climates and partial shade in the warmer southern climates. Make sure the soil is moist, well drained, and fertile — and space the plants about 10 inches apart. Marigolds wilt quickly when exposed to intense sun, so a little shade is nice.

If you are planning to add marigolds to your homemade medicine cabinet, make sure to pick ones that haven't been treated with herbicides or pesticides. As I always say, if in doubt, leave them out!

Marigolds are easy to grow. But keep a close eye on them, because they are vulnerable to a host of plant diseases (especially stem rot, downy mildew, and leaf spot) and pests (especially slugs, snails, and aphids).

Try to give them good air circulation and drainage, and keep mulch away from the stems to reduce the risk of diseases. A regular light bath with my All-Season Clean-Up Tonic will put a damper on the desires of most marigold-munching pests.

HARVESTING TIPS

With marigolds, a pinch in time makes nine. To build up your marigold medicine chest, snap off whole flower tops regularly between early summer and early fall — you'll be rewarded with even more blooms! Make sure you do your harvesting in the morning after the dew has dried.

The cut flower heads are best dried by separating the petals and laying them between sheets of brown

Jerry Baker's Anti-Alligator-Skin Fix

Here's another one of my favorites: Fill a glass jar with dried marigold blossoms. Douse the flowers with olive oil and stick the jar (sealed with a lid) on a windowsill that will get plenty of sunshine.

After 2 weeks, strain out the blossoms, leaving the oil. Refill the jar with a new batch of dried blossoms. You may need to add a tad more olive oil. Reseal the lid, but this time put it inside a brown paper bag, and then back on the sunny windowsill for another 2 weeks. Strain out the blossoms and store the rest in a dark glass bottle.

Add the contents of a vitamin E gel capsule (800 IUs) and store it in a dark place until you're ready to use it on irritated or dried skin. You won't believe how well this concoction works!

paper (a cut-up grocery bag will do just fine) in a shady spot. Give them plenty of elbowroom because touching petals can discolor them.

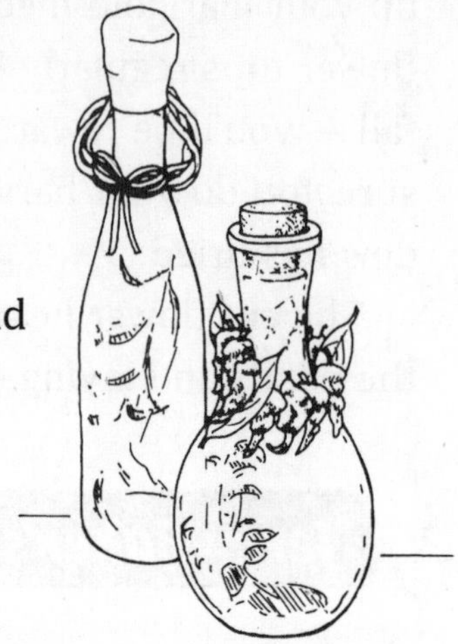

STORAGE TIPS

Here's a nifty way to chase away the winter blues. Put some dried marigold flowers in a glass jar, and display them in your kitchen as a little bit of "winter sunshine."

Marigold Salve

To relieve the pain of sore, burning feet after a long, hard day in the garden, Grandma Putt rubbed a bit of her magic Marigold Salve on her feet. It provided fast, soothing relief. One thing to remember when you use this salve — put on a pair of soft socks to prevent the grease from staining your sheets.

1 cup of marigold petals
½ cup of petroleum jelly

Grandma Putt mixed the petals and petroleum jelly in a pan, and then cooked the mixture over low heat for about 30 minutes. She strained the mixture through cheesecloth until it was clear, and stored it in a jar until her tired old dogs were a-barkin'.

Marsh Mallow

(Althaea officinalis)

Herbal ID

This hardy perennial, also known as white mallow, has woolly stems; gray, velvety, heart-shaped leaves; and fruits that are known as cheeses. Pink and white blossoms appear during late summer and early fall, followed by round seedpods (the cheeses) that turn brown when ripe.

That's Historical!

Marsh mallow comes from the Greek word *altho,* which means "to cure." Ever since ancient Greek times, this herb has been used to help generations of people all over the globe. As far back as 2,000 years ago, marshmallow was used to ward off diarrhea, bladder infections, and incontinence.

Marsh mallow also gained a reputation as a great dessert in Europe a few centuries ago. The elite at highbrow dinner parties would often cap off their meals with a popular dessert called *pâté de guimauve.* Ground marsh mallow root was combined with sugar and egg whites to create this spongy, sweet delight.

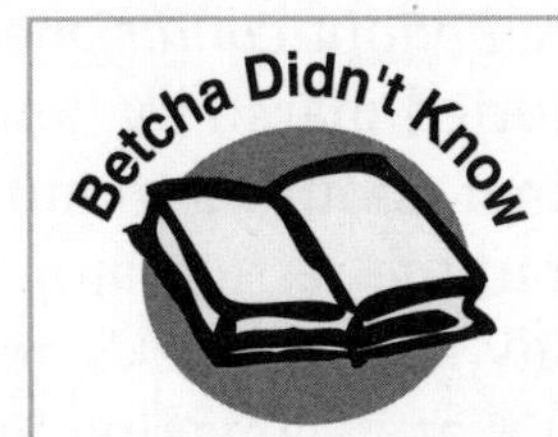

Marsh mallow is related to hollyhocks and hibiscus.

MEDICINAL USES: COMFORT YOUR SORE THROAT

Who doesn't enjoy toasting marshmallows over a campfire? But here's a bit of news: The white, spongy cubes you buy in the supermarket are related to the actual marsh mallow plant in name only. The real McCoy contains properties that help dry up congestion, stop nagging coughs and colds, aid in relieving irritable bladder conditions such as cystitis, soothe burns, speed the healing of skin wounds, and stop the pain and itch of insect bites. It's also been used to treat ulcers, heartburn, and hernias. Unfortunately, it doesn't make a great s'more!

BEST MEDICINAL FORMS

Just about all of the marsh mallow plant is used medicinally. Leaves, flowers, and even roots are used in teas, syrups, tinctures, poultices, and ointments.

An infused tea (using leaves and flowers) works great for bronchitis and bladder problems. Put 2 teaspoons of the leaves and flowers into a cup of boiling

Mother Nature's Hair Care

Marsh mallow makes a great natural moisturizer for dry hair. Instead of using a store-bought conditioner, try this rinse:

Put 2 teaspoons of dried marsh mallow root into a cup of boiling water. Let simmer about 15 minutes. Strain out the herb and let the liquid cool in the refrigerator before using it to rinse your hair. You can easily keep a week's supply in the refrigerator without it losing any of its amazing moisturizing abilities.

water and let simmer 10 minutes. Strain out the herb before drinking. As a decoction tea (roots only), it tames sore throats. Just chop a teaspoon of marsh mallow root, add it to a cup of water on the stove, and let it boil for 15 minutes. Strain out the herb before drinking. Either way, you can safely drink up to 3 cups of marsh mallow tea a day.

Marsh mallow syrups are ideal for coughs. Tinctures are commonly used to get rid of excess mucus in the lungs. The daily dose for adults is 1 to 4 ml in a glass of water or juice, up to 3 times a day. Poultices are used directly on the skin to reduce swelling and take the itch and sting out of insect bites.

Ointments can successfully draw out stubborn, deep-rooted splinters. My Grandma Putt taught me to dab some marsh mallow ointment on the sore splinter site, cover it with a bandage, and leave it alone for a few hours. When I removed the bandage, the splinter had inched close enough to the surface for me to easily pluck it out with a pair of tweezers. That grandmother of mine — she knew it all!

Growing Tips

This wild-growing perennial can easily be tamed and brought into your garden. Climate-wise, marsh mallow thrives from Zones 5 to 8.

Give marsh mallow full sun. Soil-wise, it does best in light soil that stays damp. And if you've got a problem wet area, marsh mallow is one of the few herbs that will actually thrive there, growing up to 5 feet tall.

Sow the seeds shallowly in the spring, spacing them about 2 feet apart. You'll need to stake these plants to prevent them from falling over. As your mama said, "Stand up straight! Posture is important!"

Marsh mallow doesn't win many friends among the bug and disease crowd because it is a very healthy plant. Its lovely blossoms, however, will catch the eye of many a passing butterfly.

Harvesting Tips

For the freshest leaves, collect them during the summer months right after the plant flowers. To harvest the roots, wait until they are 2 years old; then dig them up anytime into late fall. Scrub the roots thoroughly to clean them. If you're going to dry them, slice or boil them the way you would potatoes.

Look, Ma, No Toothbrush!

Marsh mallow root also makes a nifty natural substitute for toothpaste. My Grandma Putt gave me this recipe to keep my pearly whites shiny and healthy:

Cut a handful of marsh mallow root into 5-inch pieces. Peel the ends and boil them in water on the stove. Toss in some cloves and cinnamon sticks and boil until the sticks are tender and pliable. Carefully place the pieces in a glass bowl that has about a cup of brandy in it. Let them soak overnight.

The next morning, remove the pieces and let them air-dry on paper towels. Right before you're ready to use them, soak the ends in hot water. Then give your teeth and gums a good going-over for a naturally fresh and clean feeling!

Mints: Spearmint and Peppermint

(Mentha spicata and *Mentha* x *piperita)*

Herbal ID

These hardy perennials grow straight and tall, hitting heights of about 2 feet at maturity. It's easy to tell the difference between these cousins: Peppermint sports dark green leaves and a reddish stem, while spearmint features light green, pointy leaves.

Flower-wise, both spearmint and peppermint have lilac-pink blooms, and they both deliver a warm, spicy scent when their leaves are crushed or bruised.

That's Historical!

Folks have been using this dynamic mint duo as a general digestive tonic since the late 1700s. But if you're really into folklore, here's a wild tale. During ancient Greek days, Persephone — the wife of Pluto — discovered a creature named Minthe hanging around her husband. In a jealous rage, she crushed it with her feet. Pluto reacted by changing Minthe into the aromatic plant we now know as mint.

Greek soldiers would rub their weapons with mint before heading into battle because they believed it brought them good luck. And ancient Hebrews used to cover their synagogue floors with mint leaves.

MEDICINAL USES: REDUCE STOMACH ACID

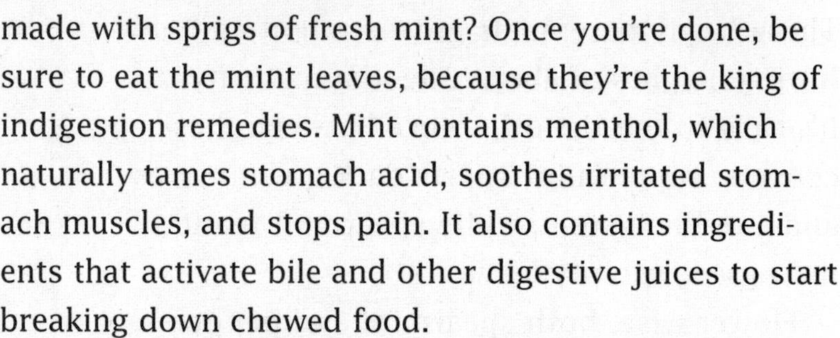

You'll find the mighty medicine in mint's leaves, petals, and flowers. Got a tummy ache? Having trouble digesting Aunt Minnie's stroganoff? Why not cap off the meal with a glass of iced tea, made with sprigs of fresh mint? Once you're done, be sure to eat the mint leaves, because they're the king of indigestion remedies. Mint contains menthol, which naturally tames stomach acid, soothes irritated stomach muscles, and stops pain. It also contains ingredients that activate bile and other digestive juices to start breaking down chewed food.

There is even some talk that mint also relieves gassy feelings and tension headaches and can treat that

Jerry Baker's Terrific Tummy Tamer

I always treat upset stomachs caused by acid indigestion or too much food with this tempting tea:

1 tsp. of dried peppermint (or spearmint) leaves

1 tsp. of dried catnip

1 tsp. of dried sweet marjoram

1 tsp. of dried lemon balm

In a bowl, mix all of the herbs thoroughly. Then scoop out 2 teaspoons of the mix and add it to a cup of boiling water. Let steep 15 minutes. Strain out the herbs and sip the tea slowly. Keep the rest of the herbs in an airtight glass container so you're ready to roll the next time your tummy has a tantrum!

dreaded gum disease known as gingivitis. Need fresh breath after eating a plate of garlic-laden pasta? Pop a few mint leaves into your mouth, and chew on that cud for a while.

BEST MEDICINAL FORMS

Spearmint and peppermint work well when used as hot teas. You can stir a teaspoon of dried (or fresh) leaves into a cup of boiling water and let it simmer for 10 minutes. Strain out the herbs and drink up to 3 cups a day between or after meals for stomach woes.

You can also buy mint in tablet, capsule, and liquid extract forms at health food stores. The recommended daily dose for these forms is 3 to 6 g.

To stop a throbbing headache dead in its tracks, mix 3 drops of peppermint (or spearmint) oil and 3 drops of eucalyptus oil with a teaspoon of vegetable oil. Dab some on your temples as soon as a headache kicks in — and then every hour or so until the pain is gone.

To relieve hot, itchy skin, make a real strong batch of mint tea and use it on your skin as a healing, cooling lotion. I love this soothing remedy after a long, hot day in the garden.

Using fresh mint leaves in teas and salads is fine, but if you want to use mint as a medicine (in capsule or tablet form), don't take it every day for more than 2 weeks. If your condition hasn't improved by then, check with your doctor for an alternative treatment. And don't, under any circumstances, give mint tea to children younger than two. The menthol in it can make them choke.

GROWING TIPS

Here's a hint for growing mint: Relax. That's right, peppermint and spearmint cater to beginning gardeners because they are super easy to grow. They do best in Zones 5 to 9, but mint can be grown indoors as a container plant in any climate.

If you're sticking with outdoor planting, be forewarned: Mint is a real garden hog and likes to spread its runners all over the place. I usually keep my mints in their own private bed and let them flourish freely. Mint also makes an excellent ground cover; you can even run your lawn mower over it to form a nice, thick carpet!

When you're ready to plant mint, use soil that is moist and rich, in a location with full sun or partial shade. Propagate by cuttings or divisions. Space plants about 15 inches apart and weed well. After that, renew

Sticky Goo That's Good for You

Sweeten up hot and cold teas with this secret mint syrup recipe:

1 cup of granulated sugar

Zest from 1 small lemon or orange

6 sprigs of fresh peppermint or spearmint leaves (or mix 'em!)

2 cups of water

In a pan, heat the sugar in the water, stirring until the sugar is dissolved. Add the mint leaves and citrus zest. Remove the pan from the heat and let the syrup steep for about 30 minutes. Strain out the herbs and pour the liquid into a container with a lid. Add syrup to your next cup of tea; it'll satisfy even the sweetest tooth.

your mint bed about every 4 years (maybe every leap year to help you remember) by dividing the plants. Take a shovel and chop the tangled roots into foot-size clumps. If you water them thoroughly and cover them with a light layer of enriched soil, new and improved mint plants will appear before you know it.

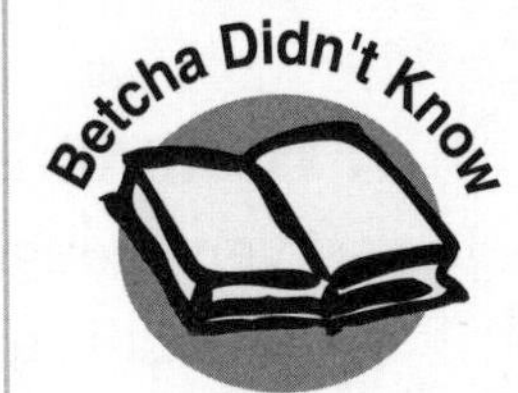

Peppermint is actually a hybrid of watermint and spearmint.

HARVESTING TIPS

There is nothing finer on God's green earth than a few fresh peppermint or spearmint leaves added to a chilled glass of iced tea. It gives tea just the right zip, and will quench even the hardest-working gardener's thirst! You can harvest the leaves throughout the season as needed for teas and salads. In the fall, be sure to cut the entire stems down to an inch above the soil.

Cut mint stalks just above the first layer of leaves as soon as flower buds poke their heads out; then hang them up to dry for a couple weeks. Carefully strip the leaves from the stems with your fingers. The leaves crumble easily, but still retain their fragrance.

STORAGE TIPS

Air-dry or microwave-dry mints and store them in airtight, dark glass containers. Do not freeze mint, or it'll lose its flavor and its medicinal value!

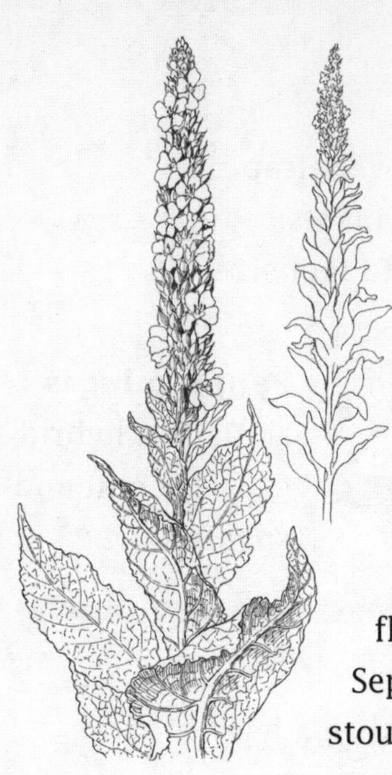

Mullein

(Verbascum thapsus)

Herbal ID

Even though it rhymes with *sullen*, mullein is a fine, fuzzy friend. Its velvety leaves give way to thick spikes of yellow flowers that bloom brightly from June to September. This hardy biennial boasts tall, stout stalks that can reach a height of 6 feet.

That's Historical!

Got a light? Ancient Greeks and Romans were centuries away from electricity, so they would dip the flower heads of the dried mullein stalks in tallow and use them as torches. Generals serving Caesar Augustus also believed that mullein's fragrance would deter demons.

Europeans crossing the Atlantic Ocean to settle in America brought mullein along with them. They made dye with the roots of this herbs and candlewicks from the stems.

Medicinal Uses: Use Mother Nature's Phlegm-Fighter

Inside mullein leaves and flowers are active ingredients called saponins and mucilages. They act like Mother Nature's expectorants, making this plant absolutely ideal for conditions like asthma, bronchitis, colds, sore throats, laryngitis, coughs, hemorrhoids, and recurrent ear infections. Well, someone's got to do it, and mullein's claim to fame is that it clears away sticky phlegm and excess mucus.

It also makes a great natural bandage to protect minor scrapes and cuts and hasten healing. In addition, mullein helps soothe skin irritated by sunburn or minor rashes.

Here's a special bonus: Two drops of mullein flower–infused oil, mixed in a little orange juice or apple juice, seems to help children overcome bedwetting. For best results, have the child drink up to 3 glasses a day.

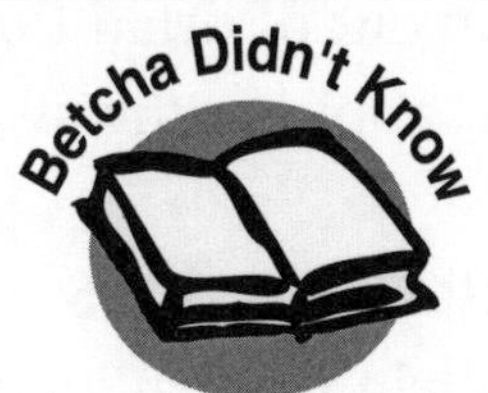

Mullein was first called bullock's lungwort because it cured lung diseases in cattle. Truth be told, there are at least 30 common names for mullein, including lady's foxglove, velvet plant, shepherd's herd, and my favorite: old man's flannel! Just talk about being the salt of the earth!

BEST MEDICINAL FORMS

Mullein comes in many forms. You can drink your medicine in a tea by pouring a cup of boiling water over 2 teaspoons of dried leaves or flowers and letting it steep 15 minutes. If you want a slightly sweet tea, use the leaves. If you want a slightly bitter tea, stick with the flowers. Strain out the herb, and drink up to 3 cups a day.

Or you can go the speedy route: a tincture. Drop 1 to 4 ml of mullein tincture into a glass of water or juice, and drink up to 3 glasses a day. In capsule form, the daily dosage is 1 or 2 g up to 3 times daily.

For minor cuts and boo-boos, crush a fresh mullein leaf to extract its medicinal oils and then lay it right on the spot. Relief is only moments away!

To shrink painful hemorrhoids, try making an infusion out of dried flowers and leaves, make a compress, and apply to the swollen spot. Ahhhhhhh!

GROWING TIPS

Mullein likes full sun and actually prefers poor, dry soil. Plus, it's an easy self-sower. Just sow the seeds in spring or fall, spacing them about 3 feet apart. Because of its basketball player–like height, plant mullein toward the back of your garden so it doesn't block your view of shorter plant friends.

Now 'ear This!

Ear infections that keep coming back can be a pain in the you-know-what, especially for young children. Here's a way to end the pain:

Crush a couple of mullein leaves in a sieve and collect the juice. With a dropper, put 2 drops of mullein juice right in the painful ear and seal it up with a cotton ball.

This method also works with bottled mullein flower oil (made by steeping flowers in olive oil), which you can keep in the refrigerator. The only thing you do differently is warm the dropper by rubbing it in your hands first, so your ear isn't shocked by the cold! Mullein oil helps kill the bacteria that causes the ear infection. But if the pain persists, it could signal a bigger problem than a routine ear infection. In that case, have a doctor examine your ear.

HARVESTING TIPS

Harvest mullein leaves when the flowers are in full bloom. Dry them in the shade. Harvest flowers as they bloom during dry weather, and, likewise, dry them in a shady place.

STORAGE TIPS

Mullein should be kept in a cool, dry place, but don't let it chill out too much. But remember: It should never be frozen!

It's best to use mullein only when you need it — it's not like a multivitamin that you take every day. In fact, it's best not to take it for more than a 2-week stretch. If your condition doesn't improve by then, you may need to chat with your doctor for an alternative treatment.

One final word of warning: Mullein leaves and flowers are perfectly safe; but avoid eating the seeds — they're poisonous!

Nasturtium

(Tropaeolum majus)

Herbal ID

This annual bushy herb, also known as Indian cress, produces long, trailing stems. Its round, green leaves give way to funnel-shaped red, yellow, white, or orange flowers from midsummer to the first frost. And best of all, its peppery-flavored leaves and flowers are just loaded with vitamin C.

That's Historical!

Pssst! Want in on a need-to-know national secret? Former President Dwight D. Eisenhower was famous for his vegetable soup. This commander-in-chief waited years before sharing his culinary secret. Turns out he added a tablespoon of chopped nasturtium leaves and stems near the end of cooking, just before serving his honored guests.

If you travel south of Ike's place — quite a bit south — you'll find nasturtium's hometown: It was born and raised in South America, specifically Bolivia and Peru.

Medicinal Uses: Heal Cuts and Lift Spirits

Because nasturtium leaves can fight germs and fungi, you can use them as a compress to help heal cuts and scrapes. You can also use a nasturtium leaf tea when you're down in the dumps with a cold or urinary troubles.

GROWING TIPS

Nasturtiums add a dazzling dose of color to any herb garden. They are also one of the easiest "no-fuss" herbs to grow. When you're ready to sow, make sure the garden soil is tilled and clear of rocks and debris. Truth be told, nasturtiums will grow even in poor soil; and they will tolerate full sun, if the soil is moist. Pick a date

Jerry's Jigglin' Gelatin

Try one of my favorite, flavor-filled summer desserts that's also low in calories:

12 nasturtium blossoms

6-oz. package of gelatin (pick your favorite flavor)

1 cup of cabbage, finely shredded

Wash the nasturtium blossoms and snip off the stems. Prepare the gelatin as indicated on the package directions, then let it cool in the refrigerator until it gets syrupy-thick. Take a 4-cup ring mold and run it under cool water. Pour the gelatin into the mold to a ½-inch depth. Return this to the refrigerator and let it chill until firm. Keep the rest of the syrupy gelatin on the counter. Layer the nasturtium blossoms on the chilled ring mold. Pour in half of the remaining gelatin. Put the ring mold back into the refrigerator and allow it time to chill completely. Bear with me, you're in the homestretch! Now, spread the shredded cabbage evenly on top of the ring mold and pour in the rest of the gelatin. Stick it back into the refrigerator to chill one last time.

When it's time for dessert, remove the mold ring and place it on a plate. Now you're ready to serve a jigglin' gelatin delight!

when you're sure that the last spring frost has come and gone. Then sow the seeds in the soil, no more than ½ inch down. Space them about a foot apart. Use a hose with a fine-mist spray (or a watering can) to keep the ground moist and prevent the seeds from washing away.

Nasturtiums make a great addition along any border or garden edge as well as in window boxes and hanging baskets.

Summer Salad Pleaser

If you're bored by the same old iceberg lettuce salad time after time, try this creative green mix that's easy to make and delivers a zesty flavor:

36 fresh nasturtium leaves
2 cucumbers
½ tsp. of dry mustard
6 tsp. of salad oil
2 tsp. of wine vinegar
2 tsp. of fresh tarragon, chopped finely
6 fresh nasturtium flowers with leaves

Wash the nasturtium leaves, plucking them off the stems. Peel and thinly slice the cucumbers. In a blender, mix all of the other ingredients except for the nasturtium flowers with leaves. Using a wooden spoon, stir in the cucumbers and fresh nasturtium leaves and toss gently. Dress up the salad with the nasturtium flowers and leaves, and you've got yourself a winner! *Serves 4.*

Wherever you plant them, know that you can count on them to repel cabbage loopers, squash bugs, Colorado potato beetles, cabbage moths, and whiteflies. Talk about double duty!

Plenty of Vim and Vinegar!

No kitchen should be without a supply of homemade herbal vinegar. Nasturtium leaves work best when mixed with white wine vinegar to deliver a mild flavor that will enhance sauces, marinades, and stews. Here's an easy recipe to try if you're new to making herbal vinegars:

2 cups of fresh nasturtium leaves
4 cups of white wine vinegar

Wash and dry the nasturtium leaves. Then tuck them into hot, sterilized glass jars using a wooden spoon so you don't burn yourself. Fill each jar with white wine vinegar, to within an inch of the top. With the wooden spoon, lightly bruise the leaves. Place a piece of plastic wrap on top of each jar before relacing the metal lids — this prevents a chemical reaction between the metal and vinegar.

Store the jars in a warm, dry spot in your house for 6 weeks. At the end of that time, pour the flavored vinegar through paper coffee filters into clean jars. Add a few more nasturtium sprigs for decoration and seal the jars. That's all there is to it!

HARVESTING TIPS

As soon as the plant reaches 6 inches tall, you can snip off leaves throughout the growing season as needed — for salads, plate garnishes, and other uses. As for the flowers, time your picking for just as they open.

Next time you eat the last pickle in the jar, save the pickle juice (which is mostly vinegar, sweetener, and spices). Then, in the fall, pluck unopened nasturtium buds and plunk them into the pickle juice! The buds make a tasty addition to salads and pasta dishes.

STORAGE TIPS

Since both nasturtium leaves and flowers are edible, I like to stick whole stems in a glass of water and refrigerate them until I'm ready to add a little zip to a sandwich or salad.

You can also store the seeds in a heat-proof jar and pour some vinegar over them. Reseal the jar and stick it in the refrigerator for about a week before using the mix.

Nasturtium seeds make suitable substitutes for capers if you pickle a peck of them.

Oregano

(Origanum vulgare)

HERBAL ID

Oregano has won the heart of many a cook. Through the years, it has also been called knotted oregano, garden oregano, and sweet oregano. Whatever you call this tender perennial, you know it immediately by its telltale downy stem, wiry side branches, velvety, grayish green leaves, and clumps of white and rose-red flowers that bloom from midsummer to early fall. And mama mia! Its inviting aroma makes it one of the herbs that put the pizzazz in pizza!

THAT'S HISTORICAL!

According to Greek folklore, the goddess Aphrodite was so touched by oregano that she bestowed upon it its inviting sweet scent. Through the ages, oregano was known as a symbol of happiness and eternal bliss, and it was woven into garlands for brides and bridegrooms. If this herb grew on a tomb, folks believed that meant the dearly departed was happy in the afterlife. It was also used as a magic charm to ward off the perceived evils of witchcraft during the Middle Ages.

Go easy on using oregano as a medicine until you're sure there are no side effects. Although regarded as a safe herb, oregano does trigger an allergic reaction in a small percentage of the population.

MEDICINAL USES: SETTLE YOUR STOMACH

Herbalists give oregano four stars and two thumbs up when it comes to performance. Oils in oregano leaves contain vitamins A and C as well as important minerals, including calcium, phosphorus, iron, and magnesium. All of these compounds make it a powerful antioxidant, carminative, antispasmodic, antiseptic, and sedative inside the body. This "pizza herb" also has the backing of scientific studies to prove that it helps the body repair cells and tissues damaged by free radicals, which are highly unstable oxygen molecules that steal electrons from other molecules and wreak havoc on membranes and other cellular structures.

✓ Quickie Quiz for Pizza Lovers

Q: In what year was oregano first sprinkled on pizzas in America?

A: The date was 1895, in a New York pizza restaurant.

BEST MEDICINAL FORMS

A cup of oregano tea is just the thing to calm you down after a long, hectic day. Essential oil of oregano, when rubbed on the skin, stops the spread of some bacteria and fungi; it also aids in healing minor burns, bruises, and even menstrual cramps.

Of course, the easiest form of oregano to use is fresh from the garden or grocer. I like to get my oregano medicine by adding fresh leaves to salads, soups, stews, stuffings, and steamed vegetables. Talk about dee-licous!

GROWING TIPS

Oregano grows best in soil that is moist, slightly acid, and not too rich. Expect it to grow no more than 2 feet tall. You can easily sow seeds in the spring, but don't be tapping your foot, expecting plants to push through the surface right away: Oregano is a real slo-o-o-w grower. Find a nice sunny, but sheltered, place for the seeds and set them out about a foot apart. You'll need to cultivate and weed oregano plants frequently until they have matured and are big enough to claim their rightful spot in your garden.

For you folks living in places that get all four seasons of weather, you can enjoy oregano year-round by

Flavorfully Refreshing!

You can cool a hot sweat and quench a parched throat after toiling in the garden by keeping a pitcher of this tea-pleaser in your refrigerator:

1 tsp. of dried oregano leaves
1 tsp. of dried hyssop leaves
1 tsp. of dried mint leaves, peppermint or spearmint
1 tsp. of dried sage leaves
1 tsp. of dried rosemary leaves
2 tsp. of dried thyme leaves

Blend all of these aromatic leaves together in a bowl. Scoop a teaspoon of the mix into a cup of boiling water. Let simmer 5–10 minutes. Strain out the herbs, then enjoy a hot cup of this sweet, warm, and mellow-flavored tea as your cares seem to fade away.

planting some seeds indoors. True, the indoor versions won't be as tall as their outdoor cousins, but they'll still give you an ample supply of healthy leaves to brew into medicinal teas or use to flavor your cooking. Indoor oregano grows well in hanging baskets and containers that are at least 10 inches across.

HARVESTING TIPS

Don't bother setting your alarm — you can sleep in and still be on time for harvesting oregano. The best time to harvest its leaves is midmorning, right after the dew has evaporated and the sun is shining.

A BLAST FROM THE PAST

Ancient Greeks liked to rub oil containing oregano into their foreheads and hair after bathing to improve blood flow to those areas. Hmmm, maybe oregano was one of the earliest tonics for baldness! If only I had known about this when I was in my 20s!

I tell my gardening chums to cut oregano stems, just before the blossoms form. This guarantees you the greatest amount of natural oils (concentrated in the leaves), and, therefore, the fullest possible flavor. Remove the leaves, discarding those that are discolored.

After you've picked the best leaves, gently (I said gently) wash them thoroughly in clean, cold water. Then pat them dry with a towel and let them dry in a warm place, out of direct sunlight and the reach of hungry insects or rodents.

STORAGE TIPS

To prolong the flavor of dried oregano leaves as much as possible, store them in airtight glass bottles or metal containers, out of direct light, heat, and moisture. Oregano does all right in the freezer as long as you wash and pat dry the whole leaves first, and then stick them in sealed plastic bags.

Muscles Sore No More!

All of that bending and squatting and yanking and pulling while gardening can leave a fella or gal with achy, sore muscles — I know! So do what I do: Keep a bottle of infused oil of oregano on hand. At the end of the day, treat your tired muscles by soaking in a warm bath that contains a bit of oil. Here's how to make your own handy supply:

Steep ½ cup of dried oregano leaves (or 1 cup of fresh leaves) in 2 quarts of boiling water on the stove. Let boil 10–15 minutes. Strain out the herbs and let this liquid cool down a bit before storing in a glass container with a lid. Then, when it's bath time, pour the liquid into the running water, ease your achy body into the tub, and feel your muscles relax and rejuvenate. You'll soon be saying, "Ahhhhh!"

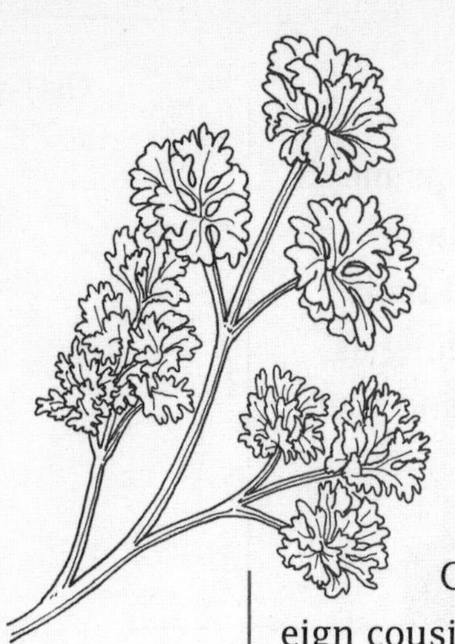

Parsley

(Petroselinum crispum)

Herbal ID

You may not know this, but there are actually two types of parsley: curled and Italian. Curled parsley is distinguished from its foreign cousin by its tightly woven, crisp foliage. Although both can be used in cooking, curled types are chiefly used as garnish. Italian parsley has broad, flat leaves and yields a more pungent flavor. This is the one chefs (like me) prefer in their soups, stews, vegetables, salads, meats, and poultry dishes.

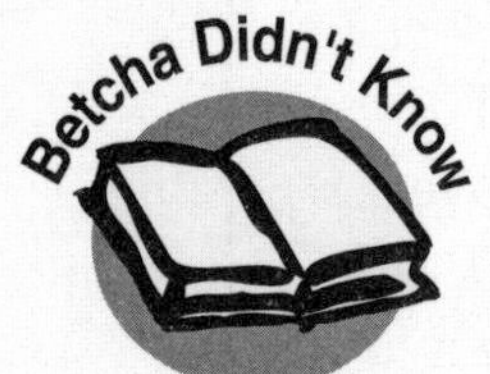

Move over, orange juice! One cup of parsley contains nearly twice as much vitamin C as a whole orange or glass of OJ. Granted, it doesn't taste quite the same, but the benefits don't stop there. A cup of parsley contains more beta-carotene than a large carrot, more calcium than a cup of milk, and a whopping 20 times more iron than a single serving of liver!

You also may not know that parsley has tiny, greenish yellow flowers that appear between June and August before producing brown seeds.

That's Historical!

Parsley has been a favorite herb for many civilizations. The ancient Romans proudly wore parsley garlands around their necks at major banquets — in hopes the herb would soak up wine fumes and keep them from getting drunk! The ancient Greeks adorned war horses and tombs with parsley. During the Middle Ages, folks believed that wearing parsley on Good Friday, under a rising moon, would ward off wickedness. Kind of makes you wonder where they got that idea, doesn't it?

MEDICINAL USES: RELIEVE BLOATING

Parsley's role in life goes far beyond being a mere plate garnish. Its high chlorophyll content helps explain why it makes for such a great natural breath freshener. Herbalists have relied on parsley leaves and seeds for three main therapeutic needs: ridding the body of excess water, stimulating the menstrual process, and easing gas pains.

Bruise News: Parsley Makes Headlines

I don't know about you, but sometimes coffee tables just seem to jump out and nail me right on the shin. Or that corner of the wall near the laundry room connects with my thigh. Before I know it, I'm sporting all colors of the rainbow on my tender little body. Well, here's how I restore the natural, healthy color to my skin — pronto:

Toss a handful of fresh parsley leaves into a blender. Add ½ cup of water. Blend the parsley and water until it looks like green slush. Pour this mix into an ice-cube tray and stick it in the freezer.

The next time you get a bruise, grab a parsley ice cube, wrap it in a thin cloth, and put it right on the sore spot for about 15 to 20 minutes. Do this 3 to 4 times a day. The ice helps keep the swelling down and the parsley goes to work on the discoloration, repairing the tiny capillaries that were burst by the crash.

It may surprise you to learn that parsley is a mild diuretic. Eating parsley leaves and seeds regularly seems to help a lot of women who are bothered by bloating during menstruation and menopause. It also helps folks with kidney and bladder problems.

Finally, parsley is also known for its ability to shrink small blood vessels and repair capillaries battered by bruises. That means no more rainbow of woe!

BEST MEDICINAL FORMS

It's difficult to determine exactly how much actual medicine you'll get from munching fresh sprigs of parsley. But I can guarantee that you'll get a healthy dose if you take it in tincture form. The recommended dose is 2 to 4 ml in a glass of water or juice, up to 3 times daily.

Parsley tea is also a good way to reap the therapeutic effects of this herb. Add 2 teaspoons of dried parsley (fresh leaves don't work as well) to a pan of boiling water (1 cup). Put a lid on the pan, turn off the heat, and let it steep 10 minutes. Then strain the herbs, and pour the tea into your favorite mug.

Jerry's Words of Wisdom

"I hate it when I'm out in my garden and suddenly come under attack from some pesky bugs. How do I spell relief? P-A-R-S-L-E-Y! Crush up some parsley leaves and use them as a poultice directly on the bite site."

One relaxing way to get rid of that annoying water retention is to take a parsley bath. Forget the bubbles and try this instead: Put 2 drops of parsley tincture, 3 drops of fennel tincture, and 3 drops of geranium tincture into a running bath. Stir it up, using your hand like a paddle, before stepping into the tub. Then soak 5 to 10 minutes every day.

GROWING TIPS

Parsley is a biennial that is usually grown as an annual. Sound confusing? Well, it's really not. Parsley typically produces a rosette of leaves during its first year of life, and then by age 2 sends up a flower stalk that yields seed. Then it dies.

To ensure a productive parsley crop, soak the seeds in water with just a touch of dish soap for a full day before planting. Plant them in early spring, in an area that gets partial to full sun and where the soil is medium-rich. Space plants about a foot apart; parsley tends to grow about 2 feet high.

Parsley is perfectly safe as a garnish or in food dishes, but hold off on using it as an herbal medicine if you're pregnant. It's best to check with your doctor first before using parsley tinctures. Also, if you've been diagnosed with kidney problems, don't eat a huge amount of parsley; it may irritate your kidneys.

HARVESTING TIPS

You can snip away at the leaves as soon as the plant is 6 inches tall. Be sure to harvest the outer leaves to give the inner ones time to mature.

In fall, I like to transplant two of my best parsley plants into pots and bring them indoors for the winter.

As long as you use a deep enough container to accommodate parsley's long taproots, you'll be rewarded with fresh parsley all winter long and well into next spring.

STORAGE TIPS

The great thing about parsley is that it stores well fresh or dried. To keep a steady supply of fresh parsley on hand, store the cleaned leaves (patted dry with a paper towel) in an airtight plastic bag or glass jar in the refrigerator. Store dried leaves in sealed glass jars away from sun and heat. Be advised, though, that dried parsley tastes kind of papery, so it's best to use it only as a seasoning.

Make Your Bladder Gladder

Try this herbal blend if you've got minor bladder and urinary problems:

1 tsp. of dried parsley leaves

1 tsp. of dried bearberry (also known as uva-ursi) leaves

1 tsp. of dried mint leaves

Mix all of the herbs together. Scoop a teaspoon of the mix into a cup of boiling water and let steep 15 minutes. Then strain out the herbs, and your tea is ready for sippin'!

Passionflower

(Passiflora incarnata)

Herbal ID

This beautiful perennial dresses up any garden with its white and lilac flowers and yellow, edible fruits. Lots of folks like to grow passionflower as an ornamental because of its unique blossoms, without regard to any of its healing properties. It's also known as apricot vine and maypop.

Passionflower is native to southeastern North America, but is now cultivated worldwide, especially in Europe. There are about 400 different New and Old World species.

That's Historical!

Passionflower got its name not from starry-eyed lovers pining away over its beauty but from Spanish missionaries. It seems that the plant's fringed petals reminded them of the crown of thorns worn by Christ during the crucifixion. Passionflower refers to spiritual suffering and, as a result, has been dubbed the Holy Trinity flower.

Long before drugstores, Native Americans would pound and boil passionflower's twining roots into poultices to treat boils, cuts, earaches, and even liver problems. Members of the Cherokee tribe regarded the leaves and sweet, yellow fruits as food treats.

MEDICINAL USES: BEAT STRESS

Passionflower is one of Mother Nature's best tranquilizers. This herb contains alkaloids and flavonoids that deliver sedating effects — it can be the perfect herb to rescue you when you feel anxious or stressed. As a side benefit, it also wards off hot flashes, tension headaches, migraines, high blood pressure, heart palpitations, and other physical problems associated with stress. An added bonus: Passionflower's natural calming ability comes without the "narcotic" hangover that's commonly associated with prescriptive tranquilizers.

Other wonders of passionflower include easing tense muscles and fatigue, boosting moods, soothing upset stomachs, and helping some people with asthma — especially when tension triggers an attack.

Some of my herbalist friends recommend passionflower for treating Parkinson's disease, a neurological disorder that's characterized by shaking and trembling. It makes sense that it helps, since the two ingredients — harmaline and harmine alkaloids — help restore muscle control. Still, anyone diagnosed with Parkinson's should be under a doctor's care and should check with him or her first before taking this herb.

WHOA! **Passionflower** is one of those use-as-needed herbs. Even though it's generally regarded as safe, you shouldn't take it every day for more than 2 weeks at a time without checking first with your herbalist or natural medicine physician. Also, don't take this herb if you are pregnant — or think you may be.

BEST MEDICINAL FORMS

The leaf, stem, or vine of passionflower can be used when brewing a tea; these ingredients are also present in store-bought tinctures.

If you need some quiet time to relax and unwind, reward yourself with a cup of passionflower tea, which acts as a mild, but safe, sedative. Just steep 1 or 2 teaspoons of the dried herb in a cup of boiling water. Wait about 20 minutes, then strain out the herbs before drinking — a perfect choice before you head for bed! You can drink up to 3 cups a day.

To use passionflower to ease muscle tension, the daily recommended dose is 20 to 30 drops of tincture in a glass of water or juice. Drink up to 3 glasses a day.

GROWING TIPS

Passionflower likes milder weather, so it is best suited for Zones 7 to 11. Give it a place in your garden that gets full sun, and make sure the soil is deep, fertile,

Jerry's Words of Wisdom

"Don't be fooled by this rather innocent-looking plant — you've got to keep an eye on it. Passionflower can soar more than 30 feet high and sprawl its roots underground throughout your entire garden. This squeeze play is not very neighborly! But if you keep this herb trimmed down to size, you will enjoy healthy passionflower plants year after year — and still have room to grow other plants in your garden!"

and well drained. Each spring, till a new layer of rich compost into the soil before planting. You can propgate this herb either by seed or cuttings. In June or July, look for its delightful, sweet-scented flowers to be in full bloom.

HARVESTING TIPS

Gather the fruit in the summer — when it's ripest. The fruits turn yellow when they're ripe.

STORAGE TIPS

Obviously, fresh fruit won't last more than a week or so in your refrigerator crisper drawer. As for store-bought tinctures and teas, keep your supply in airtight containers in a cool, dry place. Don't try to freeze passionflower.

Dreamy Dream Maker

If you find yourself unable to get a good night's sleep because something is weighing heavily on your mind, try this helpful herbal nightcap:

1 oz. of passionflower tincture
1 oz. of catnip tincture
1 oz. of hops tincture
1 oz. of skullcap tincture
1 oz. of wood betony tincture

Put all of the tinctures together in a glass container. Cap it with a lid and give it a few shakes to blend. Then take an eyedropper and fill it with the liquid. Put 20 drops of this mix into a glass of water and drink it right before you go to bed. Reseal the bottle and store it in a cool, dry place in your house — maybe in your nightstand!

Pennyroyal

(*Hedeoma pulegioides* — American;
Mentha pulegium — European)

Herbal ID

This card-carrying member of the mint family comes in many species. I'll focus on the two most popular ones: American and European. American pennyroyal, nicknamed squawmint, is an annual that grows about 15 inches tall. The European type, also known as pudding grass, is a perennial that grows a foot tall. Both feature square leaves and tubular, lavender-blue flowers that bloom during the heart of summer. American pennyroyal tends to stand tall like a soldier, while English pennyroyal typically sprawls out like a low carpet.

That's Historical!

Way back in the first century A.D., the Greeks discovered that European pennyroyal effectively fought off fleas. Maybe that's why it has earned such nicknames as fleabane, tickweed, and mosquito plant.

Pennyroyal can produce a skin rash in sensitive people and it shouldn't be used by pregnant women. And be sure never to take the essential oil internally — it's poisonous!

Medicinal Uses: Bug and Flea Fighter

Pennyroyal's main attraction is its green-yellow aromatic essential oil known as pulegium. The fact of the matter is that we like it and bugs hate it. That's why pennyroyal is a perfect natural bug repellent when you're gardening, hiking, picnicking — anytime you're outdoors during the summer. So if you're planning an outdoor cookout, keep the bugs from crashing your party by adorning the table with a pennyroyal bouquet. Every so often, crush the leaves to release their pest-be-gone fragrance.

For all you animal lovers, stick some dried leaves here and there on your dog or cat's bed. It'll make the fleas flee like they've got a hotfoot!

Beyond warding off winged warriors in the yard, pennyroyal also tames flatulence and promotes menstruation and perspiration. Some natural physicians suspect that this herb also aids digestion, relieves spasms, fights colds, and purifies the blood.

BEST MEDICINAL FORMS

Rub-a-dub-dub. The easiest way to use pennyroyal is to snag a few leaves and rub them right on your skin. Its strong and penetrating odor keeps pests far away.

The tops and leaves (before flowering) should be used in making tea, which has a minty, sweet taste and amber color. It's easy to make: With fresh pennyroyal, put about 3 teaspoons of tops and leaves into a cup of boiling water. If you're using dried herbs, you only need 1 teaspoon. Either way, cover the pot and let steep 10 minutes. Strain out the herbs, and sweeten up the tea with honey to taste.

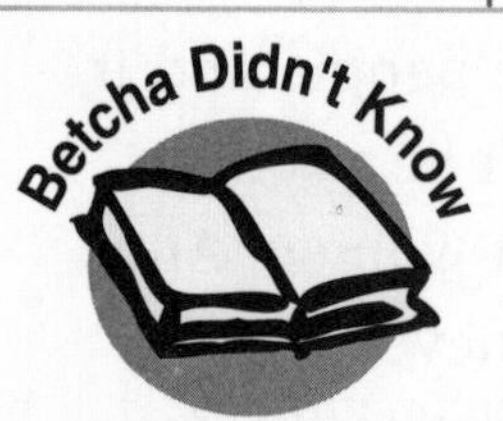

If you check the labels carefully, you'll notice that pennyroyal is one of the ingredients used in some commercial insect repellents.

GROWING TIPS

European pennyroyal tends to hug the ground with stems that can stretch up to 14 inches long. For best results, plant pennyroyal in moist, well-drained soil, and give it full sun or partial shade. It grows well in Zones 5 to 9.

For the best medicinal herbs, purchase small plants. The sprawling stems will root where they touch the ground — more free plants! Keep the scissors handy, and give the plants regular trimmings to prevent straggly stems. The top inch of soil should be dry to the touch before the plant's ready for more water. You should see flowers appearing by July.

If you like relaxing on the back porch or deck at dusk, I want you to consider placing some hanging baskets of pennyroyal nearby. The plants' aroma will help

A Cent-sible Stomach Settler

When teamed with catnip and gingerroot, pennyroyal makes a potent potion that'll get rid of excess gas — fast! Here's all you need:

1 tsp. of dried pennyroyal leaves
1 tsp. of gingerroot, ground
1 tsp. of dried catnip leaves

Mix the herbs together then infuse them in a cup of boiling water. Let steep 10 minutes, and strain out the herbs before drinking. This is a good tea to sip after a hardy meal, before you head off to sleep.

keep insects away so you can enjoy a picture-perfect, buzz-free sunset.

Indoors, treat yourself to an aromatic, wintertime houseplant. Simply transplant pennyroyal into containers in the fall, and bring them indoors to a bright, sunny window to enjoy all winter long.

HARVESTING TIPS

When your plants reach 8 inches high, it's time to harvest the leafy stems. Cut them off a few inches above the ground (or you can snip off the tips) for individual sprigs. Hang the stems upside down in bunches to air-dry.

Hiker's Delight

For those times when you have to brave a humid, thick forest (or maybe it's just your backyard), arm yourself with a little pennyroyal.

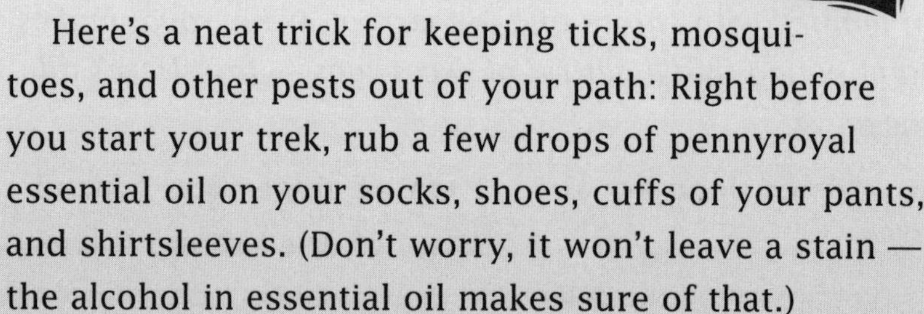

Here's a neat trick for keeping ticks, mosquitoes, and other pests out of your path: Right before you start your trek, rub a few drops of pennyroyal essential oil on your socks, shoes, cuffs of your pants, and shirtsleeves. (Don't worry, it won't leave a stain — the alcohol in essential oil makes sure of that.)

Pack the bottle of pennyroyal in your knapsack and reapply about every half hour. Avoid putting the essential oil of American pennyroyal directly on your skin, especially your face, as it can cause a rash.

Plantain

(Plantago major)

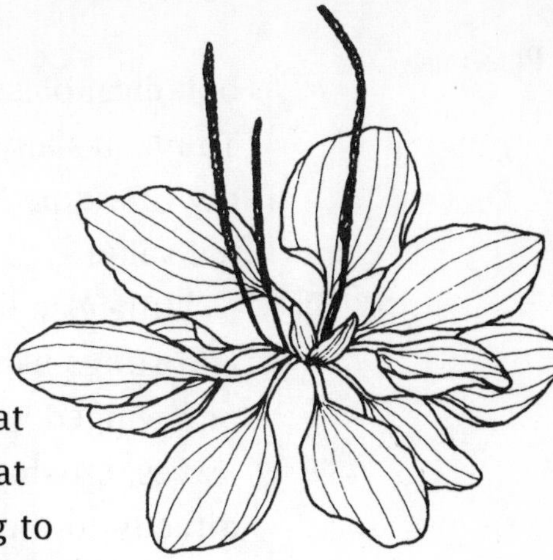

Herbal ID

Plainly speaking, this herb is a weed! That aside, plantain has broad, oval leaves that hover close to the ground. By mid-spring to early fall, clusters of tiny, white or purplish green flowers bloom off its slender central stalk.

That's Historical!

Talk about power! Pliny in ancient Greece believed boiling plantain in a pot and then laying it on the skin (cooled first, of course) would help heal wounds. The Anglo-Saxons nicknamed this herb waybread and considered it to be an important healer. In fact, they deemed it to be one of their nine sacred herbs.

According to English folklore, plantain would cure snakebites and mad dogs. (Hmm, I wonder about Englishmen in the midday sun?) Europeans brought plantain to this country, where Native Americans called it white man's foot because it grew wherever the white settlers lived.

Medicinal Uses: Soothe Bug Bites and Stings

Snubbed as a weed by lawn perfectionists, plantain is loved by herbalists because it delivers a bouquet of botanical blessings in its leaves and flowering parts. To me, it's anything but a nasty old weed — because my Grandma Putt taught me to appreciate its medicinal value.

Little else in nature takes away the itch of bug bites and stings like plantain does. If you've been the target of a winged warrior, just grab a fistful of plantain leaves, crush them up, and apply the healing juice directly to the fast-swelling spot. Ahhhh — talk about quick relief!

In its role as an astringent, plantain helps shrink itchy hemorrhoids, treats bladder infections, and hastens the healing of cuts and bruises. It also acts as a gentle expectorant — a perfect medicine for coughs, mild bronchitis, and nagging sore throats.

Beat the Bumps

You can use plantain to treat the bumps and blisters caused by poison ivy, oak, and sumac; it stops the swelling and kills bacteria.

For years, Grandma Putt relied on plantain to stop toothaches. Whenever one of us had a sore tooth, she would dab some juice from the leaves on a wad of cotton and stick it right on the tender area to tame the pain. She also grabbed a root, scrubbed it clean of dirt, and had us chew on it to ease the ache.

BEST MEDICINAL FORMS

Plantain is plentiful in backyards across the United States, but most folks wouldn't recognize it as a medicinal herb even if it bit them on the toes! If you're sure your lawn is free of pesticides and herbicides, you can use fresh plantain leaves in teas and poultices. You can even eat plantain for an extra healthy salad. Young, small leaves are the tastiest; the older, larger ones are generally bitter, and the tough, fibrous strands need to be removed before eating.

The benefits don't stop there; they just keep on coming. You'll get plenty of medicinal punch from dried leaves, ointments, and tinctures of plantain, which are available at health food stores.

GROWING TIPS

Plantain isn't picky — it'll grow just about anywhere. As a matter of fact, I've never seen it deliberately planted in a garden, but you'll see plenty of it in backyards and parks.

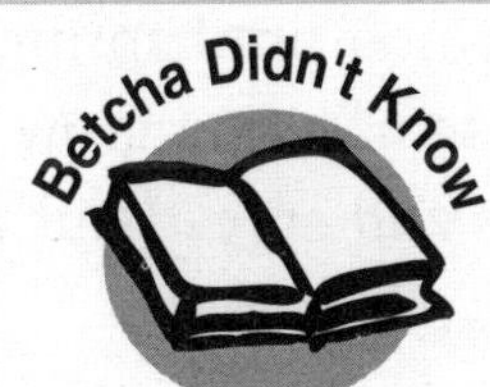

Plantain, when made into a strong tea brew, helps get rid of dandruff. Just rinse the tea right into your hair. The allantoins in this herb will make those embarrassing flakes disappear like magic!

It grows well in full sun and partial shade just about anywhere. It spreads readily in all types of soil, and its unattractive flower stalks can be as much as 18 inches high when mature. This is one hardy plant — unusually invincible against common garden pests and diseases.

HARVESTING TIPS

You can harvest plantain leaves anytime during the growing season and add them to garden salads. In the fall, dig up the roots, give them a good scrubbing, and allow them to dry until they are brittle to the touch.

Rosemary

(Rosmarinus officinalis)

Herbal ID

This is a late-flowering, woody evergreen bush that has a beckoning aroma similar to pine. It sports flashy, silvery green, needlelike leaves and pale blue flowers that usually bloom from late winter until spring.

Rosemary can grow up to 6 feet tall in warm climates and spread out just as wide. So give it lots of room, pardner!

That's Historical!

Greek students believed rosemary would keep their memories sharp so that they could make good grades. In medieval times, rosemary was thought never to grow in the gardens of evil people. That explains why some folks carried sprigs of rosemary in their pockets — to ward off evil spirits. They'd even tuck some under their pillows to shoo away nightmares!

Before the advent of electric refrigerators and freezers, hunters preserved and flavored venison and other wild game with many herbs, including rosemary.

In Europe, sprigs of rosemary symbolized love and remembrance — and supposedly fought off the plague.

In China, rosemary has been revered for its abilities to curb headaches and stop baldness (by waking up the hair follicles).

Medicinal Uses: Rejuvenate Aching Muscles

The real medicine in this herb is in its twigs, flowers, and leaves — they're packed with volatile oils including eucalyptol, flavonoids, and other healing goodies. Rosemary can work wonders, making tension headaches, gas, and even blue moods disappear. When you put it on your skin, it eases achy muscles and arthritic joints by increasing circulation to those areas. I love to soak my tired aching "dogs" in a rosemary bath after a long day in the garden!

Best Medicinal Forms

Rosemary works just dandy in teas, tinctures, and compresses. Just put 2 teaspoons of dried rosemary leaves in a cup of boiling water, let it steep 15 minutes, strain, and it's teatime! The recommended daily dose for tinctures is 2 to 5 ml in a glass of water or juice at each meal.

Rosemary is a powerful disinfectant when it's made into an herbal vinegar. The best part is that it's simple to make this germs-go-away recipe. Just put an ounce of rosemary essential oil (or a few stalks of fresh rosemary) and 2 pints of cider vinegar in a glass jar with a lid. Seal the jar and let the mix mingle for about 2 weeks. If you're using fresh rosemary, strain out the herbs. Shake

A Blast from the Past

Rosemary just may have religious ties. As a child, I loved hearing my Sunday school teacher tell this story: To hide baby Jesus from Roman soldiers on their way to Egypt, Joseph and Mary supposedly tossed a blue cloak over a rosemary bush and hid underneath it. When they took the cloak off the bush, the white flowers had turned blue!

vigorously before using. Dab some of this vinegar mix on a sponge, and those dad-blasted germs that hang out on countertops and other places won't know what hit 'em.

GROWING TIPS

Rosemary grows best in Zones 8 to 11, but it can thrive in colder climates as an annual or a container plant. Make sure the soil is sandy or gravelly and well drained. Give it full sun or light shade. You can try growing it from seed, but I've had better luck starting with small plants. Space them about 4 feet apart.

WHOA! **Rosemary is a** fairly safe herb, but it shouldn't be used if you're pregnant or if you're being treated for epilepsy or high blood pressure.

Fertilize the soil the first of each month, using a well-balanced, organic fertilizer like fish emulsion. At the end of each growing season, cover the soil surface with ½ inch of compost to give the plants something to grow on next year.

Don't let Old Man Winter keep you from enjoying this wonderful plant. Move it indoors in the fall, and your house will sing with the scent of spring all year 'round! Just a few quick pointers: Make sure you use a pot that is 6 inches or more in diameter; don't overwater (the soil should dry out between waterings); and remember that rosemary needs at least 5 hours of direct sunlight every day. No sun? No problem! Fluorescent grow-lights will do. With adult rosemary plants, you may need to transplant them into rather large 10-gallon pots to give them enough elbowroom.

HARVESTING TIPS

When you want some fresh rosemary, simply snip off a few of the leaves or stems. If you want more than a day's supply, cut the stems back by about one half. That way, you'll be able to snip another day. Allow the leaves to dry until they crumble easily.

For a winter's supply of seasoning for your favorite meat dishes, dry the stems and leaves on screens or in a dehydrator.

Herbal Hair Care

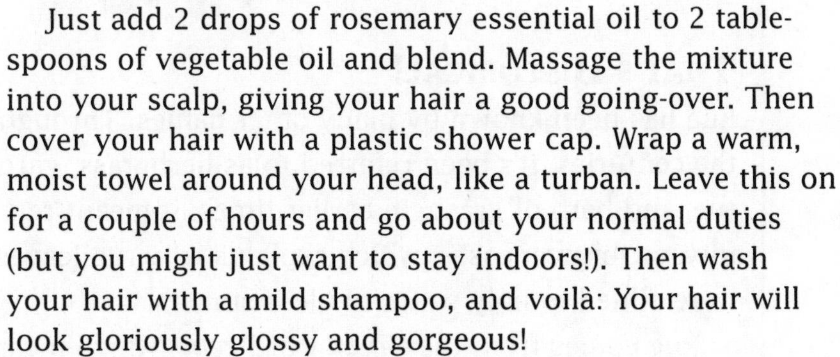

Don't get your dander up! Rosemary works terrifically as a hair rinse. In fact, some store-bought shampoos list rosemary as one of their ingredients. Even if you don't have dandruff, your hair still deserves to be treated to a good herbal massage every once in a while. (I know mine does, even with the little hair I've got left.)

Just add 2 drops of rosemary essential oil to 2 tablespoons of vegetable oil and blend. Massage the mixture into your scalp, giving your hair a good going-over. Then cover your hair with a plastic shower cap. Wrap a warm, moist towel around your head, like a turban. Leave this on for a couple of hours and go about your normal duties (but you might just want to stay indoors!). Then wash your hair with a mild shampoo, and voilà: Your hair will look gloriously glossy and gorgeous!

Rue

(Ruta graveolens)

Herbal ID

In a word or two — no regrets! Rue is a uniquely blue-green, woody perennial that has a soft texture. Its foliage erupts into colors of silver, white, and purple, and its 5-inch leaves are sometimes dusted with a whitish powder. By midsummer, expect to see clusters of blooming yellow button flowers. Rue grows up to 3 feet tall.

If you plan on sniffing rue, don't say I didn't warn you! Be ready to hold your nose because it delivers a pungent, skunklike odor! The good news is that the smell does seem to make flies high-tail it far away.

That's Historical!

Rue has been known by many other names. Through the centuries, it's been referred to as herbgrass, garden rue, and herb of grace. In earlier times, it meant regret, pity, or forgiveness — which explains why rue leaves were added to holy water to bless sinners.

Rue comes from the Greek word *reuo,* which means "to set free," as in freeing you from disease. Speaking of Greeks, generations ago they relied on it as an antidote for poison. In fact, King Mithridates supposedly drank tiny sips of rue to make himself immune to assassination attempts!

During the 16th century, courtrooms kept pots of rue to shield and protect magistrates from jail fevers and other maladies they might catch from prisoners. Now, that's one for the law books!

Years ago during High Mass, priests blessed churchgoers with holy water containing sprigs of rue.

Here's a blast from the past: Lots of my relatives on the Mason-Dixon line used to boil rue in wine with pepper and apply this mix directly on warts. Why, in no time at all, the warts disappeared without a trace! Jumpin' jiminy!

MEDICINAL USES: FLUMMOX FLEAS

The entire rue plant is like having nature's medicine cabinet at your disposal. Scientists have discovered that it contains oodles and oodles of good stuff, including tannins and volatile oils. Rue is a powerful medicinal herb, so it's important to respect it, and use it wisely. When it's good, it's very good, but when it's bad . . . watch out!

Rue should never be used during pregnancy, because it can trigger contractions before the baby is due. Because of the risk of overdoing it when taking it internally, I use it only occasionally, for bad coughs, for instance, or tension headaches.

WHOA!

Many folks are sensitive to rue's oils, and may develop a skin rash or small blisters. If you're sensitive to rue, just wear gloves and long sleeves when working in the garden. And only occasionally use rue medicinally. Pregnant women should not use this herb at all.

BEST MEDICINAL FORMS

Rue should only be taken as needed, and it's best in tea and tincture form. Infuse the tea by putting 2 teaspoons of dried rue into a cup of boiling water and letting it simmer for 15 minutes. Strain out the herbs, and the tea is ready to do its healing stuff. You can safely drink up to 3 cups a day.

Or here's a quicker way to get going. Put 1 to 4 ml of rue tincture in a glass of water or juice. Three glasses a day should do the trick!

Well, doggone it! If you tuck a handful of dried rue leaves into your pet's bedding, you'll keep fleas and other pesky pests far away. They'll rue the day they ever came your way!

GROWING TIPS

Rue grows best in Zones 4 to 9; just be patient. Rue seedlings take their own sweet time to grow, so you may want to start with a plant instead. Or you can start your seeds indoors about 2 months before the expected final frost date. When the seedlings reach 3 inches high, that's your signal to move them to the great garden outdoors.

Rue likes plenty of sun. There are no particular soil requirements, except that it must be well drained. Leave about 2 feet

A BLAST FROM THE PAST

Do you like playing cards? Great! The next time you sit down for a game of poker or bridge, take a close look at the clubs suit. Folklore has it that this suit was patterned after the leaves of a rue plant!

of space between plants, and keep them a good 10 to 12 feet away from sage, basil, and cabbage — otherwise, you'll rue the day you planted them so closely! Why? Because rue contains a substance that can actually interfere with their growth.

Rue in a Row

You can plant rue to create a low hedge, or stick it in containers to decorate your back porch. However you plant it, keep a watchful eye out: Rue is prone to root rot if overwatered or placed somewhere that has poor drainage.

HARVESTING TIPS

Before the flowers bloom, harvest the stems with leaves. Hang the stems upside down to air-dry in a shady spot. In late summer, you can harvest the seedpods for dried floral arrangements; just don't wait until they turn brown.

STORAGE TIPS

This one doesn't take well to the chill — so don't try storing it in the freezer.

Sage

(Salvia officinalis)

Herbal ID

With so many varieties of sage, there's one for just about everything under the sun. Sage is a woody perennial with lilac-blue flowers on spiky stalks that rise above lovely, gray-green foliage. It can reach about 2 feet tall and can spread 18 inches or more on the ground. It usually blooms in early to midsummer. And you guessed right if you thought that sage is a member of the mint family!

That's Historical!

Sage is the rage in many kitchens today because of its seasoning aroma and taste. I personally supervise the stuffing of the turkey at Thanksgiving, and I make darn sure that there's sage in my stuffing. But years ago, folks depended on sage to not only flavor but also preserve their meats and cheeses.

In Arabia, folks believed that sage would make them live longer. In fact, there is an old Arab proverb that asks, "How can a man die who has sage in his garden?" In China, folks were willing to trade three chests of tea for one chest of sage.

Through the years, new moms have relied on sage to help dry up milk supplies when they no longer needed to breast-feed. And women going through menopause have used sage to help control sweats triggered by hot flashes.

My Grandma Putt used to say that you could tell who ruled the roost simply by looking at what was thriving in the garden. Households where sage grew well were said to be ruled by the man, while those where thyme grew well were said to be ruled by the woman.

Honey, you can attract bees to your garden by planting lots of sage. Bees love it, and as a bonus, an industrious beekeeper gets very tasty honey!

Here's one to share with your friends: *Sage* is derived from the Latin word *salvus,* meaning "safe" or "well." No wonder folks throughout history have come to believe that sage will save them from various ills.

MEDICINAL USES: CONDITION YOUR GUMS

If you're a big science fan, you'll be interested to know that sage's medicinal lineup includes such ingredients as cineole, limonene, terpinene, and volatile oils. Put in simpler terms, these ingredients kill germs and act as antioxidants to keep your cells and tissues healthy. Sage helps restore vitality and strength, fights fevers, eases muscle spasms, and even keeps your central nervous system humming.

You shouldn't take sage if you're pregnant. Also, sage seems to interfere with iron medications taken by folks with anemia — so check with your doctor before you take it.

It's best known as a classic remedy for sore gums, mouth ulcers, sore throats, and even laryngitis. The volatile oils go right to work to soothe the swollen mucous membrane in the mouth. It's also a common remedy for excess gas, it repels insects, and it fights cold viruses. And you thought it was just for flavoring the turkey!

BEST MEDICINAL FORMS

Like most health-helping herbs, sage can be taken as a tea or tincture. Steep 3 teaspoons of fresh sage leaves (or about 1 teaspoon dried) in a cup of hot water (covered with a lid) for about 15 minutes. Then strain out the herbs. The tea can be used as a gargle for sore throats or swallowed to treat gingivitis, menopausal hot flashes, or anxiety. Drink up to 3 cups a day.

As a tincture, the recommended daily dose is 4 ml in a glass of water or juice, 3 times a day.

You can squeeze the juice from fresh sage leaves and use it as a compress for minor cuts, wounds, and insect bites and stings. These nicks and dings will heal more quickly without leaving any telltale scars.

You can also make a great poultice using sage and vinegar. Just run a rolling pin over a handful of freshly picked sage leaves, bruising them along the way. Put the leaves in a pan and cover them with cider vinegar; simmer on low until they soften. Remove the leaves,

Jerry's Words of Wisdom

"If you're a new gardener or don't have a lot of time, you may want to consider getting a head start by picking up some young sage plants at your local nursery or garden center."

carefully wrap them in a washcloth, and place it on stings, swellings, and bruises for instant relief.

GROWING TIPS

To keep this kitchen spice feeling nice, be sure to plant it in a sunny spot that has good drainage. You can start sage from seed, cuttings, or divisions.

Come planting day, space the sage plants about 2 feet apart because they are floppy. You may consider planting sage near lavender, silvery thyme, or lady's mantle — all of which make good neighbors. Sage likes dry, sandy, poor soils.

And once it makes itself at home, it's remarkably drought-resistant — so when the rest of your garden plants have their tongues out and are droopy with thirst, sage will still sport a healthy stance! Just be careful how much water you give sage; too much will

Fight Mouth Rage with Sage

It's a jungle in there, so keep your breath fresh and free from germs by gargling with sage!

Just put 2 teaspoons of fresh leaves (or a teaspoon of dried) in a pint of water on the stove. Bring to a boil, then turn off the heat and cover the pan with a lid. Let steep about 15 minutes. Strain out the herbs, and you now have your very own custom-made mouthwash!

Let it cool down before using it; then swish, spit, and say good-bye to bad breath! (This gargle also works really well to soothe a sore throat.)

makes its leaves liable to powdery mildew. Properly pampered, sage plants can live up to 4 years without having to be replaced.

HARVESTING TIPS

For a fresh supply of sage leaves for cooking and medicinal teas, snip the leaves before the flowers start to bloom. When fall arrives, cut leafy stems about 8 inches long and let them air-dry on screens. When the leaves crumble easily, that's your cue that they are completely dry and ready for storage.

STORAGE TIPS

Try not to crumble the dried leaves until you're ready to use them because they'll get stale, even in airtight containers. And keep sage from the freezer cage! Besides losing their therapeutic qualities in that cold, dark box, the leaves tend to get mushy when they thaw. Then you'll have a yucky mess!

Natural Moth Repellent

Here's another one of Grandma Putt's secrets — a natural moth repellent made out of equal parts of dried sage, rosemary, and thyme leaves in a mixing bowl. She'd place half a handful of the mixture in a loosely woven cotton bag and then sew the bag shut. She'd hang the bags in closets or lay them in the drawers among our clothes to keep these pesky little critters away.

St. John's Wort

(Hypericum perforatum)

Herbal ID

This herb is an aromatic perennial that can grow to about 2 feet tall. By midsummer, St. John's wort bears sunny yellow flowers. Each flower has three clusters of stamens that may look like a little pincushion.

That's Historical!

How did such a lowly plant get such a saintly name? Well, it turns out that it takes its name from the highly revered Knights of St. John's of Jerusalem, who acted like medics for wounded soldiers on the Crusade battlefields. Others say the name came because this plant blooms around June 24, the Feast of St. John the Baptist. I'll let you decide!

In ancient Greek days, St. John's wort treated everything from poisonous-snake bites and sciatica to wounds and melancholy moods. For many generations, this herb has been used as a folk remedy for lung and kidney problems.

Medicinal Uses: Lighten Dark Moods

A lot of folks (including me) call St. John's wort the happy herb. Both its flowers and petals have been scientifically proved to contain natural medicines that lift the spirits and lighten up moods. That's why St. John's wort is often regarded as nature's Prozac — it helps treat mild depression without the risk of addiction or side effects found in prescription medicines. Be patient, though — it may take 2 to 6 weeks before you notice a lift in your mood. If you think you may be suffering from depression, be sure to see a doctor before using St. John's wort.

This is one saintly herb when it comes to safety! About the only word of caution I can give you is that it can make some fair-skinned folks a little more sensitive to sunlight. So make sure you wear some sunblock when you go outdoors.

It seems like you almost have to have a PhD in pharmacy to figure out all of the fancy-sounding, helpful chemicals that are packed inside this herb. So I'll try to make it simple: This herb protects your brain's feel-good chemicals — serotonin and norepinephrine. It's been proved time and time again by studies conducted all over the world.

Not only does St. John's wort treat mild depression, but it also puts anxious, tense minds at ease and helps those who fret get a good night's sleep. Studies show that it relieves nerve pain caused by sciatica. When used externally, the red infused oil made from its yellow flowers is used for burns, bruises, sprains, minor cuts, and rheumatoid arthritis — just about anything that ails you.

BEST MEDICINAL FORMS

This herb comes in many helpful forms: tinctures, tablets, and creams. As a tincture, it's best to take

1 to 2 ml every day for at least 2 months if you're exhausted due to nervous tension. The recommended daily dose for tablet or capsule form is 500 mg, taken at mealtime.

If you rub a little St. John's wort cream on, it helps relieve the pain of strains, muscle cramps, and nerve aches; it also acts as a germ-fighter on minor scrapes and sores. Folks suffering from tennis elbow or other swollen joints can find relief if they dab a little essential oil of St. John's wort on the tender spot.

A BLAST FROM THE PAST

The word wort (no, not wart!) is actually Old English for *plant.*

When herb shopping, look for St. John's wort products that have been standardized to 0.3 percent hypericin; that way you're guaranteed uniform strength every time.

Hear Ye! Hear Ye!

Here's a quick and easy remedy for aching ears. St. John's wort works to reduce pain and swelling in the ear canal and also kills viruses.

Just mix a solution containing equal amounts of essential oils of St. John's wort and mullein flower. Using an eyedropper, put 2–3 drops in the affected ear and seal it with a cotton ball. Replace the cotton ball and add new drops (and a fresh cotton ball) about every 8 hours, until the symptoms disappear.

A Saintly Salve

I always keep a jar of homemade St. John's wort salve in my kitchen, so I can treat minor burns right on the spot! This salve also works nicely on minor cuts and skin rashes.

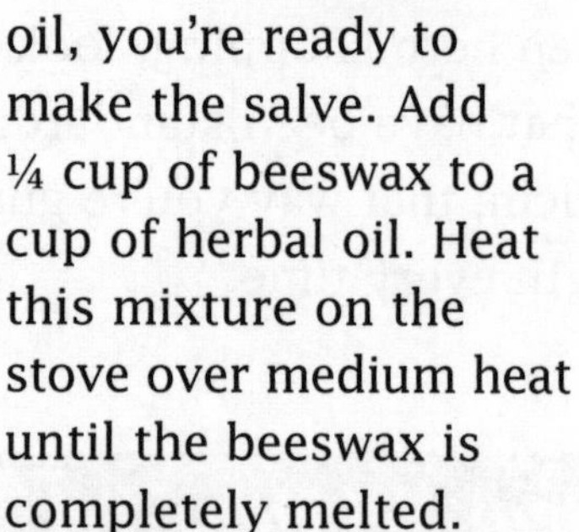

1 handful of St. John's wort leaves and flowers

1 handful of calendula flowers

1 handful of comfrey leaves

½ cup of vegetable oil

Stick the fresh herbs and vegetable oil in a double boiler. Simmer on low for about an hour. Take care to keep an eye on it to make sure that the oil doesn't overheat.

Lay a cheesecloth or muslin bag over a large stainless-steel strainer. Carefully pour the herbal mix from the double boiler into the strainer. Store the oil in a glass container in a cool, dry, dark place.

Now you're in the homestretch! Once you have made the herbal oil, you're ready to make the salve. Add ¼ cup of beeswax to a cup of herbal oil. Heat this mixture on the stove over medium heat until the beeswax is completely melted.

Remove the pan from the heat and pour the contents into tiny glass jars. Seal them with lids, and store away from direct sunlight and heat. Then the next time bacon grease splatters on your arm, stop your cussin' and reach for this soothing, healing salve!

Growing Tips

St. John's wort is best suited for Zones 3 to 8, where it will thrive if placed in a spot that receives a lot of sun. You can start seeds indoors about 8 to 10 weeks before it's safe to put plants in the ground outdoors. Just make sure that the soil is cool, well drained, and slightly acidic before planting. Set the plants about a foot apart. St. John's wort is a good plant for the middle of your garden.

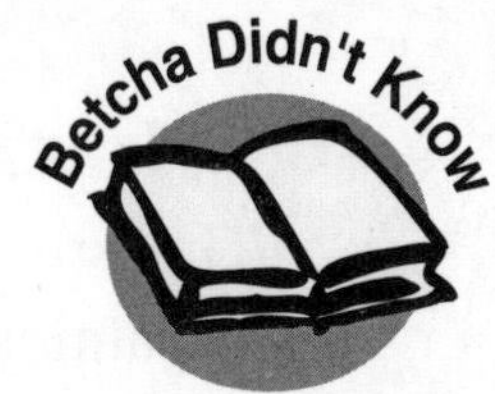

You don't have to worry about spraying St. John's wort with insect repellent, studying up on companion planting, or picking off critters, because diseases and garden pests rarely bother this herb.

Harvesting Tips

Harvest just the flowers, or the whole stem, flowers, and leaves, in summer. Infuse the flowers in oil and use the oil to soothe aches and burns. You can also dry the leaves and flowers to use for tea. It's great when you're feeling tense or grumpy!

Saw Palmetto

(Serenoa repens)

Herbal ID

This small, low-to-the-ground, scrubby fan-palm is also known as sabal. It has lots of protruding, spiky, green fronds and produces clusters of creamy white flowers and black berries from September through January. Saw palmetto reaches heights of up to 15 feet even though its stems may be partially or completely underground.

Saw palmetto grows in warm, humid climates like those typically found in the southeastern United States.

That's Historical!

Seminole Indians living in the Florida Everglades would eat saw palmetto seeds as food. Only later did they discover why they didn't have any urinary problems — it was because of something they ate.

In the early 1900s, this native North American plant was brewed into a berry tea by men who believed it would increase their sex drive and sperm production!

Medicinal Uses: Tone Male Reproductive System

Saw palmetto has a reputation for being a man's herb. That's because a lot of its ingredients help tone and strengthen the male reproductive system — and, when used safely, even boost testosterone, the male sex hormone. Studies show that it works successfully as a remedy for enlarged prostate glands (the FDA even declares so) and to treat a condition called early-stage benign prostatic hyperplasia (BPH) when used under the supervision of a doctor. Although it can't cure prostate cancer, saw palmetto can help prevent it.

But saw palmetto can be used by women as well. Not a lot of folks realize that taking it internally can help firm sagging breast tissue.

The seeds and berries of this spiky plant contain a laundry list of ingredients that treat a whole host of other conditions as well. For instance, this herb can tame irritated mucous membranes and rid the body of excess fluid.

This is generally regarded as a safe herb, but you men should check with your doctor first before taking it if you think you have benign prostatic hyperplasia (BPH). Let your doctor make that diagnosis.

As for women, the only restriction is that you should not take saw palmetto during pregnancy, just to be on the safe side.

BEST MEDICINAL FORMS

The powdered, dried fruit can be made into a tea, but I gotta warn you: Saw palmetto won't win any taste tests among tea drinkers. If you're brave, scoop a teaspoonful into a cup of boiling water, reduce the heat, and let simmer 5 minutes. You can drink up to 3 cups a day, but take it from the voice of experience: You'll want to mask its pungent taste with honey.

The recommended daily dose for saw palmetto's tincture form is 2 ml in a glass of water or juice, up to 3 times a day.

Growing Tips

This is a tough herb to grow, unless you happen to live in Zones 9 to 11. Saw palmetto needs the warm, tropical sun and sandy soil to grow well.

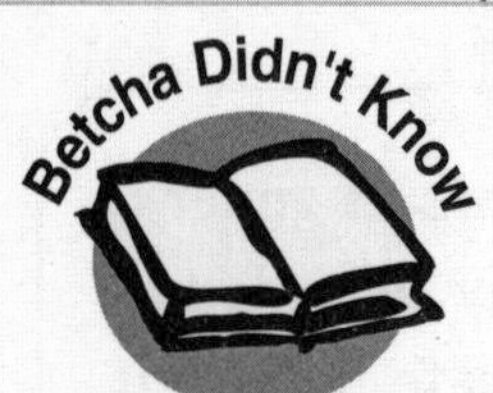

Some herbalists believe saw palmetto can treat baldness — or at least slow down hair loss for men. It seems that saw palmetto contains an ingredient that blocks DHT (dihydrotestosterone), a substance known to kill hair follicles.

Each year, the plant produces about seven spiky leaves that range in size from 1 to 3 feet wide. Honeybees keep the flowers pollinated, and many types of endangered wildlife — including the beautiful Florida panther — like to live among these plants.

Harvest Tips

The medicinal berries should be handpicked from early fall through midwinter and dried for storage.

Manly Tonic

This tea was specially created for us guys. Drinking a cup or two a day may keep prostate problems at bay!

1 tsp. of saw palmetto berries
1 tsp. of hawthorn berries
1 tsp. of fennel seeds
1 tsp. of marsh mallow root
½ tsp. of licorice root

Mix all of these herbs together, then put them in a pan with 6 cups of water. Bring to a boil and let simmer 25 minutes. Allow the tea to cool, strain out the herbs, and then bottom's up — here's to a better man!

Slippery Elm

(Ulmus rubra)

Herbal ID

Slippery elm is a medium-size hardwood tree that is native to the eastern and central United States. It also goes by such names as sweet elm, moose elm, and Indian elm. It has broad, flat leaves and rough twigs. When mature, it soars skyward — up to 60 feet high.

That's Historical!

Don't slip up on the origin of slippery elm: It's a native of North America. From what I've gathered, it seems like Native Americans had 101 uses for slippery elm. Not only did they use it for a host of medical conditions, but they also created baskets and other household goods from its inner bark.

During the 1800s, slippery elm was sold in stores as a medicinal flour as well as a cooking grain. Slippery elm gained popularity for its ability to coat and calm irritated mucous membranes and cool hemorrhoids.

Nowadays, stately elm trees of many species are much less common. The population has dwindled, thanks to the dreaded Dutch elm disease.

Stay away from slippery elm if you're pregnant. And for the trees' sake, use slippery elm sparingly — remember, there aren't many of these beauties left. To help conserve them, make sure you buy from places that use only bark from tree farms.

MEDICINAL USES: CLEAR YOUR LUNGS

You'll find a virtual medicine cabinet in the inner bark of this herb. Slippery elm contains calcium, polysaccharides, starches, tannins, and other healing ingredients that work to clear the lungs and bronchial tubes of excess, thick mucus, and act as antiseptics. The realm of elm is impressive: Herbalists brag about its soothing effect on diarrhea, colds, coughs, upset stomachs, peptic ulcers, and bladder infections. Their claims were bolstered when the FDA declared slippery elm to be a safe and effective treatment for throat and respiratory problems.

When used externally as a paste or gel, slippery elm is ideal for boils, abcesses, and skin ulcers.

Give Heartburn the Slip

Tame the burning sensation quickly with slippery elm lozenges. You can use ones available in health food stores, or make your own batch. For you adventurous souls, here's how to make them:

¼ cup of slippery elm powder
3 tbsp. of honey
4 drops of vanilla extract
Flour

In a small bowl, mix the slippery elm powder and the honey together and form it into a nonsticky dough. Then add the vanilla. On a cutting board dusted with flour, roll the dough into a long, thin shape. Cut the roll into bite-size pieces and put them on a baking sheet. Allow them to bake for an hour at 250ºF.

Cool, then place in an airtight container. Then, the next time you have a bellyache, pop one of these lozenges into your mouth!

SPRAY AWAY SORE-THROAT PAIN

Here's a nifty, natural way to get the lumps and raspies to beat a hasty retreat from your throat. First, get yourself a small spray bottle or mister. Brew a triple-strength tea with 3 teaspoons each of dried slippery elm, echinacea, and licorice in 3 cups of water. Bring it to a full boil, then reduce the heat and let simmer 10–15 minutes.

Strain out the herbs and pour the brew into a spray bottle. Open your mouth, stick out your tongue, and spray the back of your throat as needed during the day. Whether you say ahhhhh before or after you spray is up to you, but I bet my bottom dollar you'll feel relieved!

BEST MEDICINAL FORMS

Think of the three Ts: teas, tinctures, and tablets. Slippery elm works very well in all of these forms, though it's most commonly sold as a powder.

To make a tea, boil 2 g of bark in a pint of water for 15 minutes. Let cool, remove the bark, and drink up to 4 cups a day. Or you can use 2 teaspoons of powdered bark per cup of water. This tea is very nutritious and healing, but it's a bit bland. You might want to sweeten it with honey to taste.

The recommended daily dose for tinctures is 5 ml in a glass of water or juice up to 3 times daily. In tablet form, the dose is two 400 mg tablets, taken up to 4 times a day.

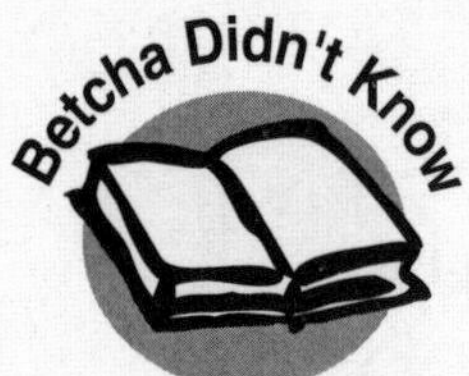

You can coax out stubborn splinters by dabbing a little slippery elm ointment on the site, covering it with a small bandage, and leaving it alone for a few hours. When you lift off the bandage, you should be able to take out the splinter easily with a pair of tweezers or a sterilized needle.

As a poultice, slippery elm helps heal skin conditions. Mix the coarse, powdered bark with just enough boiling water to form a paste, and apply it to an open wound or boil.

GROWING TIPS

Growing a slippery elm tree can be a tricky proposition because of its susceptibility to developing Dutch elm disease. It needs the rich, well-drained soil that's typically

A Dilly of a Diarrhea Remedy

As unpleasant as it is, diarrhea is your body's way of getting rid of some things that shouldn't be there — you know: bacteria, parasites, and spoiled food, to name a few. But all those trips to the bathroom can make you dehydrated and weak, and this is one herb that can make you better again.

Mix a teaspoon of slippery elm powder and a pinch of ginger powder in a cup of hot water. Drink a cup every couple of hours to help relieve the symptoms.

found in bottomlands and slopes. You need to keep a close eye out for any signs of problems. Caused by a fungus, Dutch elm disease starts off with leaf yellowing on one or several branches; before long, entire branches are infected. A professional nurseryman can sometimes treat affected trees and save them, but seriously affected trees must be cut down.

A Healthy Nightcap

To guarantee a nice, restful sleep that is uninterrupted by the gurglings and groanings of indigestion, stir a spoonful of slippery elm powder into a tall glass of milk (cold or warm: your choice). Drink it before you head for bed.

HARVESTING TIPS

When you harvest the inner bark of a slippery elm tree, be conservative. Ideally, you should wait at least 10 years before harvesting the bark. Then, collect the bark only from one side. If you remove the bark from all sides, say bye-bye to your elm tree!

STORAGE TIPS

When you have dried the bark, pound it with a mortar and pestle into a powder and store in an airtight, dark glass jar.

Strawberry

(Fragaria vesca)

Herbal ID

To me, strawberries are taste-temptin' signs that warm weather has finally arrived. Strawberry plants have three fan-shaped, sharp-toothed, dark leaves. In spring, tiny, rose-shaped, white flowers with five petals and eye-catching yellow centers appear in clusters on the plants. Then, saving the best for last, the plant proudly displays its juicy red fruits.

That's Historical!

My Grandma Putt used to tell me plenty of strawberry stories. She said the plant was a symbol of foresight. Long, long ago, folks believed the wild strawberry plant was powerful enough to fend off demons! She also told me that Anglo-Saxon children used to string the berries on straws and sell them — berry industrious!

In more recent times, Indian tribes in the Pacific Northwest would take dried, pulverized strawberry leaves and place

Betcha Didn't Know

The strawberry is actually a member of the rose family! That's right! So the next time you're in hot water, try giving your sweetheart a dozen red strawberries — see what happens! (Just be ready to duck!)

them in the navels of newborn babies to promote healing. Who needs a belly-button tattoo?!

MEDICINAL USES: RELIEVE A STUFFY NOSE

This sweet-tasting fruit harbors more than just a great fresh taste. Its berries, leaves, and roots are loaded with vitamin C, minerals, catechins, and other healthy ingredients. Permit me to take a deep breath before I tell you all it does: It helps shrink swollen tissues, eases headaches, puts the brakes on histamine growth, and enhances the role of proteins in the body. Although it hasn't been proved conclusively yet, the mighty strawberry also seems to help treat kidney stones, diarrhea, toothaches, and skin conditions such as eczema and sunburn. So the next time you're suffering with one of these ailments, reach for the strawberry shortcake!

A BLAST FROM THE PAST

We now say "strawberries," but we used to call them "hautboy" or "woodman's delight." They really don't sound too appealing, do they!

FAST FACT

Forget about comparing apples and oranges — try strawberries! Did you know that eating a cup of these tasty berries will give your body a more than ample supply of vitamin C?

BEST MEDICINAL FORMS

Teas made from strawberry leaves have been used to stimulate appetites, stop sweating, relieve anemia, and prevent miscarriages. Just crush 3 teaspoons of fresh leaves (or use a teaspoon of dried leaves) and put them in a cup of boiling water. Let steep 5 minutes. Strain out the leaves and enjoy this cooling, fruity tea.

GROWING TIPS

Strawberry plants do best when started in late spring, after the final frost has come and gone. You can sow seeds or propagate by planting the small plants that appear at the end of the runners. Whichever method you choose, make sure to plant them about 8 inches apart in rich, moist, well-drained soil. Strawberries are sun worshipers, so you'll need a wide-open area. It's very important to plant your strawberries so that their crowns are just at surface level. If the crown is too low, it will rot; if the crown is too high, the roots will dry out. Picky, picky!

Strawberry Facial

There's no need to go to a fancy spa to pamper yourself when you can do it yourself for a fraction of the cost. If you've got oily skin, try this herbal formula to leave your face looking fresh, clean, and healthy!

1 tbsp. of facial clay (available at health food stores)

1 large ripe strawberry, mashed

1 tbsp. of witch hazel tincture

1 drop of lavender essential oil

In a small bowl, combine all of the ingredients to form a paste. Apply it to your face (being careful to steer clear of your eyes), leaving this fruit mask on for 15 minutes or so. Despite how beautiful you look with the mask on (ugh!), the best is yet to come. Head for the bathroom sink and rinse off the mask with warm water. Your skin will glow, but the shine produced by overactive oil glands will be gone.

Once you've packed the soil around the plants, sprinkle a layer of straw on top.

Even though strawberries are among the easiest plants to grow, don't expect too much of them. They can't produce bushels of wonderful fruits year after year in the same spot. So rotate your stock, introducing new plants into your patch each year and getting rid of older plants once they've celebrated their third or fourth birthdays. (Don't worry about being cold-hearted; it's for the good of the patch!)

Strawberries make great friends and companions with spinach, borage, lettuce, and bush beans — so consider making them garden neighbors. But keep strawberries and away from members of the cabbage family, since they're archenemies!

Just a word of caution: If you break out in hives from eating fresh strawberries, you're also likely to be allergic to the medicinal form of this plant. When you use strawberry medicinally, don't take it every day for more than 2 weeks if your condition doesn't improve. You may need to see your doctor for a more effective treatment. And don't use the leaves until they're completely dry.

HARVESTING TIPS

This is one of my all-time favorite plants to harvest. Talk about instant gratification! Mornings make the best picking time — that's when berries are the firmest and easiest to handle.

If you want to keep from bruising these red beauties come picking time, grab the stem close to the cap. Then twist and pull, leaving as short a stem as possible still attached to the cap. Don't go hog-wild and pile a mountain of strawberries all in one basket, or you'll end up with bruised and battered berries. Collect them in several small containers instead.

STORAGE TIPS

You can store fresh strawberries in a sealed container in your refrigerator or freezer. Don't rinse them off until you're ready to use them — they'll last longer. Just remember that adding sugar or water only makes them mushier faster — so keep those berries unadulterated!

Run Relief

Try this fruity-flavored tea the next time you keep having to do the green apple shuffle to the bathroom. This good-tasting tea will replenish lost fluids and prevent you from becoming dehydrated.

1 tsp. of dried strawberry leaves
1 tsp. of dried marsh mallow leaves
1 tsp. of dried meadowsweet leaves

Blend the herbs. Scoop out a teaspoonful and add it to a cup of boiling water. Let it steep 15 minutes, then strain out the herbs before sipping. You can drink up to 3 cups a day.

Tarragon, French

(Artemisia dracunculus 'sativa')

Herbal ID

French tarragon has long, narrow leaves on upright stalks and greenish gray flowers that bloom summer to fall. It grows 2 to 3 feet tall. Length-wise, it likes to stretch and sprawl, so give it room to roam. Taste-wise, it has a strong licorice flavor.

That's Historical!

Tarragon's botanical name, *dracunculus,* means "little dragon." In Europe, this spice was once used to heal snakebites. *Tarragon* is French for "lasting involvement."

Medicinal Uses: Restore Your Appetite

Tarragon has been used as a folk remedy to stimulate appetites and to relieve colic and rheumatism. Some herbalists believe it can help lower blood pressure and restore regularity to menstrual cycles.

Growing Tips

To increase your chances that this herb will stay and thrive in your garden and not "tarra-be-gone," plant it in fertile soil and give it ample water and sunlight.

Given a choice, tarragon grows best in Zones 4 to 8. Fertilize it once with fish fertilizer during the growing season (any more than that, and you risk robbing this herb of its flavor). Health-wise, tarragon is usually pest-free, but it can be prone to root rot and mildew in poorly drained soil. So watch how you water!

Who's Who?

The French variety of tarragon packs a whole lot more flavor than the Russian variety. But how do you tell them apart? While Russian tarragon leaves have little fragrance, on the other hand French tarragon has a strong, can't-miss-it aroma.

Every 3 to 4 years, you'll need to divide the plants to make them more manageable. At the end of the season, I also recommend mulching over the roots to protect the plants from Old Man Winter.

If you plan on growing tarragon indoors, plant it in 12-inch or larger containers. Use a standard potting mix, and place the containers in a cool, bright place. Indoor tarragon tends to be shorter than its outdoor cousins, but its lack of height won't affect its leafiness or flavor.

HARVESTING TIPS

You can snip sprigs of tarragon as needed for culinary delights throughout the growing season. For the final harvest, cut the stalks a few inches above the ground. Hang small, tied bunches of tarragon upside down on drying racks in a dark, airy place. It will take tarragon about 2 weeks to dry completely;

you'll know it's ready when the leaves crumble easily in your hand.

STORAGE TIPS

Like most herbs, tarragon quickly loses its volatile oils and flavors when it's exposed to heat and light. Don't be tempted to store it atop your refrigerator — it can really get hot up there!

Freezing is an excellent storage alternative for this herb. Wash the leaves and pat them dry with a towel.

USS Tarragon

Ahoy, seafood lovers! Let "Captain Jerry" send your taste buds on a delicious seafood cruise with this tarragon-fennel vinegar recipe:

Put a small handful of fresh tarragon and fennel into a glass jar. Then pour equal amounts of heated cider and white wine vinegars over the herbs, filling the jar. Seal the jar and stash it in a place out of direct heat and sunlight for about 3 weeks. Then strain out the herbs and reseal.

Congratulations! You've just made your own batch of herbal vinegar that'll dress up your next broiled fish dish. Experiment with the ratio of herbs to cider and vinegar to suit your own taste.

Place the fresh fish filets in aluminum foil, fashioned like a rowboat. Pour on some of the tarragon-fennel vinegar, add a pat of butter or margarine, and top with fresh sprigs of tarragon. The tarragon adds a mild anise-like flavor, while the vinegar takes away the smelly fish odor! You'll be in hog, I mean fish, heaven.

You can freeze them whole or chopped, in sealed plastic bags. Don't forget to put some ID on each bag, or you'll be scratching your head, wondering which is which! You can also freeze fresh sprigs of tarragon in water, in ice-cube trays, and plop them into the pot as needed for cooking.

Terrific Twosome

Tarragon and mustard make a marvelous marinade for chicken, salmon, swordfish, or lamb. Try this delicious recipe the next time you're in the mood:

¼ cup of tarragon white wine vinegar

¼ cup of Dijon mustard

1 cup of olive oil

1 tbsp. of fresh tarragon leaves, minced

2 cloves of garlic, minced

Mix all of these ingredients in a blender until they're smooth. Pour the mix into a glass dish, and add your meat or fish. Let it all marinate 10–20 minutes before cooking.

Thyme

(Thymus vulgaris)

Herbal ID

Thyme after thyme after thyme. Cyndi Lauper or Simon and Garfunkel? Anyway, at last count there were at least 130 varieties of thyme being enjoyed in kitchens and gardens worldwide. All belong to the Labiatae family, which is native to the Mediterranean, and all feature lip-shaped flowers and small, oval-shaped leaves. These are among the best-known varieties:

- Garden thyme *(Thymus vulgaris),* a shrubby plant with pale pink blooms.
- Lemon thyme *(Thymus* x *citriodorus),* a spreading plant with deep pink flowers.
- Mother-of-thyme *(Thymus serpyllum),* a carpeting plant with pinkish lavender flowers.
- Azores thyme *(Thymus caespititius),* a mat-forming, citrus-pine-smelling plant that has pink, lilac, or white flowers.

That's Historical!

Centuries before the Cowardly Lion in *The Wizard of Oz,* thyme was grabbing attention for courage with a capital C. In fact, the Greek word *thumus* means "courage." Hippocrates, the ancient Greek dubbed the Father of Medicine, made sure that thyme was in his medicine cabinet.

Thyme is filled with other wonderful folklore. Romans burned thyme as a deodorizer and relied on it as a cure for hangovers. Sprigs of thyme were embroidered into the clothing of medieval knights before they rode off to battle. When Shakespeare referred to it, I can only guess that he had thyme on his hands. Thyme even went to war — World War I soldiers used it to clean battlefield wounds.

Small amounts in cooking are okay, but do not ingest large amounts of thyme if you have thyroid problems or high blood pressure, or if you are pregnant.

Medicinal Uses: Fight Germs Naturally

Thyme is one of nature's painkillers. Rich in volatile oils, it's a powerful antiseptic. Therapeutically, the thymol in thyme acts as a stimulant, expectorant, astringent, and diuretic. And let's not forget that this herb also contains vitamins A and D, as well as a boatload of minerals like potassium, calcium, iron, magnesium, and zinc.

In summary, this herb's thyme has come! (I couldn't help myself.) It's terrific for treating sore throats, colds, and congestion. Plus, it's a natural germ-fighter; lotions containing thyme give TLC for healing blemished skin.

Best Medicinal Forms

In no time at all, you can prepare a cup of thyme tea. Just add a teaspoon of dried thyme or 2 teaspoons of fresh leaves to a cup of boiling water. Cover, let steep 10 minutes, and then strain. A teaspoon of honey sweetens its taste.

To make a fantastic facial lotion, put 2 tablespoons of dried thyme (or 4 tablespoons of fresh) leaves in a cup of boiling water. Cover, then steep 10 minutes. Cool before using, or you'll burn your skin!

I like to ease the muscle aches and pains of gardening by tossing a handful of dried thyme into my running hot bath. I soak in the tub for 10 to 15 minutes and let the aromatic oils in this herb take my aches and pains away.

GROWING TIPS

Old Man Winter can't rattle Father Thyme. This is one herb that grows quite well in containers or pots indoors year-round. Just make sure you put it in a spot that gets lots of sun. Thyme can do the neighborly thing, too, and gladly share a large container with parsley and oregano, two other terrific cooking spices.

Outdoors, thyme is an equal-opportunity herb. It grows in just about any sunny place, except for a swamp. You can propagate thyme by seeds, divisions, or cuttings.

I've found that the best place to grow thyme is in sandy, dry soil with plenty of room for it to creep and spread. Space the plants about a foot apart to

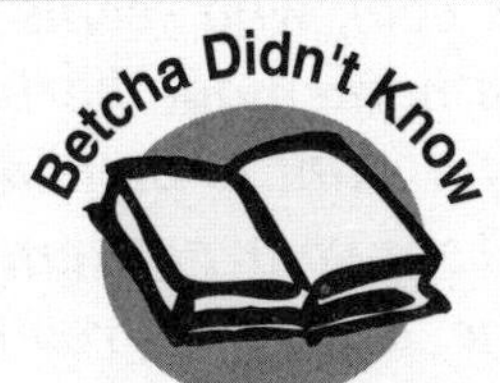

Thyme makes a very effective moth repellent. You can fill muslin bags with dried thyme and tuck them into the folds of blankets, linens, and winter clothes during the spring and summer months. I also tuck some in dresser drawers and hook a couple on hangers to keep the moths from munching on my clothes.

allow for the woody roots to stretch and grow. Some varieties also reach up to 18 inches in height, making it a nice little hedge or border planting. Thyme is also a great addition to any rock garden. In late May/early June, thyme marches on — and flowers start appearing.

Harvesting Tips

Snip leaves for salads and other immediate needs during the growing season. As with most herbs, the best time to collect thyme is on a sunny morning, after the dew has evaporated. This is when the essential oils inside thyme are their mightiest.

Give the Gift of Thyme

What can you get a cook who seems to have everything? How about a homemade herbal wreath? Not only is it a wonderful sight to behold, but it can also be used for cooking! From your garden, harvest long stems of fresh thyme, sage, and small red and green chili peppers. From the craft store, buy a small wreath frame and spool of medium-gauge green wire. Then follow these five easy steps:

1. Divide the herbs into small bunches.
2. Place a bunch of thyme against the frame. Bind the ends with the wire onto the frame. Be sure to overlap, so that the thyme covers the whole frame.
3. Repeat step 2 with sage.
4. Thread the red and green chilies onto the wire to form a circle.
5. Hold the chili circle against the wreath and wind the wire around both to fasten the chilies to the wreath.

The best end-of-season harvesttime is in early August. Take up to a third of the plant, cutting the stems just as the flowers start to open. After washing off any dirt and bugs (they're not so tasty), hang the leafy stems upside down in small bunches on drying racks. It'll be about 2 weeks before the leaves reach the dry, crumbly stage. If you're not that patient (and who is these days?), you can pop them in the microwave. Put down a double layer of paper towels, and then microwave the herbs on high for 1 or 2 minutes.

STORAGE TIPS

You can keep a year-round supply of fresh thyme leaves handy by freezing some bundles. Tuck freshly cleaned thyme into plastic bags as soon as it's cut. Seal the bags, label and date them, and toss them into the freezer. When it's thyme, you can easily chop the leaves while they're still frozen. It's that simple!

Fresh thyme can also be stored for a week or so in a sealed plastic bag in the refrigerator.

If you're storing dried thyme, you know the drill: Pick a dry, dark, and cool place. Mark the date on the container, because dried thyme rarely lasts longer than 7 months. After that, you can say good-bye to any flavor or aroma.

Jerry's Words of Wisdom

"If you don't have the thyme, stay out of the kitchen!"

Valerian

(Valeriana officinalis)

Herbal ID

This vanilla-smelling perennial is also called all-heal, garden heliotrope, capon's tail, vandal root, and St. George's herb. It grows to about 5 feet tall with fern-like leaves and white, flat-topped flowers. In some cases, the flowers are pink or lavender. Whatever their color, valerian blooms in clusters at the ends of the stems.

That's Historical!

Valerian comes from the Latin word *valere,* which, appropriately, means "to be in good health." Through the ages, it's been a symbol for protection, purification, sleep, and love. The virtues of valerian were known in the days of ancient Greek physician Dioscorides, who relied on this herb to treat nausea, weak bladders, tummy aches, and liver problems.

In the Middle Ages, valerian was prized both as a spice and as a perfume. It wasn't until the 18th century that folks discovered valerian was a great nighty-night herb. And in more modern times, soldiers in World War I and II were given valerian to counter shell shock and nervous stress brought on by battle.

MEDICINAL USES: RELIEVE RESTLESSNESS

Valerian is a natural choice for those times when you feel anxious, nervous, or restless — it has sedative, hypnotic, antispasmodic, and carminative properties. A lot of folks use it to get a good night of zzzzs because it gently slips you into a healthy slumber.

Valerian also helps relax tense muscles, soothes stomach upsets, and reduces high blood pressure. Oh, did I mention that it can tame the tickle of a nagging cough and strengthen the heart? Put them all together, and you have to agree that this is quite a checklist of feats!

Valerian's therapeutic powers are deep-rooted — where else but in its roots! They contain the essential oils that provide the calming, relaxing qualities of this herb.

BEST MEDICINAL FORMS

You can take a teaspoonful of valerian tincture up to 3 times a day. It won't win any taste contests, so be sure to camouflage its "dirty old sock" smell in a glass of juice. Valerian's awful taste has been well known since the ancient Greek days. In fact, it was nicknamed *phu* (as in phew!) by the ancient Greek physician Galen.

The best way to use fresh valerian is to soak about 2 teaspoons of chopped root in a cup of cold water for 10 hours. Then put a couple of drops of peppermint water in the cup to mask valerian's odor. Remove the root, and sip away.

Teatime, anyone? Another way to sip this herb's medicine is to add 2 teaspoons of dried valerian root to a cup of boiling water. Let it steep a good 15 minutes. Strain out the herbs, and the tea is ready.

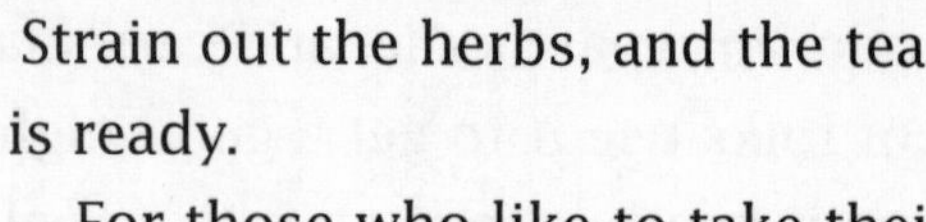

For those who like to take their medicine in tablet or capsule form, the daily dose is 300 to 500 mg. Insomniacs should take it right before bedtime; and don't fret — valerian is not addictive. In fact, it's a whole lot safer than Valium or other prescriptive medications!

Got muscle cramps from pickin' weeds all day? Loosen up those muscles quickly by soaking a damp washcloth in valerian tincture and placing it right on the tight tendon.

GROWING TIPS

Voilà! Valerian grows wild all over France and the rest of Europe. In the United States, it thrives in Zones 4 to 8. This is one herb that you can easily start indoors. About 8 weeks before the last predicted frost date, sow the seeds in rich soil — without covering them — in peat or newspaper pots. Keep the soil moist but not overwatered, using a gentle-misting sprayer. Set the container on a windowsill that gets plenty of sun.

Once all threat of frost has come and gone, introduce these young seedlings to the great outdoors — and to your garden! Since they grow up to 5 feet tall, stick them in the back of the garden so they don't overshadow your smaller plants. Work a little manure into the soil, then plant these tiny tots about 2 feet apart. Although valerian prefers a location that gets full sun, it has been known to tolerate partial shade.

Get Some Welcome Zzzzzs

Ever had one of those restless nights when you toss and turn, aware of each passing hour? The terrific herbal trio of valerian root, chamomile flower, and cinnamon blend nicely into a sleeping remedy that'll put an end to the restlessness. Try this easy recipe, and you can't lose — you'll snooze!

20 drops of valerian root tincture (or 1 tsp. of dried valerian root)

1 tsp. of dried chamomile flowers

Pinch of cinnamon

Mix all of the ingredients together in a bowl. Put a teaspoon of this herbal mix into a cup of boiling water and steep 10 minutes. Strain out the chamomile flowers, and your bedtime drink is ready and waiting. Before you know it, you'll be waking up the next morning feeling refreshed!

This is a fairly hardy plant that is resistant to most diseases and pests, but it can fall prey to a pet — namely, the neighbor's roaming feline. Cats consider this a purr-fect herb to munch on when they want to feel frisky! So much for catnip!

HARVESTING TIPS

Valerian needs to be at least 2 years old before it's mature enough for you to harvest its root. Your cue to start digging will come at the end of the second growing season, just about the time the leaves are turning colors. Use a spading fork, and dig up the roots on a dry day.

Cut the roots into 2-inch pieces, clean them free of dirt, and dry them in a dehydrator or on screens in the shade.

It probably goes without saying, but you shouldn't take valerian when drinking alcohol — heed the drowsy factor! Don't use it for more than 3 months.

STORAGE TIPS

This is one herb that should not be stockpiled; it loses its punch quicker than an aging prizefighter! As usual, store cleaned and dried roots in glass containers, far away from heat and light.

Violet

(Viola odorata)

Herbal ID

Best known as sweet violet (but also known as garden violet, English violet, and florist's violet), this low-growing perennial starts out with a short rootstock that sends out stolons. These stolons are modified stems that produce nifty new plants at their tips. So cool your jets and be patient! Its downy leaves can be heart-shaped or kidney-shaped. Each spring, usually around April or May, these plants burst forth with fragrant purple, violet, white, or pink flowers.

That's Historical

Some forms of violet have been used for centuries in love potions. In ancient Greek mythology, violet was called heartsease. Here's the scoop: It seems Zeus had a mistress, the goddess Io. When his wife, Hera, discovered this, she erupted into a jealous rage and turned Io into a cow! To counter his wife's udder foolishness, Zeus gave Io pastures of sweet-tasting violets to eat.

Drift back with me for a minute, to history class (you know, the one you had to take over). Remember Napoleon, the little general with the funny hat, hand in his jacket, and his plans to conquer the world? Well, he used violet as his emblem so that his soldiers could identify each other as friend, not foe, during the heat of battle.

You've heard of the term "shrinking violet"? Well, among old-time herbalists, *violet* means "modesty."

MEDICINAL USES: TREAT SKIN PROBLEMS

You'll find violet's medicine inside leaves and flowers. Sweet violet has been used for years to treat a whole host of skin problems, like eczema, as well as bronchitis. But it may surprise you to learn that this herb also has a reputation to fight the big C: skin cancer. A lot of holistic physicians are making sure their skin-cancer patients get plenty of sweet violet in addition to their other treatments.

Violet has both antiseptic and expectorant properties. The leaves are rich natural sources of vitamins A and C, too.

BEST MEDICINAL FORMS

A nice cup of tea is one of the most relaxing and enjoyable ways to take sweet violet. Just add a teaspoon of this dried herb (or 3 teaspoons of fresh leaves) to a cup of boiling water. Let simmer for 15 minutes. Remove the herb by straining, and the tea is ready. You can drink up to 3 cups a day. It also makes a terrific therapeutic gargle for scratchy throats!

If you want to try the tincture route, the recommended daily dose is 2 ml of sweet violet in a glass of water or juice, 3 times a day.

GROWING TIPS

Violet prefers the mild climates of Zones 5 to 8. It's a low-rider in the garden, reaching only 6 inches in height; so make sure you put it front and center — in rich, humusy, moist soil and a place that gets partial shade. Leave about a foot of space between plants.

Violets tend to bloom in early spring, adding a welcome touch of color to an otherwise dreary landscape. You'll be glad to know that this plant self-sows very easily and spreads rapidly. I doubt if you'll ever have to worry about having enough violets, because once they take root, they're off to the races! But keep your eyes open for red spider mites, which can shrink your violets in a hurry! Show who's mite-ier by spraying with insecticidal soap or Plant Shampoo. Mulching the plants before winter sets in will help keep mites away.

In late winter or early spring, you can propagate violets by dividing them or transplanting runners. Thick crops need to be thinned, and there's no better way to show you care than sharing with a friend. Cutting off the runners will also allow the violets' crowns to flourish.

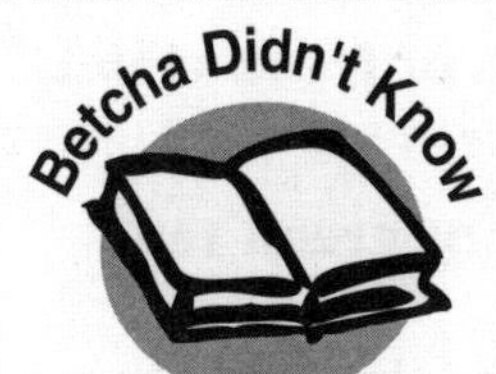

Violets are cultivated in commercial gardens for the perfume industry all over the world. Ever wonder how the term "shrinking violet" came to be? The violet's downturned ear and fleeting fragrance is the perfect image for shy people!

HARVESTING TIPS

Gather up your violets when the flowers are still wide open. Cut each flower or leaf, keeping

its stem attached. You can dry violets by pressing them between sheets of absorbent paper in a big, thick book, like an encyclopedia or dictionary (I stick mine under "flower" or "violet" to help me remember the place where I stashed them!).

STORAGE TIPS

To keep violets colorful as long as possible, store the dried flowers in dark, airtight containers. A lot of folks (me included) like to use dried violet flowers in candies, jams, and fruit salads.

Viva la Violet

Treat your special summertime guests to this vitality-packed tea:

1½ cups of fresh violet flowers

1 tsp. of green tea

6 cups of boiling water

1 tbsp. of brandy

Mix the violet flowers and green tea in a 6-cup teapot (or you can make do with a glass coffeemaker). Add the boiling water and let it steep a good 10 minutes. Then add the brandy. Stir it up, and you can almost feel the energy before this tea reaches your lips. When it does, you may want to add a little honey or lemon to counter violet's slightly bitter taste.

Vitex (Chastetree)

(Vitex agnus-castus)

Herbal ID

Depending upon where you live, this perennial flowering shrub may be called vitex or chastetree. To add to the confusion, this herb has a couple of other nicknames: monk's pepper and agnus-castus. As I said earlier, in this herb business you really can't tell the players without a scorecard!

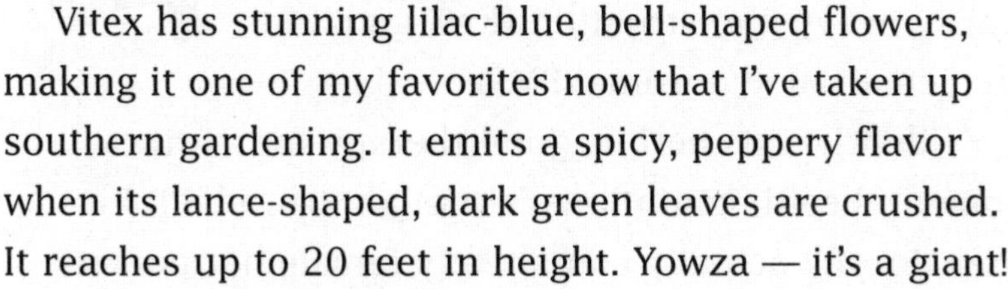

Vitex has stunning lilac-blue, bell-shaped flowers, making it one of my favorites now that I've taken up southern gardening. It emits a spicy, peppery flavor when its lance-shaped, dark green leaves are crushed. It reaches up to 20 feet in height. Yowza — it's a giant!

That's Historical!

Vitex, whose Latin roots mean "pure," "innocent," or "chaste," has been valued as a natural medicine for centuries. Check your history books, and you'll see it mentioned by some great physicians, like Hippocrates and Dioscorides. In ancient Greece, some women used vitex to curb their sexual

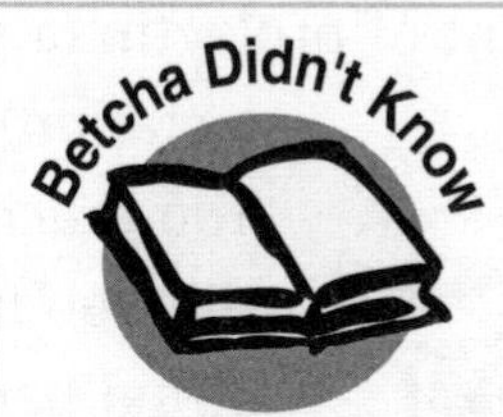

In Germany, doctors have been in the forefront of prescribing vitex to treat PMS symptoms in their female patients.

desires. This herb was also sacrificed as a symbol of chastity to the goddess Ceres. In the 1800s, women in France drank vitex syrup to calm down their libidos.

But guess what? Modern herbalists say all this chastity power is pure nonsense. In fact, they argue that vitex actually enhances one's sexual desire! Viagra, move over!

MEDICINAL USES: BLAST PMS

Vitex berries are the natural pharmacy for this herb. Commonly thought of as a "women's herb," it's been used to treat fibrocystic disease, infertility, menopause, heavy menstruation flow, and premenstrual syndrome (PMS).

Evidently, this herb is good therapy for many women's health conditions, although, truth be told, vitex doesn't actually contain any female hormones. It does its job by working on the pituitary gland, prodding it to produce more progesterone in order to balance and regulate a woman's cycle.

At the same time, vitex berries keep tabs on the amount of prolactin (a protein hormone that induces lactation) produced in a woman's body. Too much prolactin can make her infertile; too little can cause irregular menstrual periods. Vitex helps maintain a healthy balance of prolactin.

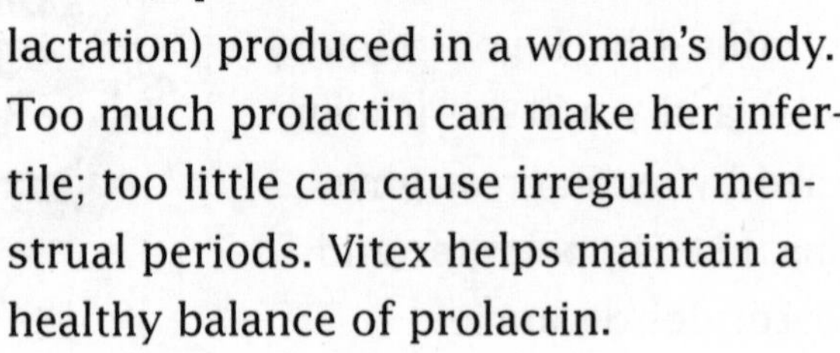

BEST MEDICINAL FORMS

Vitex is available in teas, tinctures, tablets, and capsules. The best way to make a cup of tea is to pour a cup of boiling water over a teaspoonful of ripe berries. Let steep 10 to 15 minutes; then remove the berries and sip. You can drink up to 3 cups a day.

As a tincture, put 40 drops (or 1 ml) in a glass of water or juice and drink it every morning. (Other forms of vitex are also best taken first thing in the morning.)

Don't expect a quick fix; vitex is slow-acting. Women may need to take it daily up to 6 months before feeling results.

GROWING TIPS

Although vitex is native to western Asia and southern Europe, it can grow here in the South, particularly in Zones 6 to 9. It grows best in well-drained but moist soil.

Vitex needs plenty of water. To help keep in moisture, place a thick layer of pine straw or pine bark mulch around the shrub. If there is no rain for a week, get out the hose and give vitex a good dousing!

Look for the plant to flower from June to December. I swear, its berries smell just like peppercorns (minus the sneeze factor, of course)!

As far as maintenance goes, this deciduous shrub may need a little trimming each year to keep it from becoming too bushy. That's about it.

HARVESTING TIPS

The dark berries of vitex are best harvested when ripe, usually in late fall. It really doesn't matter if you dry them in the sun or the shade.

This is a very safe herb. But to err on the side of caution, steer clear of it during pregnancy. Also, check with your doctor before taking vitex if you're on the pill — this herb can counteract the effectiveness of the contraceptive.

STORAGE TIPS

The leaves can also be gathered, dried, and used as a spice. Vitex is a favorite flavoring in many Moroccan recipes. Store the dried herb in dark, airtight glass containers. You can store the berries the same way but put them in a separate container.

Wild Yam

(Dioscorea villosa)

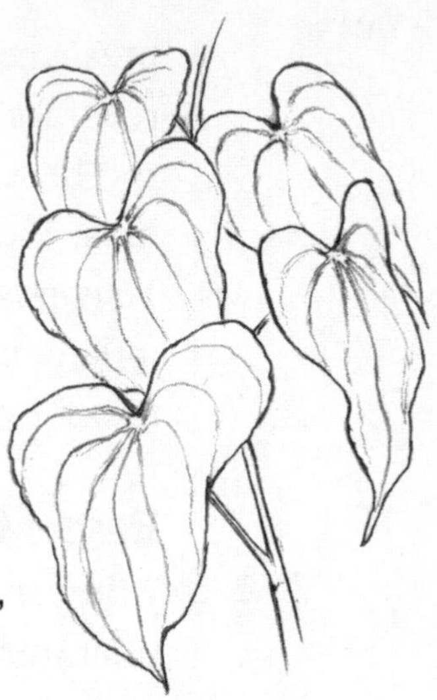

Herbal ID

Wild yam is a twining perennial, which means it wraps its little self around the branches of any neighboring plants. Also known as rheumatism root or colic root, it features large, heart-shaped leaves and tiny flowers.

That's Historical!

"I yam what I yam, and that's all that I yam," in the words of my favorite philosopher, Popeye.

Native Americans often used wild yam to relieve the pain caused by childbirth. And if infants suffered from colic, wild yam came to the rescue again.

Medicinal Uses: Relax Muscles

No wonder herbalists and natural physicians are wild about yams. It seems like every day, more and more benefits are discovered from using them as medicine.

The roots, leaves, and fruits contain hormonal ingredients similar to progesterone, which means big benefits for women going through menopause.

Through the years, wild yams have been used to relax muscles, stop spasms, treat colic, kill germs, lower high blood

Taking fresh wild yam can cause vomiting and other side effects, so avoid it altogether. And if you're pregnant, consult your doctor first.

pressure, soothe urinary tract infections, and provide relief for acute rheumatic conditions. Wow!

The wild yam is loaded with alkaloids, saponins, tannins, and phytosterols — a mighty medicinal melody! They possess antioxidant, antispasmodic, and anti-inflammatory properties. In a medical school classroom, I yam sure they'd earn straight As!

BEST MEDICINAL FORMS

Wild yam works its medicinal magic best in teas and tinctures. The recommended daily dose for the tincture is 2 to 3 ml in a glass of water or juice; drink up to 4 glasses a day.

Or you can take 1 or 2 capsules or tablespoons of the dried root up to 3 times daily.

Folks nursing achy, arthritic joints can benefit from a tincture drink of wild yam, celery seeds, angelica, and meadowsweet.

Tame Arthritis with Wild Yam

A warm cup of wild yam and willow bark tea works wonders on the aches, pains, and swelling associated with arthritis.

Just place an ounce of wild yam root and an ounce of willow bark into 3 pints of water in a saucepan on the stove. Allow the herbs to simmer for 20–25 minutes. Then remove the herbs and pour the tea into a pitcher with a lid on it.

You can drink this tasty tea hot or cold. It can be stored in the refrigerator for up to 3 days. The recommended daily dose is 3 cups.

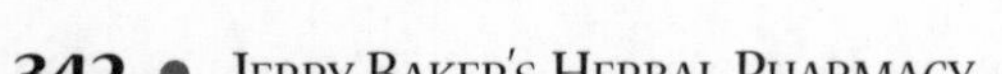

GARDENING TIPS

Believe it or not, this is an easy one to grow. All it needs is some healthy, well-drained soil and a sunny spot in your garden. It can also tolerate light shade.

HARVESTING TIPS

Fall is the best time for digging up wild yam roots and for harvesting its leaves and fruits.

STORAGE TIPS

Good news! This herb's dried roots keep their medicinal potency for up to a year, if you store them in airtight containers out of direct sunlight.

Wild yam is used in the production of birth-control pills and natural progesterone (found in prescriptive menopause creams).

It appears on the United Plant Savers at-risk list. This nonprofit group is dedicated to making sure that native American medicinal plants are preserved and not recklessly overharvested in their native habitats.

For this reason, they ask that folks buy wild yam only from organic sources. I agree!

Divert Diverticulitis

Use wild yam to stop the pain and swelling caused by the unsettling digestive condition diverticulitis.

The best way I know to calm your stomach is to put a couple of tablespoons of wild yam into a quart of boiling water. Reduce the heat and let simmer 20 minutes. Drink up to 3 cups daily.

You can enhance this brew's medicinal might by adding some valerian, peppermint, and black haw.

Witch Hazel

(Hamamelis virginiana)

Herbal ID

This native North American deciduous small tree ranges in size from 8 to 15 feet by the time it's an adult. It has yellow, spidery petals and black nuts. It's also known as snapping hazelnut and spotted alder.

That's Historical!

Native Americans were the first to recognize the medicinal value of witch hazel. They would make poultices out of the leaves and bark and treat a wide range of ailments — from insect bites and minor cuts to hemorrhoids, ulcers, and even tumors.

When European settlers arrived on our shores, they went native and used witch hazel as a pain reliever and astringent.

Medicinal Uses: Shrink Whatever Swells

Put to practical use, witch hazel is a top herb choice for folks with diarrhea, hemorrhoids, varicose veins, a bleeding cut, bruises, sprains, sore eyes, and sunburn.

The best medicine in the herb is found in the bark, leaves, and twigs. These contain bitters, calcium oxalate, tannins, and volatile oils. Quite simply, the ingredients found in witch hazel shrink tissues and act as mild, but safe, sedatives. Witch hazel is also an analgesic and antiseptic.

This herb's therapeutic abilities are backed by scientific studies and Commission E, a prestigious government-appointed team of scientists from Germany who scrutinize the value of botanical medicines.

BEST MEDICINAL FORMS

Hold off on taking witch hazel if you're pregnant. And it's best to check with your doctor first before using witch hazel if you've ever had lower intestinal problems or stomach ulcers.

For treating arthritis, sprains, or bruises, drink 2 to 3 cups of tea made with either the leaves or roots. Brew witch hazel tea (minus any spooky spells!) by scooping a teaspoonful of dried leaves or 2 inches of root into a cup of boiling water. Let it steep for 10 to 15 minutes.

The fastest way to take witch hazel is by tincture: Drop 1 to 2 ml into a glass of water or juice, stir, and drink up to 3 glasses a day. However, witch hazel works most of its healing magic from the outside. To treat varicose veins, add distilled witch hazel to a damp washcloth or compress, and apply it both in the morning and at night.

For those nasty hemorrhoids, just tuck a fresh witch hazel leaf in the sore spot, and literally sit tight(!). Replace it a couple of times a day.

The eyes have it: Witch hazel also makes a terrific cleansing wash for swollen and sore peepers. Dilute 1 part witch hazel in 20 parts boiled water. Let the mixture cool before pouring it on a clean washcloth and placing it over your closed eyes for 5 to 10 minutes.

Did you spend a little too much time in the sun and now (ouch!) you're paying the price with lobster-colored skin? Relief is on its way! Just combine a teaspoon of honey, a teaspoon of witch hazel, and a whipped egg white. Gently dab this mix right on the reddened skin a couple of times a day, and let its cooling, healing actions go to work.

In health food stores and other places that sell herbs, witch hazel comes in two commercial preparations: alcohol extract (called witch hazel tincture) and water extract (appropriately called witch hazel water). I've found that either one works well.

A Chilling Brew

On those scorching, humid summer afternoons, anyone who is outdoors runs the risk of overheating. If you ignore the symptoms, you can develop a more dangerous condition — heatstroke. So before the first hot blasts of summer, make like a Boy or Girl Scout and BE PREPARED. Whip up this cooling medicinal spray, and keep it handy.

2 tsp. of witch hazel tincture
10 drops of peppermint essential oil
12 drops of lavender essential oil

Fill an 8-ounce plastic spray bottle nearly full with water (distilled, if you have it). Then add the herbs. Give it a good shake. When the weather heats up, keep yourself and others around you cool by occasionally misting face, arms, neck, and legs while outdoors.

GROWING TIPS

Witch hazel grows best in Zones 3 to 9. Be sure to give it rich, moist soil, and locate it in a place that gets full sun to partial shade.

This low-growing tree will dress up any garden with its slightly fragrant, spidery flowers that bloom in late fall and early winter. Plus, it's easy on the pocketbook, since it's invincible to most garden pests and diseases.

A BLAST FROM THE PAST

This herb isn't really named after the ugly old broom-flyers in black pointy hats. Witch hazel actually comes from the Middle English word *wich*, which means "flexible."

HARVESTING TIPS

The leaves should be gathered in early- to midsummer. You can pick the twigs and bark as needed; just don't damage the shrub by overpicking.

For next year's crop, you can harvest the seeds in the fall and store them in a warm room indoors for 5 months. Then move them into a cooler room for 3 months before planting them outdoors the following spring.

STORAGE TIPS

Stash bottles of witch hazel (your choice: bark, leaves, and/or twigs) in a cool, dry place out of direct heat and light. Don't freeze it, or it will lose its potency.

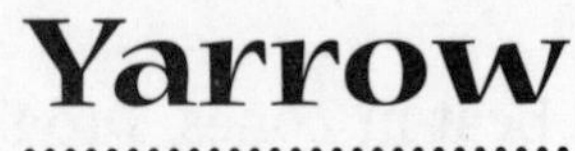

Yarrow

(Achillea millefolium)

Herbal ID

This hardy perennial has feathery, fern-like leaves and clusters of small, white flowers. The flowers like to bloom early and often, sticking around for a long time during the season. Yarrow typically grows to be 2 to 3 feet tall; you've probably seen it along roadsides. Your nose knows yarrow by its distinctive pungent smell.

That's Historical!

Take a good close look at yarrow's botanical name, and it will give you a big clue about its origin. This herb was named after Achilles, the mighty Greek hero who was anything but a heel! He used yarrow to stop the bleeding among his troops during the Trojan War. In fact, yarrow was used to treat wounded soldiers all the way up through the Civil War.

My Grandma Putt told me when I was a tyke that yarrow used to be called the "nosebleed" plant because folks reached for its leaves to stop the bleeding and form a clot. They would stick a pinch of crushed yarrow leaf in the nostrils and continue breathing — through their mouths, of course! This old-fashioned first-aid remedy is still used today.

> **A BLAST FROM THE PAST**
>
> **Dried yarrow stems were** first used in the ancient Chinese fortune-telling system known as the I Ching, before they were replaced with coins.

Native American women relied on yarrow for a wide assortment of female conditions, including irregular periods, childbirth, and breast pain. In many cultures, yarrow is highly regarded as a sacred plant. Unfortunately, in the United States today, many folks regard it as a weed.

MEDICINAL USES: BOOST YOUR IMMUNITY

Yarrow is a wonderful natural cold medicine because it helps you sweat. That's particularly important when you need to break a fever. Yarrow works a lot like the popular cold-fighting herb echinacea. Take yarrow at the first sniffle or sneeze, rather than waiting till your cold (and your nose) gets full blown.

Yarrow, however, does more than combat colds. Why, folks in my family have relied on yarrow for many years to get rid of urinary tract infections and painful hemorrhoids, stop nosebleeds, tame heartburn, and soothe achy, inflamed joints. Some women use it to keep their emotions on an even keel during menopause, too.

Ready for a little science? Turns out that yarrow contains sesquiterpene lactones, tongue-twister chemicals that can boost your immune system. Two other chemicals, achillein and azulene, act like a roadblock to stop bacteria and viruses from infiltrating mucous membranes. They also help cool a fever.

Yarrow can cause a minor skin rash — but that's only in folks who are extremely sensitive to light. Just to be cautious, though, don't take it if you're pregnant. And don't take it internally for prolonged periods.

All told, yarrow contains more than 120 medicinal compounds, making it a powerful medical helper. This versatile herb is astringent, bitter, cooling, drying, and pungent.

BEST MEDICINAL FORMS

When a cold or the flu has you on the ropes, treat yourself to a healing cup of yarrow tea. Stir 2 teaspoons of dried yarrow leaves into a mug of boiling water. Let it steep 15 minutes. Strain out the herbs, and drink up to 4 cups a day.

If you've got a urinary tract infection, make the tea the same way, but wait until it's lukewarm to drink it; my herbalist buddies tell me that's the best temperature to treat the condition.

A faster way to take yarrow is by tincture. The recommended daily dose is 3 to 4 ml in a glass of water or juice. You can drink up to 3 glasses a day.

What about hemorrhoids? You can tame the pain and ditch the itch by making a yarrow compress. Just pour yarrow tea onto a clean washcloth or cotton pad and apply it directly on the hemorrhoid. Do this several times a day. You can also soak in a warm bath. Simmer a handful of fresh yarrow leaves in a saucepan of water for 15 minutes. Strain out the withered leaves and add the herbal water to

Don't Go Ape Over Scrapes

The next time you scrape yourself doing outdoor chores, slap a fresh yarrow leaf on the wound. It'll stop the bleeding and kill germs right on the spot until you can wash it up with soap and water and put a proper bandage on it.

your tub. As I always say, with yarrow you'll no longer care-o about those nasty old hemorrhoids!

GROWING TIPS

Take a look around, and you'll be surprised at all the places wild yarrow grows. I've seen it in meadows, parks, roadsides, seashores, and even empty city lots. Climate-wise, it grows best in Zones 3 to 9 — almost anywhere, in other words.

I usually sow the seeds indoors during the late winter months or outdoors in the late spring. Either way works fine; just give it a super sunny location.

Since yarrow tends to grow in clumps, leave it plenty of room to roam, year after year. But watch out, because it spreads rather quickly and will soon take

Make a Fever Flee

Inside our bodies, yarrow is like the gatekeeper of the dam. Its volatile oils help open the pores and cause sweating — an essential action needed to break a fever. For those times when you're a little under the weather, try my sure-fire one-two fever fighter:

Sip a cup of hot yarrow tea while soaking in a bathtub that has a few drops of yarrow tincture sprinkled in it. Over the next 10–15 minutes, watch the sweat flood out of your pores.

Just be sure to towel yourself off thoroughly before climbing into bed.

over its neighbors' turf. Also, yarrow is prone to powdery mildew, so keep the soil well drained and the plants clean with a weekly soapy-water shower. Yarrow, you'll find, is a hardy plant and isn't bugged by many garden pests.

HARVESTING TIPS

You can gather flower clusters from late spring through early fall. The best snipping time is right before full bloom. You can clip the leaves one by one or snip the entire stem and strip the leaves later. Spread the leaves on a fine-mesh screen and dry in a well-ventilated, shady spot for a few days. When the leaves crumble easily, transfer them to dark glass, airtight containers. If you wish to dry the blossoms for dry arrangements, collect the entire stems when the flowers are almost fully open. Before you hang the bunches up to dry, strip the foliage off the stems. Yarrow is a neat choice for dried flower arrangements.

The Remedy Finder

Here is a quick reference to help you find the herbs that may soothe your symptoms, whatever they are. For further information, refer to the entries for specific herbs in chapter 6. Be sure to note the precautions we've included for many of the herbs (the "Whoa!" box that occurs from time to time), especially if you are pregnant, have allergies, or notice any unpleasant reactions to the herbs, such as dizziness or an upset stomach. Check with your physician before using herbs as medicine regularly, especially if you are taking any prescription drugs. And always be sure to follow the guidelines for dosage.

ACHES AND PAINS: Cayenne, kava, licorice, and thyme

ANXIETY: Basil, ginseng, kava, lemon balm, passionflower, and St. John's wort

ARTHRITIC PAIN: Bay, cayenne, clover, and wild yam

ASTHMA: Echinacea, German chamomile, mullein, and thyme

ATHEROSCLEROSIS/HIGH BLOOD PRESSURE: Chives, evening primrose, garlic, ginger, ginkgo, licorice, tarragon, and wild yam

BAD BREATH: Cilantro and parsley

BLADDER INFECTION: Slippery elm, wild yam, and yarrow

BRONCHITIS: Echinacea, garlic, licorice, mullein, and thyme

BUG BITES AND STINGS: Aloe, basil, calendula, plantain, and St. John's wort

CIRCULATION, POOR: Ginkgo and hyssop

COLD SORES: Echinacea, garlic, ginger, lemon balm, sage, and St. John's wort

COLDS AND FLU: Catnip, echinacea, garlic, ginger, horseradish, lemon balm, slippery elm, thyme, and yarrow

CONGESTION: Catnip, eucalyptus, mullein, and thyme

COUGHS: Clover, echinacea, garlic, licorice, rue, thyme, and valerian

CUTS AND ABRASIONS: Aloe, calendula, witch hazel, and yarrow

DEPRESSION: Lemon balm and St. John's wort

DIABETES: Evening primrose and garlic

DIARRHEA: Blackberry, ginger, and witch hazel

DIGESTION, POOR: Angelica, anise hyssop, blackberry, caraway, dill, fennel, ginger, mints, slippery elm, and valerian

EAR INFECTION: Echinacea, garlic, and mullein

ECZEMA: Evening primrose, violet, and witch hazel

Best Germ Fighters

These herbs are nature's SWAT team! They fight germs, so include them in your diet regularly.

- Basil
- Bay
- Eucalyptus
- Garlic
- Horseradish
- Thyme
- Wild Yam

ENLARGED PROSTATE GLAND: Saw palmetto

FEVER: Borage and yarrow

GAS: Bee balm, fennel, ginger, rosemary, and sage

HANGOVER: Dandelion

HEADACHE: Feverfew, rosemary, and rue

HEARTBURN: Angelica, anise hyssop, bee balm, fennel, ginger, parsley, and sage

HEMORRHOIDS: Slippery elm and witch hazel

HIGH BLOOD PRESSURE: Chives, garlic, licorice, tarragon, and wild yam

HORMONAL PROBLEMS: Calendula, evening primrose, and vitex (chastetree)

IMMUNE DEFICIENCIES: Calendula, ginseng, and lemon balm

INDIGESTION: Anise hyssop, blackberry, caraway, chamomile, cilantro, dill, fennel, and mints

INFECTION: Basil, bay, and oregano

INSOMNIA: Hop, oregano, and passionflower

LAXATIVE: Chicory

MENTAL CLARITY: Ginkgo

MIGRAINE HEADACHE: Feverfew

MOOD ENHANCER: St. John's wort

MUSCLE RELAXANT: Catnip, horehound, kava, lavender, valerian, and wild yam

NAUSEA: Blackberry, cilantro, dill, and ginger

POISON IVY, OAK, AND SUMAC: Plantain

PREMENSTRUAL SYNDROME: Evening primrose, rosemary, valerian, and vitex (chastetree)

SEDATIVE: Oregano

SKIN PROBLEMS: Aloe, plantain, and violet

SORE THROATS: Anise hyssop, echinacea, lemon balm, and sage

ULCERS: Calendula, marigold, and slippery elm

UPSET STOMACH: Mints, slippery elm, and valerian

URINARY TRACT INFECTIONS: Slippery elm, wild yam, and yarrow

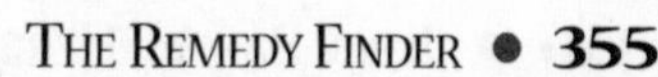

Herbal Resources

American Botanical Council
P.O. Box 144345
Austin, TX 78714-4345
(512) 926-4900; (800) 373-7105
Fax: (512) 926-2345
e-mail: abc@herbalgram.org
Web site: www.herbalgram.org

Publishes a magazine, booklets, and scientific reprints.

American Herb Association
P.O. Box 1673
Nevada City, CA 95959
(530) 265-9552
Fax: (530) 274-3140

Publishes a newsletter and focuses on medicinal herbs.

The American Herbalists Guild
P.O. Box 70
Roosevelt, UT 84066-0070
(435) 722-8434
Fax: (435) 722-8452
e-mail: ahgoffice@earthlink.net
Web site: www.healthy.net/herbalists

Produces a quarterly publication and emphasizes the practice of herbal medicine in North America.

Herb Growing & Marketing Network
P.O. Box 245
Silver Spring, PA 17575-0245
(717) 393-3295
Fax: (717) 393-9261
e-mail: herbworld@aol.com
Web site: www.herbworld.com

Publishes a trade journal as well as an annual resource guide.

Herb Research Foundation
1007 Pearl Street, Suite 200
Boulder, CO 80302
(303) 449-2265
Fax: (303) 449-7849
e-mail: info@herbs.org
Web site: www.herbs.org

A nonprofit research and educational organization.

The Herb Society of America, Inc.
9019 Kirtland Chardon Road
Kirtland, OH 44094
(440) 256-0514
Fax: (440) 256-0541
e-mail: herbs@herbsociety.org (general);
membership@herbsociety.org (membership)
Web site: www.herbsociety.org

Dedicated to promoting the knowledge, use, and delight of herbs through educational programs.

International Herb Association
910 Charles Street
Fredericksburg, VA 22401
(540) 368-0590
Fax: (540) 370-0015
e-mail: members@iherb.org
Web site: www.iherb.org

A professional trade association providing education, services, and development for members.

United Plant Savers
P.O. Box 98
East Barre, VT 05649
e-mail: info@plantsavers.org
Web site: www.plantsavers.org

The group's mission is to protect native medicinal plants of the United States and Canada.

Index

C

D

E

F

I

J

K

N

O

P

R

S